SIGNPOSTS

HARRY VERPLOEGH has published or compiled the following works.

The Epistles of Paul and Hebrews, a paraphrase by George Barker Stevens, 1898; Verploegh Editions, 1980.

A.W. Tozer, An Anthology, Christian Publications, 1984.

The Gospel of Mark, Verploegh Editions, 1985.

The Set of the Sail, A.W. Tozer, Christian Publications, 1986.

Oswald Chambers, The Best from All His Books, Oliver-Nelson, A Division of Thomas Nelson, 1987.

The Next Chapter after the Last, Christian Publications, 1987.

SIGNPOSTS

A Collection of Sayings from
A.W. Tozer

Compiled by Harry Verploegh

VICTOR BOOKS®

A DIVISION OF SCRIPTURE PRESS PUBLICATIONS INC.
USA CANADA ENGLAND

RECOMMENDED DEWEY DECIMAL CLASSIFICATION: 248.08

SUGGESTED SUBJECT HEADING: QUOTATIONS

LIBRARY OF CONGRESS CATALOG CARD NUMBER: 88-60218

ISBN: 0-89693-583-3

Grateful acknowledgment is made to Harper & Row for permission to
quote from *The Knowledge of the Holy* © 1964, and to Christian Publications
for permission to quote from the other books.

FOREWORD

The quotations in this book are like nuggets mined from a rich vein of gold, or like a cup of refreshing water from a deep and sweet well. These words are distilled from the mind and heart of Dr. A.W. Tozer, whose life was given to worship, prayer, reading, writing, and preaching. They are the confluence of numerous rivers: the Scriptures, the classics, the mystics, and the poets, to name a few. They are the result of long thought and observation by a superb mind that penetrated the obvious and uncovered Christian motives and practices with profound insight. They are clear and incisive. They are pointed and convicting. They are practical and helpful. They are touched with a feeling of loneliness, of longing, of holy dissatisfaction.

Tozer's writings are all the more remarkable for the author had no formal education beyond grade school. After moving to Akron, Ohio, from a small town in Pennsylvania, he heard a street-corner preacher, which led to his conversion. Shortly after that, he received the gift of discernment from the Holy Spirit. Along with these deep spiritual experiences, his fine mind awakened and he began to read everything in sight. Shakespeare, Milton, Wordsworth, and Emerson became his companions, as did, of course, the Bible. He once observed that it was to his advantage that he never attended university or seminary, since this allowed him to be like a hungry bee gathering nectar from any flower. Eventually his finely educated mind and gifts were recognized by two colleges that granted him honorary doctorates. Wheaton College gave him the Litt. D. and Houghton College the D.D.

You will notice that Dr. Tozer was always thoughtful. His mind sat in judgment on all things. His preaching and writing were controlled by his thinking. He didn't make rash statements, and he didn't try to use clever phrases. One favorite statement of his was: "You get into the Kingdom heart first, but that doesn't mean you cut your head off."

That agile mind seemed always at work. In the inside pocket of his jacket he carried a ten-cent-store spiral notebook and several ballpoint pens. Wherever he was, he would jot down thoughts and ideas. He was usually in the midst of writing an editorial for the *Alliance Witness*, working on a book, or preparing a sermon.

To many, Dr. Tozer was known as a preacher and pastor. He preached twice on Sundays and spoke at the Wednesday evening prayer meeting. For some years he spoke on Saturday mornings on radio station WMBI from Chicago's Moody Bible Institute. He enjoyed and promoted the singing of great hymns and his church choir was of great importance to him. It was in his preaching that he would state the ideas and concepts that later found their way into his books and editorials. In fact most of his best-known books first appeared as sermons—*The Pursuit of God, The Divine Conquest,* and *The Knowledge of the Holy.*

It must not be thought that his writings are from sermon tapes. Dr. Tozer would take his sermon notes as seeds for articles or books and carefully and painstakingly rework them into the literary form he wanted. It was his thesis that hard writing meant easy reading. He would sit in his study bent over his portable typewriter with a green eyeshade to protect his light-sensitive eyes, wearing a sweater with the elbows out, and pound out editorials and books with Webster's *Unabridged Dictionary* within easy reach.

Another important part of Dr. Tozer's life was his sense of humor. If humor may be defined as the perception of the incongruous, it enjoyed a heightened awareness in him. You may catch a breath of it now and again in these pages, but those of us who knew him knew how sharp his perceptions were. He was never a clown and seldom a storyteller. But he was brilliantly witty. He thought in similes and metaphors, and his conversations abounded in these figures. He could convulse a congregation by a mere aside. He struggled at abandoning much of his humor during sermons, though some would sneak through, much to the delight of his hearers. It is a pity more of it didn't get into his writings.

The most central part of this amazing person was his deep desire to worship Jehovah. To Tozer the supreme activity of man was worship, and he practiced that. He became a disciple of mystics like Meister Eckart, Fénelon, Bernard of Cluny, Bernard of Clairvaux, and Julian of Norwich (whom he affectionately called a girlfriend). He had a superb collection of hymnbooks, and he knew many hymns from memory. He often suggested that the hymnbook should be our constant companion in devotion and worship, but he would warn that the hymnbook ought to be at least 100 years old. As he got older, the Bible became more and more his basic reading. He would insist that the way to spiritual progress was to read a plain-text Bible and diligently apply the knees to the floor.

Sometimes Dr. Tozer was criticized for his mystical bent. What he took from the mystics was their great emphasis on the truth that God could be known and experienced in a very intimate way. He never questioned that the Scriptures were the final authority in matters of faith and practice. But he insisted that this truth must become internally real and move us to an awareness of God in every practical way.

These quotations are to be considered just that—quotations. Elton Trueblood once pointed out that the problem with quotes is that we don't hear or read the whole argument. That doesn't dilute their effectiveness, but to see them in context often clarifies the author's full intention.

You may disagree with some of Tozer's ideas. There is a sense of *ipse dixit* in the writings of a man who saw himself as a prophet to the Christian church, a sense of certainty that he was right. However, this certainty rested in the confidence of his calling. But God works in "earthen vessels," and this is evidenced by the humanity of Tozer that shows up on the pages of his work. Allow him to be the human he was and enjoy him.

I spent from 1943 to 1959 with Dr. Tozer on the staff of the Chicago church where he preached and pastored. No other person has had such an influence on my mind and life. May the Spirit who breathes in these pages be the means of conforming us more and more into the likeness of the Christ whom Dr. Tozer worshiped and served.

Raymond McAfee
Ocean City, New Jersey
January 1988

INTRODUCTION

IN THIS COLLECTION from the works of A.W. Tozer, I have attempted to present excerpts that do not require a context for interpretation. There has been no editing of the material. Each citation, indicating the source of a statement, refers to the first edition.

The quotations demonstrate Tozer's sensitive use of the English language in communicating his discernment of the state of the church in his time. I read him appreciatively because he has been for me one of those men who, as Oswald Chambers observed, "can express for us what we feel inarticulate about." I hope that this anthology will not only provide a valuable introduction and reference to A.W. Tozer but also invite further discovery of the treasures to be found in his writings.

Harry Verploegh

This Book
Is Dedicated To
The Memory Of
Aiden Wilson Tozer
(1897-1963)

This collection has been
compiled from the following A.W. Tozer works:

A   The Pursuit of God, *1948*

B   The Divine Conquest, *1950*

C   The Root of the Righteous, *1955*

D   Born After Midnight, *1959*

E   Of God and Men, *1960*

F   The Knowledge of the Holy, *1964*

G   That Incredible Christian, *1964*

H   Man: The Dwelling Place of God, *1966*

K   God Tells the Man Who Cares, *1970*

L   The Set of the Sail, *1986*

M   The Next Chapter after the Last, *1987*

The source of the citations is indicated by a letter-number code following each excerpt. The letter represents the corresponding book from the key above. The number is the book's page number; all are taken from the first editions.

A C T I O N

In this world men are judged by their ability to do. D56

Any act done because we are afraid not to do it is of the same moral quality as the act that is not done because we are afraid to do it. E94

Never seek the leading of the Lord concerning an act that is forbidden in the Word of God. To do so is to convict ourselves of insincerity. L76

A C T I V I T Y

We are under no spiritual obligation to aid any man in any activity that has not upon it the marks of the cross. C19

Be concerned not with what you have accomplished but over what you might have accomplished if you had followed the Lord completely. C29

The desire to be dramatically active is proof of our religious infantilism; it is a type of exhibitionism common to the kindergarten. C76

Aimless activity is beneath the worth and dignity of a human being. Activity that does not result in progress toward a goal is wasted; yet most Christians have no clear end toward which they are striving. D101

One of the most popular current errors, and the one out of which springs most of the noisy, blustering religious activity being carried on in evangelical circles these days, is the notion that as times change the church must change with them. K18

It is altogether possible to serve our own interests with poured-out devotion. It is possible to serve the flesh even while engaged in the most intense sort of religious activities. The very fact that our activities are religious will sometimes disguise the presence of the rankest kind of selfishness. M56

The great weight of exhortation these days is in the direction of zeal and activity. "Let's get going" is the favorite watchword for gospel workers, with the result that everyone feels ashamed to sit down and think. M69–70

It would be a shock to most of us to learn just what God thinks of our breathless activity, and a greater shock to many to find out the true quality of our service as God sees it. M70

A D V I C E

No man has any right to offer advice who has not first heard God speak. C18

No man has any right to counsel others who is not ready to hear and follow the counsel of the Lord. C18

A T H E I S M

Were every man on earth to become atheist, it could not affect God in any way. He is what He is in Himself without regard to any other. To believe in Him adds nothing to His perfections; to doubt Him takes nothing away. F33

B

BELIEF AND UNBELIEF
(see also FAITH)

Believing . . . is directing the heart's attention to Jesus. It is lifting the mind to "behold the Lamb of God," and never ceasing that beholding for the rest of our lives. A90

Since believing is looking it can be done any time. A94

Since believing is looking, it can be done without special equipment or religious paraphernalia. A94

It might shock some of us profoundly if we were brought suddenly face to face with our beliefs and forced to test them in the fires of practical living. C49

Any belief that does not command the one who holds it is not a real belief: it is a pseudo belief only. C49

It is no sin to doubt some things, but it may be fatal to believe everything. C119

In our constant struggle to believe we are likely to overlook the simple fact that a bit of healthy disbelief is sometimes as needful as faith to the welfare of our souls. C119

To believe in God is more than to believe that He exists. E56

It is not enough that we believe; we must believe in the right thing about the right One. E56

True faith requires that we believe everything God has

said about Himself, but also that we believe everything
He has said about us. Until we believe that we are as bad
as God says we are, we can never believe that He will
do for us what He says He will do. E56

If we will believe we may even now enjoy the
presence of God and the ministry of His heavenly
messengers. Only unbelief can rob us of this royal
privilege. E118

Unbelief is actually perverted faith, for it puts its trust
not in the living God but in dying men. The unbeliever
denies the self-sufficiency of God and usurps attributes
that are not his. This dual sin dishonors God and
ultimately destroys the soul of the man. F35

The unbelieving mind would not be convinced by any
proof, and the worshiping heart needs none. F59

To believe on Christ savingly means to believe the
right things about Christ. G22

Human unbelief cannot alter the character of God. G27

One enemy we must resist is *unbelief*. The temptation
is strong to reject what we cannot explain, or at least to
withhold belief till we have investigated further. This
attitude is proper, even commendable, for the scientist,
but wholly wrong for the Christian. G87

Every man during his lifetime will have to decide for
himself whether or not he can afford the terrible luxury of
unbelief. G118

The natural man must know in order to believe; the
spiritual man must believe in order to know. H29

When men believe God they speak boldly. When they
doubt they confer. H115

Unbelief judges God to be unworthy of confidence
and withholds its trust from Him. L39

The unbeliever refuses to trust God because his
conception of God is base and ignoble. L123

B I B L E
(see also SCRIPTURES, VOICE OF GOD)

The Bible is not an end in itself, but a means to bring
men to an intimate and satisfying knowledge of God.
A-Preface

The Bible assumes as a self-evident fact that men can
know God with at least the same degree of immediacy as
they know any other person or thing that comes
within the field of their experience. A50

A loving Personality dominates the Bible, walking
among the trees of the garden and breathing fragrance
over every scene. A50

Any man who by repentance and a sincere return to
God will break himself out of the mold in which he has
been held, and will go to the Bible itself for his
spiritual standards, will be delighted with what he finds
there. A71

God did not write a book and send it by messenger to
be read at a distance by unaided minds. He spoke a Book
and lives in His spoken words, constantly speaking His
words and causing the power of them to persist across the
years. A75

The Bible will never be a living Book to us until we
are convinced that God is articulate in His universe. A81

A new world will arise out of the religious mists
when we approach our Bible with the idea that it is not
only a book which was once spoken, but a book which
is *now speaking.* A82

If you would follow on to know the Lord, come at once to the open Bible expecting it to speak to you. Do not come with the notion that it is a thing which you may push around at your convenience. It is more than a thing, it is a voice, a word, the very Word of the living God. A82

The difficulty we modern Christians face is not misunderstanding the Bible, but persuading our untamed hearts to accept its plain instructions. B114

The most realistic book in the world is the Bible. God is real, men are real and so is sin and so are death and hell, toward which sin inevitably leads. D93

The Bible is among other things a book of revealed truth. That is, certain facts are revealed that could not be discovered by the most brilliant mind. These facts are of such a nature as to be past finding out. E26

The Word of God well understood and religiously obeyed is the shortest route to spiritual perfection. E67

The Bible . . . is more than a volume of hitherto unknown facts about God, man and the universe. G27

The Bible, to be understood by its readers, must condescend to tell of eternal things in the language of time. G27

God's Word is true whether we believe it or not. G27

Whatever keeps me from the Bible is my enemy, however harmless it may appear to me. G82

The Bible is not addressed to just anybody. Its message is directed to a chosen few. H26

Some believe and some do not; some are morally receptive and some are not; some have spiritual capacity and some have not. It is to those who do and are and have that the Bible is addressed. Those who do not and are not and have not will read it in vain! H27

The saving power of the Word is reserved for those for whom it is intended. H28

The impenitent heart will find the Bible but a skeleton of facts without flesh or life or breath. H28

The Bible is a supernatural book and can be understood only by supernatural aid. H29

Seen one way, the Bible is a book of doom. H112

We find the Bible difficult because we try to read it as we would read any other book, and it is not the same as any other book. H112

A growing acquaintance with the Holy Spirit will always mean an increasing love for the Bible. H127

Christ is in the Bible as no one can be in a mere portrait, for the Bible is a book of holy ideas and the eternal Word of the Father can and does dwell in the thought He has Himself inspired. H127

A true lover of God will be also a lover of His Word. Anything that comes to us from the God of the Word will deepen our love for the Word of God. H127

The Bible is the book of supreme love, but it is at the same time altogether frank and downright. K110

The Bible is a book of controversy. L116

The Bible was called forth by the moral emergency occasioned by the fall of man. L165

The purpose of the Bible is to bring men to Christ, to make them holy and prepare them for heaven. In this it is unique among books, and it always fulfills its purpose when it is read in faith and obedience. L168

B L E S S E D N E S S

Only the conquered can know true blessedness. B84

It is doubtful whether God can bless a man greatly until He has hurt him deeply. C137

B O O K S

The function of a good book is to stand like a signpost directing the reader toward the Truth and the Life. B-Preface

The work of a good book is to incite the reader to moral action, to turn his eyes toward God and urge him forward. Beyond that it cannot go. B-Preface

To seek our divinity merely in books and writings is *to seek the living among the dead;* we do but in vain many times seek God in these, where His truth too often is not so much enshrined as entombed. B25

To think without a proper amount of good reading is to limit our thinking to our own tiny plot of ground. The crop cannot be large. H147

The best book is not one that informs merely, but one that stirs the reader up to inform himself. H147

To observe only and neglect reading is to deny ourselves the immense value of other people's observations; and since the better books are written by trained observers the loss is sure to be enormous. H147

Extensive reading without the discipline of practical observation will lead to bookishness and artificiality. H147

Reading and observing without a great deal of meditating will fill the mind with learned lumber that will always remain alien to us. H147

B R O T H E R H O O D

It is ironic that this generation which more than any other in history preaches the brotherhood of man is also the generation most torn by unbrotherly strife. D108

Always it is more important that we retain a right spirit toward others than that we bring them to our way of thinking, even if our way is right. E92

We human beings were made for each other, and what any of us is doing at any time cannot be a matter of indifference to the rest of us. On the human plane all men are brothers. M35

C

CHANGE

God cannot change for the better. F49

In God no change is possible; in men change is impossible to escape. F50

In a world of change and decay not even the man of faith can be completely happy. F51

CHARACTER

Whatever a man wants badly enough and persistently enough will determine the man's character. C116

Not the naked Word only but the character of the witness determines the quality of the convert. E34

A man is the sum of his parts and his character the sum of the traits that compose it. F114

As the excellence of steel is strength and the excellence of art is beauty, so the excellence of mankind is moral character. L122

A God who lies is a God without character, and where there is no character there can be no confidence. This is the moral logic of unbelief. L123

CHASTISEMENT

God never chastens a perfectly obedient child. Consider the fathers of our flesh; they never punished us for obedience, only for disobedience. G114

God chastens us not that He may love us but because He loves us. G114

When we feel the sting of the rod we may be sure we
are temporarily out of the right way. G114

C H O I C E

However deep the mystery, however many the
paradoxes involved, it is still true that men become saints
not at their own whim but by sovereign calling. B48

The right of determination must always remain with
God. B49

God has indeed lent to every man the power to lock
his heart and stalk away darkly into his self-chosen night,
as He has lent to every man the ability to respond to
His overtures of grace, but while the "no" choice may be
ours, the "yes" choice is always God's. B49

"If any man will," said our Lord, and thus freed
every man and placed the Christian life in the realm of
voluntary choice. E38

One of the marks of God's image in man is his ability
to exercise moral choice. F29

We must all choose whether we will obey the gospel
or turn away in unbelief and reject its authority. Our
choice is our own, but the consequences of the choice
have already been determined by the sovereign will of
God, and from this there is no appeal. F113

Where there is no freedom of choice there can be
neither sin nor righteousness, because it is of the nature of
both that they be voluntary. G30

Where there is no moral knowledge or where there is
no voluntary choice, the act is not sinful; it cannot be, for
sin is the transgression of the law and transgression
must be voluntary. G30

If a man chooses the will of God he is not denying but exercising his right of choice. G131

Some things are not debatable; there is no other side to them. There is only God's side. H114

The choices of life, not the compulsions, reveal character. H158

Any nation which for an extended period puts pleasure before liberty is likely to lose the liberty it misused. H159

It is the free nation that reveals its character by its voluntary choices. H159

The man or woman who is wholly and joyously surrendered to Christ cannot make a wrong choice. Any choice will be the right one. L77

CHRIST

Jesus does not offer an opinion for He never uttered opinions. He never guessed; He knew, and He knows. A110

To many Christians, Christ is little more than an idea, or at best an ideal: He is not a fact. Millions of professed believers talk as if He were real and act as if He were not. C49

Christ is God acting like God in the lowly raiments of human flesh. C59

The meek and lowly Jesus has displaced the high and holy Jesus in the minds of millions. The vibrant note of triumph is missing in our witness. A sad weeping Jesus offers us His quiet sympathy in our griefs and temptations, but He appears to be as helpless as we are when the pressure is on. His pale feminine face looks at us from the "holy picture" of the Catholic and the Easter card of the Protestant. We give Him our sympathy, but scarcely our confidence. The helpless Christ of the crucifix and the vacuous-countenanced Christ that looks out in sweet innocence from the walls of our evangelical homes is all one and the same. The Catholics rescue Him by bringing a Queen of Heaven to His aid. But we Protestants have no helper. So we sing pop choruses to cheer our drooping spirits and hold panel discussions in the plaintive hope that someone will come up with the answer to our scarce-spoken complaint. C72

Christ must be Lord or He will not be Saviour. C86

The Christ of popular Christianity has a weak smile and a halo. He has become Someone-up-There who likes people, at least some people, and these are grateful but not too impressed. If they need Him, He also needs them. F36

For every man it must be Christ or eternal tragedy. F42

Christ in His atonement has removed the bar to the divine fellowship. Now in Christ all believing souls are objects of God's delight. F101

The trouble is that the whole "Accept Christ" attitude is likely to be wrong. It shows Christ applying to us rather than us to Him. It makes Him stand hat-in-hand awaiting our verdict on Him, instead of our kneeling with troubled hearts awaiting His verdict on us. It may even permit us to accept Christ by an impulse of mind or emotions, painlessly, at no loss to our ego and no inconvenience to our usual way of life. G18

To accept Christ is to form an attachment to the Person of our Lord Jesus altogether unique in human experience. The attachment is intellectual, volitional and emotional. G18

To accept Christ is to know the meaning of the words "as he is, so are we in this world." We accept His friends as our friends, His enemies as our enemies, His ways as our ways, His rejection as our rejection, His cross as our cross, His life as our life and His future as our future.

If this is what we mean when we advise the seeker to accept Christ we had better explain it to him. He may get into deep spiritual trouble unless we do. G19

To accept Christ it is necessary that we reject whatever is contrary to Him. G74

There are disadvantages to the life in Christ. G74

While Christ was the perfect example of the healthy normal man, He yet did not live a normal life. He sacrificed many pure enjoyments to give Himself to the holy work of moral rescue. His conduct was determined not by what was legitimate or innocent, but by our human need. He pleased not Himself but lived for the emergency; and as He was so are we in this world. G104

What had Christ to offer to us that is sound, genuine and desirable? He offers forgiveness of sins, inward cleansing, peace with God, eternal life, the gift of the Holy Spirit, victory over temptation, resurrection from the dead, a glorified body, immortality and a dwelling place in the house of the Lord forever. These are a few benefits that come to us as a result of faith in Christ and total committal to Him. Add to these the expanding wonders and increasing glories that shall be ours through the long, long reaches of eternity, and we get an imperfect idea of what Paul called "the unsearchable riches of Christ." G117

Whatever makes Christ dear to us is pretty sure to be from God. G125

The love of Christ both wounds and heals, it
fascinates and frightens, it kills and makes alive, it draws
and repulses, it sobers and enraptures. There can be
nothing more terrible or more wonderful than to be
stricken with love for Christ so deeply that the whole
being goes out in a pained adoration of His person, an
adoration that disturbs and disconcerts while it purges
and satisfies and relaxes the deep inner heart. G129

The Christ of fundamentalism is strong but hardly
beautiful. G129

Christ is not one of many ways to approach God, nor
is He the best of several ways; He is the only way, "the
way, the truth and the life." G135

Jesus Christ is a Man come to save men. H12

Much that is being done in Christ's name is false to
Christ in that it is conceived by the flesh, incorporates
fleshly methods, and seeks fleshly ends. H124

One thing is certain: the call of Christ is always a
promotion. H124

Christ has been explained, humanized, demoted.
Many professed Christians no longer expect Him to usher
in a new order; they are not at all sure that He is able to
do so; or if He does, it will be with the help of art,
education, science and technology; that is, with the
help of man. This revised expectation amounts to
disillusionment for many. And of course no one can
become too radiantly happy over a King of kings who has
been stripped of His crown or a Lord of lords who has
lost His sovereignty. H155

Christ is every man's contemporary. K17

The Christ of the tentative smile and air of puzzlement
is not the Christ of God. L55

Christ is enough. To have Him and nothing else is to
be rich beyond conceiving. To have all else and have not
Christ is to be a cosmic pauper, cut off forever from all
that will matter at last. L89

Christ stands alone, above and outside of every
ideology devised by man. He does not join any of our
parties or take sides with any of our great men except
as they may come over on His side and try to follow Him
in righteousness and true holiness. M45

Christ will be standing upright, tall and immortal,
after the tumult and the shouting dies and the captains and
the kings lie stretched side by side, the "cause" that
made them famous forgotten and their whole significance
reduced to a paragraph in a history book. M47

One thing the Bible teaches very plainly is that Christ
is the sum of all virtues and the essence of all beauty. M58

Christ is God shining through the personality of a
man, and *shining unhindered.* His sacred humanity does
not veil His divine beauty in any degree. M58

The Christ who lived among men showed forth the
nature of God as certainly as if He had still been with His
Father in the preincarnate state. M58

C H R I S T I A N

The true Christian ideal is not to be happy but to be
holy. B100

The Christian is strong or weak depending upon how
closely he has cultivated the knowledge of God. C11

One of the most stinging criticisms made against
Christians is that their minds are narrow and their hearts
small. C113

Christians have often been accused of being reactionary because they cannot get up any enthusiasm over the latest scheme that someone thinks up to bring in the millennium. C156

A real Christian is an odd number anyway. He feels supreme love for One whom he has never seen, talks familiarly every day to Someone he cannot see, expects to go to heaven on the virtue of Another, empties himself in order to be full, admits he is wrong so he can be declared right, goes down in order to get up, is strongest when he is weakest, richest when he is poorest, and happiest when he feels worst.

He dies so he can live, gives away so he can keep, sees the invisible, hears the inaudible and knows that which passes knowledge. C156

The average Christian is so cold and so contented with His wretched condition that there is no vacuum of desire into which the blessed Spirit can rush in satisfying fullness. D8

We Christians are left in the world to witness, and while we have breath we must speak to men about God and to God about men. D35

The most godly Christian is the one who knows himself best, and no one who knows himself will believe that he deserves anything better than hell. D36

The Christian should look well to his pleasures for they will ennoble or debase him, and this by a secret law of the soul from which there is no escape. D129

A Christian is a born-one, an embodiment of growing life, and as such may be retarded, stunted, undernourished or injured very much as any other organism. E11

It might be well for us Christians to listen less to the news commentaries and more to the voice of the Spirit. E36

The Christian is a man of heaven temporarily living on earth. E40

The only true Christian is the practicing Christian. E58

The Christian who has dedicated his life to God and has shouldered his cross need not be surprised at the conflict in which he at once finds himself engaged. Such conflict is logical; it results from the nature of God and of man and of Christianity. E61

A free Christian should act from within with a total disregard for the opinions of others. If a course is right he should take it because it is right, not because he is afraid not to take it. And if it is wrong he should avoid it though he lose every earthly treasure and even his very life as a consequence. E98

We Christians must simplify our lives or lose untold treasures on earth and in eternity. E103

We of the Christian faith need not go onto the defensive. The man of the world is the dreamer, not the Christian. E108

Surely the days are evil and the times are waxing late, but the true Christian is not caught unawares. He has been forewarned of just such times as these and has been expecting them. E131

Christians today appear to know Christ only after the flesh. They try to achieve communion with Him by divesting Him of His burning holiness and unapproachable majesty, the very attributes He veiled

while on earth but assumed in fullness of glory upon
His ascension to the Father's right hand. F36

The Christian believes that in Christ he has died, yet
he is more alive than before and he fully expects to live
forever. G11

The true Christian should be, indeed must be, a
theologian. He must know at least something of the
wealth of truth revealed in the Holy Scriptures. G21

There are many . . . happy exchanges we Christians
may make if we will, among them being our ignorance
for His knowledge, our folly for His wisdom, our
demerit for His merit, and our sad mortality for His
blessed immortality and faith for sight at last. G34

What the Christian used to be is altogether the least
important thing about him. What he is yet to be is all that
should concern him. G44

The Christian is saved from his past sins. G44

The average Christian these days is a harmless enough
thing, God knows. He is a child wearing with
considerable self-consciousness the harness of the
warrior; he is a sick eaglet that can never mount up with
wings; he is a spent pilgrim who has given up the
journey and sits with a waxy smile trying to get what
pleasure he can from sniffing the wilted flowers he has
plucked by the way. G72

If God sets out to make you an unusual Christian He is
not likely to be as gentle as He is usually pictured by the
popular teachers. G122

A Christian is one who believes on Jesus Christ as
Lord. H60

Christians have fallen into the habit of accepting the
noisiest and most notorious among them as the best and
the greatest. They too have learned to equate
popularity with excellence, and in open defiance of the
Sermon on the Mount they have given their approval
not to the meek but to the self-assertive; not to the
mourner but to the self-assured; not to the pure in
heart who see God but to the publicity hunter who seeks
headlines. H96

Under the scornful attack of the religious critic real
Christians who ought to know better are now
"rethinking" their faith. H153

He [the Christian] must come with the understanding
that he will not be popular and that he will be called to
stand where Jesus stood before the world: to be
admired by many, loved by a few and rejected at last by
the majority of men. K39

The Christian knows a thing to be true, not because
he has verified it in experience but because God has said
it. His expectations spring from his confidence in the
character of God. K136

That we Christians modify the moral teachings of
Christ at our convenience to avoid the stigma of being
thought different is a proof of our backsliding, and the
shame of it will not be removed until we have repented
and brought our lives completely under the discipline
of Christ. K144

No man, no home, no nation is the worse for the
presence of a real Christian. L81

It is of far greater importance that we have better
Christians than that we have more of them. L154

We who follow Christ are men and women of
eternity. We must put no confidence in the passing scenes

of the disappearing world. We must resist every
attempt of Satan to palm off upon us the values that
belong to mortality. Nothing less than forever is long
enough for us. M9

The Christian will find slim pickings where professed
believers play and pray all in one breath. He may be
compelled sometimes to travel alone or at least to go
with the ostracized few. To belong to the despised
minority may be the price he must pay for power. But
power is cheap at any price. M21–22

We Christians are Christians first and everything else
after that. Our first allegiance is to the kingdom of God.
Our citizenship is in heaven. M45

CHRISTIANITY

Christianity takes for granted the absence of any self-
help and offers a power which is nothing less than the
power of God. B88

Deity indwelling men! That, I say, is Christianity and
no man has experienced rightly the power of Christian
belief until he has known this for himself as a living
reality. B98

Christians must hear again the doctrine of the
perturbing quality of faith. People must be told that the
Christian religion is not something they can trifle
with. C48

Many of us have become extremely skillful in
arranging our lives so as to admit the truth of Christianity
without being embarrassed by its implications. C49

The superiority of Christianity to every other religion
lies in the fact that in Christianity a *Person* is present,
active, filling, upholding and supporting all. That
Person, of course, is Jesus Christ. C70

Christianity is rarely found pure. Apart from Christ
and His inspired apostles probably no believer or
company of believers in the history of the world has
ever held the truth in total purity. D76

Large and influential sections of the world of
fundamental Christianity have gone overboard for
practices wholly unscriptural, altogether unjustifiable
in the light of historic Christian truth and deeply
damaging to the inner life of the individual
Christian. E12

Much that the church—even the evangelical church—
is doing these days she is doing because she is afraid not
to. E15

Much that passes for New Testament Christianity is
little more than objective truth sweetened with song, and
made palatable by religious entertainment. E28

Christianity will always reproduce itself after its
kind. E34

Evangelical Christianity is now tragically below the
New Testament standard. Worldliness is an accepted part
of our way of life. Our religious mood is social instead
of spiritual. We have lost the art of worship. We are not
producing saints. Our models are successful
businessmen, celebrated athletes and theatrical
personalities. We carry on our religious activities after
the methods of the modern advertiser. Our homes have
been turned into theaters. Our literature is shallow and
our hymnody borders on sacrilege. And scarcely anyone
appears to care. E36

Christianity is basically a religion of meanings, and
meaning belongs to intelligent beings only. E87

Christianity can stand on its own legs. Christ does not
need our nervous defense. E96

There is about the Christian faith a quiet dogmatism, a cheerful intolerance. E129

The Christian faith engages the profoundest problems the human mind can entertain and solves them completely and simply by pointing to the Lamb of God. E129

At the heart of the Christian system lies the cross of Christ with its divine paradox. G11

The power of Christianity appears in its antipathy toward, never in its agreement with, the ways of fallen men. G11

At the foundation of the Christian life lies vicarious atonement, which in essence is a transfer of guilt from the sinner to the Saviour. G32

Let us not be shocked by the suggestion that there are disadvantages to the life in Christ. G74

Christianity involves an acceptance and a repudiation, an affirmation and a denial. G74

Large numbers of supposedly sound Christian believers know nothing at all about personal communion with God; and there lies one of the greatest weaknesses of present-day Christianity. G83

Christianity is the religion of the heart. It searches for and finds the man under his wrappings. G89

Christianity today is man-centered, not God-centered. God is made to wait patiently, even respectfully, on the whims of men. H27

Christianity has as one of its most effective talking points the idea that God exists to help people to get ahead in this world. H57

Christless Christianity sounds contradictory but it
exists as a real phenomenon in our day. H124

There is a notion abroad that Christianity is on its last
legs, or possibly already dead and just too weak to lie
down. H137

The whole Christian family stands desperately in need
of a restoration of penitence, humility and tears. K12

The message of the cross offers eternal life and the
blessedness of the Holy Spirit indwelling the soul. These
distinguish Christianity from every other religion; and
it is significant that these distinguishing marks are of such
a nature as to be wholly above and beyond the reach of
man. They are altogether mysterious and divine and are
unaffected by race, politics, economics or education. K43

Pure Christianity, instead of being shaped by its
environment, actually stands in sharp opposition to it,
and where the power of God has been present over a
sustained period the church has sometimes reversed the
direction of things and exercised a purifying effect
upon society. K45

Christianity must embrace the total personality and
command every atom of the redeemed being. K45

The supreme purpose of the Christian religion is to
make men like God in order that they may act like
God. K56

The most effective argument for Christianity is still
the good lives of those who profess it. L16

Christianity is nothing if not moral. L26

Christianity engages to bring God into human life, to
make men right with God, to give them a heart
knowledge of God, to teach them to love and obey

God and ultimately to restore in them the lost image of God in full and everlasting perfection. L79

God's truth has never been popular. Wherever Christianity becomes popular, it is not on its way to die—it has already died. M20

Christianity's scramble for popularity today is an unconscious acknowledgment of spiritual decline. Her eager fawning at the feet of the world's great is a grief to the Holy Spirit and an embarrassment to the sons of God. M21

Christianity is bigger than any country, loftier than any civilization, broader than any human ideology. M46

C H U R C H

The Church has gained or lost power exactly as she has moved toward or away from the inwardness of her faith. B-Preface

The churches (even the gospel churches) are worldly in spirit, morally anemic, on the defensive, imitating instead of initiating and in a wretched state generally because for two full generations they have been told that justification is no more than a "not guilty" verdict pronounced by the Heavenly Father upon a sinner who can present the magic coin *faith* with the wondrous "open-sesame" engraved upon it. B37

No real union between the world and the Church is possible. When the Church joins up with the world it is the true Church no longer but only a pitiful hybrid thing, an object of smiling contempt to the world and an abomination to the Lord. B110

A church that is soundly rooted cannot be destroyed, but nothing can save a church whose root is dried up. No stimulation, no advertising campaigns, no gifts of money and no beautiful edifice can bring back life to the rootless tree. C9

The fast-paced, highly spiced, entertaining service of today may be a beautiful example of masterful programming—but it is not a Christian service. C92

There is not another institution in the world that talks as much and does as little as the church. D34

The Church is dedicated to things that matter. D75

A man may attend church for a lifetime and be none the better for it. D100

The church is called the household of God, and it is the ideal place to rear young Christians. D113

The true Church has never sounded out public expectations before launching her crusades. Her leaders heard from God, they knew their Lord's will and did it. E15

The church must examine herself constantly to see if she be in the faith; she must engage in severe self-criticism with a cheerful readiness to make amends; she must live in a state of perpetual penitence, seeking God with her whole heart; she must constantly check her life and conduct against the Holy Scriptures and bring her life into line with the will of God. E33

The first look of the church is toward Christ, who is her Head, her Lord and her All. E33

The task of the church is twofold: to spread Christianity throughout the world and to make sure that the Christianity she spreads is the pure New Testament kind. E34

If anyone is to go on the defensive it should never be the church. E97

The first step down for any church is taken when it surrenders its high opinion of God. F4

To regain her lost power the Church must see heaven opened and have a transforming vision of God. F114

We Christians are the Church and whatever we do is what the Church is doing. F114

The witness of the Christian church is most effective when she declares rather than explains, for the gospel is addressed not to reason but to faith. G11

Our churches these days are filled (or one-quarter filled) with a soft breed of Christian that must be fed on a diet of harmless fun to keep them interested. About theology they know little. Scarcely any of them have read even one of the great Christian classics. G76

Someday the church can relax her guard, call her watchmen down from the wall and live in safety and peace; but not yet, not yet. G86

A church is a living organism and is subject to attack from such enemies as prey on living things. G87

The church lives in a hostile world. Within and around her are enemies that not only could destroy her, but are meant to and will unless she resists force with yet greater force. G87

The Church has been tempted to think of God by the use of images and forms, and always when she has so done she has fallen into externalism and spiritual decay. G90

The center of attraction in a true church is the Lord
Jesus Christ. G136

The church today is suffering from the secularization
of the sacred. By accepting the world's values, thinking
its thoughts and adopting its ways we have dimmed
the glory that shines overhead. H56

One hundred religious persons knit into a unity by
careful organization do not constitute a church any more
than eleven dead men make a football team. The first
requisite is life, always. H75

The church *has* failed, not by neglecting to provide
leadership but by living too much like the world. H138

The world has never shown much disposition to listen
to the church when she speaks in her true prophetic
voice. H139

The world wants the church to add a dainty spiritual
touch to its carnal schemes, and to be there to help it to its
feet and put it to bed when it comes home drunk with
fleshly pleasures. H139

A local church can die. This happens when all the old
saints in a given place fall asleep and no young saints arise
to take their place. H140

We are in real need of a reformation that will lead to
revival among the churches, but the church is not dead,
neither is it dying. The church cannot die. H140

Almost everything the church is doing these days has
been suggested to her by the world. H166

According to the Scriptures the church is the
habitation of God through the Spirit, and as such is the
most important organism beneath the sun. She is not
one more good institution along with the home, the state,

and the school; she is the most vital of all institutions—
the only one that can claim a heavenly origin. K26

Whoever scorns the local church scorns the Body of
Christ. K27

The church is found wherever the Holy Spirit has
drawn together a few persons who trust Christ for their
salvation, worship God in spirit and have no dealings
with the world and the flesh. K27

The church is still to be reckoned with. "The gates of
hell shall not prevail against her." K27

Any belief or practice that causes the members of a
local church to separate into groups on any pretext
whatever is an evil. At first it may seem necessary to
form such groups and it may be easy enough to show
how many practical advantages follow these divisions;
but soon the spirit of separateness unconsciously enters
the minds of the persons involved and grows and
hardens until it is impossible for them to think of
themselves as belonging to the whole church. They
may each and all hold the *doctrine* of unity, but the
damage has been done; they *think* and *feel* themselves
to be separated nevertheless. K50

One place where the evil manifests itself is in the
practice of dividing the church into age groups. . . .
Neither the Hebrew worshipers of Old Testament
times nor the church of the New Testament ever divided
into age groups to worship the Lord. The practice
appears to have come in with the modern vogue of
glorifying youth and downgrading age as something a
bit disgraceful. K50

In the average church service the most real thing is the
shadowy unreality of everything. The worshiper sits in a
state of suspended mentation; a kind of dreamy
numbness creeps upon him; he hears words but they do

not register, he cannot relate them to anything on his own life-level. He is conscious of having entered a kind of half-world; his mind surrenders itself to a more or less pleasant mood which passes with the benediction leaving no trace behind. It does not affect anything in his everyday life. He is aware of no power, no Presence, no spiritual reality. There is simply nothing in his experience corresponding to the things which he heard from the pulpit or sang in the hymns. [K90]

The church's mightiest influence is felt when she is different from the world in which she lives. [L35]

One sure mark of the Church's heavenly character is that she is different from the rest of mankind; similarity is a mark of her fall. [L35]

The Church is born out of the gospel and that gospel has to do with God and man's relation to God. [L79]

The business of the church is God. [L80]

The church will never fall as long as she resists. [L114]

The church must claim again her ancient dowry of everlastingness. She must begin again to deal with ages and millenniums rather than with days and years. She must not count numbers but test foundations. She must work for permanence rather than for appearance. Her children must seek those enduring things that have been touched with immortality. [M9]

A church fed on excitement is no New Testament church at all. The desire for surface stimulation is a sure mark of the fallen nature, the very thing Christ died to deliver us from. [M13]

The historic church, while she was a hated minority group, had a moral power that made her terrible to evil and invincible before her foes. [M20]

C I V I L I Z A T I O N

One way the civilized world destroys men is by preventing them from thinking their own thoughts. E103

Modern civilization is so complex as to make the devotional life all but impossible. E103

The most ominous sign of the coming destruction of our country is the passing of the American home. E105

Future historians will record that we of the twentieth century had intelligence enough to create a great civilization but not the moral wisdom to preserve it. H49

Our Western civilization is on its way to perishing. It has many commendable qualities, most of which it has borrowed from the Christian ethic, but it lacks the element of moral wisdom that would give it permanence. H49

Were men everywhere to ignore the things that matter little or not at all and give serious attention to the few really important things, most of the walls that divide men would be thrown down at once and a world of endless sufferings ended. H116

Our science-based civilization has given us many benefits but it has multiplied our distractions and so taken away far more than it has given. L130

Time may show that one of the greatest weaknesses in our modern civilization has been the acceptance of quantity rather than quality as the goal after which to strive. M7

The Word of God ignores size and quantity and lays all its stress upon quality. M8

COMMITMENT
(see also CONSECRATION, SEPARATION)

Everything is safe which we commit to Him, and nothing is really safe which is not so committed. A28

By one act of consecration of our total selves to God we can make every subsequent act express that consecration. B121

How can we live lives acceptable to God?
The answer is near thee, even in thy mouth. Vacate the throne room of your heart and enthrone Jesus there. Set Him in the focus of your heart's attention and stop wanting to be a hero. Make Him your all in all and try yourself to become less and less. Dedicate your entire life to His honor alone and shift the motives of your life from self to God. Let the reason back of your daily conduct be Christ and His glory, not yourself, not your family nor your country nor your church. In all things let Him have the preeminence. D70

The act of committal to Christ in salvation releases the believing man from the penalty of sin, but it does not release him from the obligation to obey the words of Christ. E52

Dedication of the life to anything or anyone short of God Himself, is a prostitution of noble powers and must bring a harvest of grief and disappointment at last. L56

COMMUNION

God formed us for His pleasure, and so formed us that we, as well as He, can, in divine communion, enjoy the sweet and mysterious mingling of kindred personalities. A34

Some things may be neglected with but little loss to the spiritual life, but to neglect communion with God is to hurt ourselves where we cannot afford it. C12

The fellowship of God is delightful beyond all telling. C15

True Christian communion consists in the sharing of a *Presence.* H77

COMPETITION

God's servants are not to be competitors, but co-workers. M56

God is one; it is wholly impossible for Him to compete with Himself. M56

As long as His Spirit is in control there can be no such thing as competition among those who are under that control. The Spirit achieves cooperation, always, and makes of His servants not competitors, but co-workers. M56-57

A local church, as long as it is indwelt by the Holy Spirit, cannot entertain the psychology of competition. When it begins to compete with another church, it is a true church of God no longer; it has voided its character and gone down onto a lower level. M57

Wherever the spirit of competition between brethren rears its head, there will be found carnality, selfishness and sin. The only way to deal with it is to tag it for what it is and put it away in the sorrows of repentance. M57

We should cultivate the idea that we are co-workers rather than competitors. We should ask God to give us the psychology of cooperation. M57

COMPLACENCY

Complacency is a deadly foe of all spiritual growth. A17

Religious complacency is encountered almost everywhere among Christians these days, and its presence is a sign and a prophecy. For every Christian will become at last what his desires have made him. We are all the sum total of our hungers. C55

One of the greatest foes of the Christian is religious complacency. C55

In spite of the undeniable lukewarmness of most of us we still fear that unless we keep a careful check on ourselves we shall surely lose our dignity and become howling fanatics by this time next week. D11

The complacency of Christians is the scandal of Christianity. H38

COMPLAINING

Among those sins most exquisitely fitted to injure the soul and destroy the testimony, few can equal the sin of complaining. M15

The complaining heart never lacks for occasion. It can always find reason enough to be unhappy. The object of its censure may be almost anything: the weather, the church, the difficulties of the way, other Christians or even God Himself. M15

A complaining Christian puts himself in a position morally untenable. The simple logic of his professed discipleship is against him with an unanswerable argument. Its reasoning runs like this:

First, he is a Christian because he chose to be. There are no conscripts in the army of God. He is, therefore, in the awkward position of complaining against the very conditions he brought himself into by his own free choice.

Secondly, he can quit any time he desires. No Christian wears a chain on his leg. Yet he still continues

on, grumbling as he goes, and for such conduct he has
no defense . . . and the complaining Christian, if he but
looks closely, will see his own face peering out at him
from the background.

Lastly, the believer who complains against the
difficulties of the way proves that he has never felt or
known the sorrows which broke over the head of
Christ when He was here among men. After one look at
Gethsemane or Calvary, the Christian can never again
believe that his own path is a hard one. M15–16

We dare not compare our trifling pains with the
sublime passion endured for our salvation. Any
comparison would itself be the supreme argument
against our complaints, for what sorrow is like unto
His? M16

C O M P R O M I S E

God will not compromise and He need not be
coaxed. F54

We are sent to bless the world, but never are we told
to compromise with it. Our glory lies in a spiritual
withdrawal from all that builds on dust. M21

C O N C E P T   O F   G O D

The Church has surrendered her once lofty concept of
God and has substituted for it one so low, so ignoble, as
to be utterly unworthy of thinking, worshiping
men. F-Preface

It is impossible to keep our moral practices sound and
our inward attitudes right while our idea of God is
erroneous or inadequate. F-Preface

A right conception of God is basic not only to
systematic theology but to practical Christian living as
well. F2

To be right we must think worthily of God. It is
morally imperative that we purge from our minds all
ignoble concepts of the Deity and let Him be the God
in our minds that He is in His universe. F35

Our concepts of measurement embrace mountains
and men, atoms and stars, gravity, energy, numbers,
speed, but never God. We cannot speak of measure or
amount or size or weight and at the same time be
speaking of God, for these tell of degrees and there are
no degrees in God. All that He is He is without growth or
addition or development. F45–46

Nothing in God is less or more, or large or small. He
is what He is in Himself, without qualifying thought or
word. He is simply God. F46

CONDUCT

We modern Christians are long on talk and short on
conduct. D32

Each one should watch his ambitions, for they will
shape him as an artist shapes the yielding clay. D130

Christ-like conduct is the end of Christian faith. E60

The stream of human conduct flows out of a fountain
polluted by evil thoughts and imaginations. G37

Most Christians would be better pleased if the Lord
did not inquire into their personal affairs too closely.
They want Him to save them, keep them happy and
take them to heaven at last, but not to be too inquisitive
about their conduct or service. G105

The Lord loves the artless, the candid, the childlike.
He cannot work with those who argue or bargain or
plead or excuse themselves. G106

Tie up the loose ends of your life. Begin to tithe; institute family prayer; pay up your debts as far as possible and make some kind of frank arrangement with every creditor you cannot pay immediately; make restitution as far as you can; set aside time to pray and search the Scriptures; surrender wholly to the will of God. You will be surprised and delighted with the results. H40

To do a wrong act a man must for the moment think wrong; he must exercise bad judgment. H46

Apostacy always begins with the conduct. L30

Love alone can make our conduct acceptable to God. L120

The conscience is a bit of a pest but most persons manage to strike a truce with it quite early in life and are not troubled much by it thereafter. L144

CONFIDENCE

A blind confidence which trusts without seeing is far dearer to God than any fancied knowledge that can explain everything. M55

CONSECRATION

(see also COMMITMENT, SEPARATION)

Every soul belongs to God and exists by His pleasure. God being Who and What He is, and we being who and what we are, the only thinkable relation between us is one of full lordship on His part and complete submission on ours. We owe Him every honor that it is in our power to give Him. Our everlasting grief lies in giving Him anything less. A102

The man who surrenders to Christ exchanges a cruel slave driver for a kind and gentle Master whose yoke is easy and whose burden is light. A104

The whole course of the life is upset by failure to put God where He belongs. A107

The whole man must make the decision before the heart can know any real satisfaction. God wants us all, and He will not rest till He gets us all. No part of the man will do. A107

By one act of consecration of our total selves to God we can make every subsequent act express that consecration. A121

CONTEMPT

Contempt for another human being is an affront to God almost as grave as idolatry, for while idolatry is disrespect for God Himself, contempt is disrespect for the being He made in His own image. E82

Contempt is an emotion possible only where there is great pride. The error in moral judgment that undervalues another always springs out of the error that overvalues one's self. E83

No one for whom Christ died can be common or worthless. E84

To esteem anyone worthless who wears the form of a man is to be guilty of an affront to the Son of Man. E84

CONTENTMENT

Contentment, when it touches spiritual things, is surely a vice. C54

Contentment with earthly goods is the mark of a saint; contentment with our spiritual state is a mark of inward blindness. C55

CREATION

God dwells in His creation and is everywhere indivisibly present in all His works. A61

The primary purpose of God in creation was to prepare moral beings spiritually and intellectually capable of worshiping Him. D123

Had there been no creation there could have been no fall and no redemption. E119

In the mind of God all things occurred at once, but in the sequence of time creation comes first. E119

Everything God does is praiseworthy and deserves our deepest admiration. Whether He is making or redeeming a world, He is perfect in all His doings and glorious in all His goings forth. E119

God brought His creatures into being that He might enjoy them and they rejoice in Him. F61

God is happy in His love for all that He has made. F100

God enjoys His creation. F100

C R I T I C I S M

Don't defend your church or your organization against criticism. If the criticism is false it can do no harm. If it is true you need to hear it and do something about it. C29

Do not condemn or criticize, but seek a better way. God will honor you. H40

C R O S S

The cross is rough and it is deadly, but it is effective. A47

Who today is interested in a gloomy mysticism that would sentence its flesh to a cross and recommend self-effacing humility as a virtue actually to be practiced by modern Christians? B60

Who but someone very old and very conservative
would insist upon death as the appointed way to life? B60

Men crave life, but when they are told that life comes
by the cross they cannot understand how it can be, for
they have learned to associate with the cross such
typical images as memorial placques, dim-lit aisles and
ivy. So they reject the true message of the cross and
with that message they reject the only hope of life known
to the sons of men. B62

That life which goes to the cross and loses itself there
to rise again with Christ is a divine and deathless treasure.
Over it death hath no more dominion. B62

Whoever refuses to bring his old life to the cross is but
trying to cheat death, and no matter how hard he may
struggle against it, he is nevertheless fated to lose his
life at last. B62

The life that halts short of the cross is but a fugitive
and condemned thing, doomed at last to be lost beyond
recovery. B62

No one ever enjoyed a cross just as no one ever
enjoyed a gallows. B125

The cross of old Roman times knew no compromise;
it never made concessions. It won all its arguments by
killing its opponent and silencing him for good. It
spared not Christ, but slew Him the same as the rest. C61

The cross of Christ is the most revolutionary thing
ever to appear among men. C61

The cross effects its ends by destroying one
established pattern, the victim's, and creating another
pattern, its own. Thus it always has its way. It wins by
defeating its opponent and imposing its will upon him. It
always dominates. It never compromises, never

dickers, nor confers, never surrenders a point for the sake of peace. It cares not for peace; it cares only to end its opposition as fast as possible. C62

If we are wise we will do what Jesus did: endure the cross and despise its shame for the joy that is set before us. C63

The cross will cut into our lives where it hurts worst, sparing neither us nor our carefully cultivated reputations. It will defeat us and bring our selfish lives to an end. C63

We must do something about the cross, and one of two things only we can do—flee it or die upon it. C63

The cross stands high above the opinions of men and to that cross all opinions must come at last for judgment. C63

In every Christian's heart there is a cross and a throne, and the Christian is on the throne till he puts himself on the cross; if he refuses the cross he remains on the throne. C66

We want to be saved but we insist that Christ do all the dying. No cross for us, no dethronement, no dying. C66

The very power of the cross lies in the fact that it is the wisdom of God and not the wisdom of man. C79

It is easy to learn the doctrine of personal revival and victorious living; it is quite another thing to take our cross and plod on to the dark and bitter hill of self-renunciation. D10

The cross would not be a cross to us if it destroyed in us only the unreal and the artificial. It is when it goes on to slay the best in us that its cruel sharpness is felt. D53

It cannot be denied that the way of the cross is unpopular and that it brings a measure of reproach upon those who take it. D53

The cross of Christ creates a moral situation where every attribute of God is on the side of the returning sinner. D137

Christ calls men to carry a cross; we call them to have fun in His name. He calls them to forsake the world; we assure them that if they but accept Jesus the world is their oyster. He calls them to suffer; we call them to enjoy all the bourgeois comforts modern civilization affords. He calls them to self-abnegation and death; we call them to spread themselves like green bay trees or perchance even to become stars in a pitiful fifth-rate religious zodiac. He calls them to holiness; we call them to a cheap and tawdry happiness that would have been rejected with scorn by the least of the Stoic philosophers. D141

The man with a cross no longer controls his destiny; he lost control when he picked up his cross. That cross immediately became to him an all-absorbing interest, an overwhelming interference. No matter what he may desire to do, there is but one thing he *can* do; that is, move on toward the place of crucifixion. E38

The old self-sins must die, and the only instrument by which they can be slain is the cross. F31

To try to find a common ground between the message of the cross and man's fallen reason can only result in an impaired reason, a meaningless cross and a powerless Christianity. G11

The cross stands in bold opposition to the natural man. G11

The truth of the cross is revealed in its contradictions. G11

Christ by His death on the cross made it possible for the sinner to exchange his sin for Christ's righteousness. It's that simple. No one is compelled to accept it, but at least that is what it means. G32

The old cross slew men; the new cross entertains them. The old cross condemned; the new cross amuses. The old cross destroyed confidence in the flesh; the new cross encourages it. The old cross brought tears and blood; the new cross brings laughter. The flesh, smiling and confident, preaches and sings about the cross; before that cross it bows and toward that cross it points with carefully staged histrionics—but upon that cross it will not die, and the reproach of that cross it stubbornly refuses to bear. G59

Men have fashioned a golden cross with a graving tool, and before it they sit down to eat and drink and rise up to play. G60

The cross is the suffering the Christian endures as a consequence of his following Christ in perfect obedience. G114

The pain of the cross means that we are in "the way." G114

In coming to Christ we do not bring our old life up onto a higher plane; we leave it at the cross. The corn of wheat must fall into the ground and die. H44

The cross that ended the earthly life of Jesus now puts an end to the sinner; and the power that raised Christ from the dead now raises him to a new life along with Christ. H45

The way of the cross is still a narrow way. K59

A strange thing under the sun is crossless Christianity. L36

The cross separated between the dead and the living. L36

The cross is the essence of all that is extreme and final. L36

The cross is the symbol of Christianity, and the cross speaks of death and separation, never of compromise. No one ever compromised with a cross. L36

The cross of Christendom is a no-cross, an ecclesiastical symbol. The cross of Christ is a place of death. Let each one be careful which cross he carries. L43

The cross has been the end of a life and the beginning of a life. L43

CURIOSITY

A determination to know what cannot be known always works harm to the Christian heart. M54

Human curiosity and pride often combine to drive us to try to understand acts of God which are plainly outside the field of human understanding. We dislike to admit that we do not know what is going on, so we torture our minds trying to fathom the mysterious ways of the Omniscient One. It's hard to conceive of a more fruitless task. M54

We may as well learn (and the earlier the better) that God has no private secretaries who are on the inside of the secrets of eternity. All God wanted to say, He has said in the Scriptures. M55

D

DESIRE

In our desire after God let us keep always in mind that God also hath desire, and His desire is toward the sons of men, and more particularly toward those sons of men who will make the once-for-all decision to exalt Him over all. A107

We are all the sum total of our hungers. C55

Among the many who profess the Christian faith scarcely one in a thousand reveals any passionate thirst for God. C56

At the root of all true spiritual growth is a set of right and sanctified desires. C116

In the moral world . . . right desires tend toward life and evil ones toward death. C116

When our dominant desires are bad the whole life is bad as a consequence. When the desires are good the life comes up to the level of our desires, provided that we have within us the enabling Spirit. C116

A thing looks morally better because we want it. C117

To want a thing, or feel that we want it, and then to turn from it because we see that it is contrary to the will of God is to win a great battle. C117

The desire after God and holiness is back of all real spirituality, and when that desire becomes dominant in the life nothing can prevent us from having what we want. C117

Unsanctified desire will stop the growth of any Christian life. Wrong desire perverts the moral judgment so that we are unable to appraise the desired object at its real value. C117

For all God's good will toward us He is unable to grant us our heart's desires till all our desires have been reduced to one. D8

No Christian ever fell into sin who did not first allow himself to brood over it with increasing desire. D130

D I S C E R N M E N T

Learning will enable a man to pass judgment on our yesterdays, but it requires a gift of clear seeing to pass sentence on our own day. E22

Among the gifts of the Spirit scarcely any one is of greater practical usefulness in these critical times than the gift of discernment. G153

D O C T R I N E
(see also THEOLOGY)

Mere acquaintance with correct doctrine is a poor substitute for Christ and familiarity with New Testament eschatology will never take the place of a love-inflamed desire to look on His face. D132

There is scarcely anything so dull and meaningless as Bible doctrine taught for its own sake. Truth divorced from life is not truth in its Biblical sense, but something else and something less. E25

The purpose behind all doctrine is to secure moral action. E27

A doctrine has practical value only as far as it is prominent in our thoughts and makes a difference in our lives. G64

Love is more important than correct doctrine, though
there is no incompatibility between the two: love without
right doctrine is sentimentality and right doctrine
without love is dead. K134

The deceitful human heart would like only too well to
involve it in the fog of doctrinal argument and thus rob it
of its real meaning. M66

E

ENTERTAINMENT

For centuries the Church stood solidly against every form of worldly entertainment, recognizing it for what it was—a device for wasting time, a refuge from the disturbing voice of conscience, a scheme to divert attention from moral accountability. C32

The growth of the amusement phase of human life to such fantastic proportions is a portent, a threat to the souls of modern men. C32

Religious entertainment is in many places rapidly crowding out the serious things of God. C33

The great god Entertainment amuses his devotees mainly by telling them stories. C33

If men do not have joy in their hearts they will seek it somewhere else. If Christians are forbidden to enjoy the wine of the Spirit they will turn to the wine of the flesh for enjoyment. C69

The whole religious machine has become a noisemaker. C75

The "Christian" film that seeks to draw customers by picturing amorous love scenes in its advertising is completely false to the religion of Christ. Only the spiritually blind will be taken in by it. D38

The pure religion of Christ that flows like a crystal river from the heart of God is being polluted by the unclean waters that trickle from behind the altars of abomination that appear on every high hill and under every green tree from New York to Los Angeles. D38

The sacred has been secularized, the holy vulgarized and worship converted into a form of entertainment. D68

Much that passes for New Testament Christianity is little more than objective truth sweetened with song and made palatable by religious entertainment. E28

No nation can long endure whose people have sold themselves for bread and circuses. E105

It is now common practice in most evangelical churches to offer the people, especially the young people, a maximum of entertainment and a minimum of serious instruction. H136

It is scarcely possible in most places to get anyone to attend a meeting where the only attraction is God. H136

God's professed children are bored with Him, for they must be wooed to meeting with a stick of striped candy in the form of religious movies, games and refreshments. H136

E Q U A L I T Y

God has no favorites, except as some of His children by their loving response make it possible for Him to shower more love upon them. M97

E X I S T E N C E

God exists in Himself and of Himself. His being He owes to no one. His substance is indivisible. He has no parts but is single in His unitary being. F15

Nothing is complete in itself but requires something outside itself in order to exist. F33

Time marks the beginning of created existence, and

because God never began to exist it can have no application to Him. F39

The ancient image of God whispers within every man of everlasting hope; somewhere he will continue to exist. F41

E X P E R I E N C E

True Christian experience must always include a genuine encounter with God. B26

No spiritual experience, however revolutionary, can exempt us from temptation. C101

There are delights which the heart may enjoy in the awesome presence of God which cannot find expression in language; they belong to the unutterable element in Christian experience. C145

True Christian experience is direct knowledge of God. E86

A large part of Christian experience consists of exchanging something worse for something better, a blessed and delightful bargain indeed. G32

Conscious fellowship with Christ is by faith, love and obedience. And the humblest believer need not be without these. G67

This new doctrine, this new religious habit, this new view of truth, this new spiritual experience—how has it affected my attitude toward and my relation to God, the Holy Scriptures, self, other Christians, the world and sin. H121

We can prove the quality of religious experience by its effect on the self-life. H128

True spiritual experience must be shared. L52

F

F A I T H
(see also BELIEF AND UNBELIEF)

Faith enables our spiritual sense to function. Where faith is defective the result will be inward insensibility and numbness toward spiritual things. A52

At the root of the Christian life lies belief in the invisible. The object of the Christian's faith is unseen reality. A56

Faith in a risen Saviour is necessary if the vague stirrings toward immortality are to bring us to restful and satisfying communion with God. A79

Faith will get me anything, take me anywhere in the Kingdom of God, but without faith there can be no approach to God, no forgiveness, no deliverance, no salvation, no communion, no spiritual life at all. A86

Faith is the gaze of a soul upon a saving God. A89

Faith is not a once-done act, but a continuous gaze of the heart at the Triune God. A90

Faith is not in itself a meritorious act; the merit is in the One toward Whom it is directed. Faith is a redirecting of our sight, a getting out of the focus of our own vision and getting God into focus. A91

Faith is the least self-regarding of the virtues. It is by its very nature scarcely conscious of its own existence. Like the eye which sees everything in front of it and never sees itself, faith is occupied with the Object upon which it rests and pays no attention to itself at all. A91

If faith is the gaze of the heart at God, and if this gaze is but the raising of the inward eyes to meet the all-seeing eyes of God, then it follows that it is one of the easiest things possible to do. A94

The true quality of faith is almost universally missed, viz., its moral quality. B38

Real faith must always mean more than passive acceptance. It dare mean nothing less than surrender of our doomed Adam-life to a merciful end upon the cross. B63

The only man who can be sure he has true Bible faith is the one who has put himself in a position where he cannot go back. C48

The faith of Christ will command or it will have nothing to do with a man. It will not yield to experimentation. C48

We can prove our faith by our committal to it—and in no other way. C49

For true faith, it is either God or total collapse. C50

Pseudo faith always arranges a way out to serve in case God fails it. C50

Faith never asks questions when it has been established that God has spoken. C120

Faith never means gullibility. The man who believes everything is as far from God as the man who refuses to believe anything. C120

It takes real faith to begin to live the life of heaven while still upon the earth, for this requires that we rise above the law of moral gravitation and bring to our everyday living the high wisdom of God. D98

Faith reposes on the character of God and if we believe that God is perfect we must conclude that His ways are perfect also. D117

Without faith it is impossible to please God, but not all faith pleases God. E54

True faith commits us to obedience. E57

That dreamy, sentimental faith which ignores the judgments of God against us and listens to the affirmations of the soul is as deadly as cyanide. E57

Faith in faith is faith astray. E57

Faith is not a substitute for moral conduct but a means toward it. E60

We must have faith; and let us not apologize for it, for faith is an organ of knowledge and can tell us more about ultimate reality than all the findings of science. E118

Faith is an organ of knowledge, and love an organ of experience. F9

Every man lives by faith, the nonbeliever as well as the saint; the one by faith in natural laws and the other by faith in God. Every man throughout his entire life constantly accepts without understanding. F17

Reflection upon revealed truth naturally follows the advent of faith, but faith comes first to the hearing ear, not to the cogitating mind. F19

To seek proof is to admit doubt, and to obtain proof is to render faith superfluous. F19

God's eternity and man's mortality join to persuade us that faith in Jesus Christ is not optional. F42

Any faith that must be supported by the evidence of the senses is not real faith. F62

We rest in *what God is*. I believe that this alone is true faith. F62

Faith rests upon the character of God, not upon the demonstrations of laboratory or logic. G11

True faith is not the intellectual ability to visualize unseen things to the satisfaction of our imperfect minds; it is rather the moral power to trust Christ. G70

The contemporary moral climate does not favor a faith as tough and fibrous as that taught by our Lord and His apostles. G76

When faith gains the consent of the will to make an irrevocable committal to Christ as Lord, truth begins its saving, illuminating work; and not one moment before. G93

Faith is an organ of knowledge. H24

The faith that saves reposes in the Person of Christ; it leads at once to a committal of the total being to Christ, an act impossible to the natural man. H29

In natural matters faith follows evidence and is impossible without it, but in the realm of the spirit faith precedes understanding; it does not follow it. H29

Every benefit flowing from the atonement of Christ comes to the individual through the gateway of faith.

Forgiveness, cleansing, regeneration, the Holy Spirit,
all answers to prayer, are given to faith and received by
faith. There is no other way. H29

The faith that saves is not a conclusion drawn from
evidence; it is a moral thing, a thing of the spirit, a
supernatural infusion of confidence in Jesus Christ, a
very gift of God. H29

In the divine scheme of salvation the doctrine of faith
is central. God addresses His words to faith, and where
no faith is no true revelation is possible, "Without faith
it is impossible to please Him." H31

Faith based upon reason is faith of a kind, it is true; *but
it is not of the character of Bible faith,* for it follows the
evidence infallibly and has nothing of a moral or
spiritual nature in it. Neither can the absence of faith
based upon reason be held against anyone, for the
evidence, not the individual, decides the verdict. H31

True faith rests upon the character of God and asks no
further proof than the moral perfections of the One who
cannot lie. H32

I AM THAT I AM is the only grounds for faith. To
dig among the rocks or search under the sea for evidence
to support the Scriptures is to insult the One who
wrote them. H32

To attempt the impossible God must give faith or
there will be none, and He gives faith to the obedient
heart only. H33

Faith and morals are two sides of the same coin.
Indeed the very essence of faith is moral. Any professed
faith in Christ as personal Saviour that does not bring
the life under plenary obedience to Christ as Lord is
inadequate and must betray its victim at the last. H33

Faith as the Bible knows it is confidence in God and His Son Jesus Christ; it is the response of the soul to the divine character as revealed in the Scriptures; and even this response is impossible apart from the prior inworking of the Holy Spirit. H33

Faith is a miracle; it is the ability God gives to trust His Son, and anything that does not result in action in accord with the will of God is not faith, but something else short of it. H33

True faith is not passive but active. It requires that we meet certain conditions, that we allow the teachings of Christ to dominate our total lives from the moment we believe. H61

True faith brings a spiritual and moral transformation and an inward witness that cannot be mistaken. These come when we stop believing in belief and start believing in the Lord Jesus Christ indeed. H61

The man of saving faith must be willing to be different from others. H61

Faith leaves no area of the new believer's life unaffected. H63

Faith in faith has displaced faith in God in too many places. H65

True faith is never found alone; it is always accompanied by expectation. The man who believes the promises of God expects to see them fulfilled. Where there is no expectation there is no faith. K134

Real faith is not the stuff dreams are made of; rather it is tough, practical and altogether realistic. K135

Faith sees the invisible but it does not see the nonexistent. K135

Get acquainted with God through reading the
Scriptures, and faith will come naturally. L39

The faith of the Christian rests upon Christ Himself.
On Him we repose and in Him we live. L98

FAITHFULNESS

God, being who He is, cannot cease to be what He is,
and being what He is, He cannot act out of character with
Himself. He is at once faithful and immutable, so all
His words and acts must be and must remain faithful. F79

The faithfulness of God is a datum of sound theology
but to the believer it becomes far more than that: it passes
through the processes of the understanding and goes
on to become nourishing food for the soul. F80

Upon God's faithfulness rests our whole hope of
future blessedness. Only as He is faithful will His
covenants stand and His promises be honored. Only as
we have complete assurance that He is faithful may we
live in peace and look forward with assurance to the
life to come. F81

FALL OF MAN

The fall of man has created a perpetual crisis. It will
last until sin has been put down and Christ reigns over a
redeemed and restored world. D28

The Fall was a moral crisis but it has affected every
part of man's nature, moral, intellectual, psychological,
spiritual and physical. D29

Man's moral fall has clouded his vision, confused his
thinking and rendered him subject to delusion. D29

Since the fall of man the earth has been a disaster area
and everyone lives with a critical emergency. Nothing is
normal. Everything is wrong and everyone is wrong

until made right by the redeeming work of Christ and the effective operation of the Holy Spirit. G104

Had there been no Fall there would have been no incarnation, no thorns, no cross. These resulted when the divine goodness confronted the human emergency. G104

From man's standpoint, the most tragic loss suffered in the Fall was the vacating of his innermost being by the Spirit of God. H10

F E A R

No one can know the true grace of God who has not first known the fear of God. C38

Not death but sin should be our great fear. E131

When men no longer fear God, they transgress His laws without hesitation. F71

The moment we come under the protection of one of good will, fear is cast out. F99

The saving power of the Word is reserved for those for whom it is intended. The secret of the Lord is with them that fear Him. H28

If a man has not cast his fears on Christ, he must bear them himself. L86

Only that man has a right to be unafraid who has fled for refuge to the mighty Saviour. L86

To dismiss fear while the danger still exists is little short of insanity. L86

F E E L I N G S
(see also MOOD)

It is much more important that we think godly

thoughts and will to do God's will than that we feel "spiritual." L73

Religious feelings may and do vary so greatly from person to person, or even in the same person they may vary so widely from one time to the next, that it is never safe to trust them. L74

FLESH
(see also COMPROMISE, WORLD)

We may sow to the flesh if we will. There will be no interference from above. M86–87

FORGIVENESS

The idea that God will pardon a rebel who has not given up his rebellion is contrary both to the Scriptures and to common sense. C43

The chronic unhappiness of most Christians may be attributed to a gnawing uneasiness lest God has not fully forgiven them, or the fear that He expects as the price of His forgiveness some sort of emotional penance which they have not furnished. G99

To be forgiven, a sin must be forsaken. H164

FREEDOM

God has made us in His likeness, and one mark of that likeness is our free will. B49

Only God is free. F108

The casual indifference with which millions of Protestants view their God-blessed religious liberty is ominous. H16

It is the Son who is the Truth that makes men free. H24

The important thing about a man is not where he goes
when he is compelled to go, but where he goes when he
is free to go where he will. H158

The true character of a people is revealed in the uses it
makes of its freedoms. H159

Freedom is liberty within bounds: liberty to obey holy
laws, liberty to keep the commandments of Christ, to
serve mankind, to develop to the full all the latent
possibilities within our redeemed natures. K149

True Christian liberty never sets us free to indulge our
lusts or to follow our fallen impulses. K149

Freedom is priceless. Where it is present almost any
kind of life is enjoyable. When it is absent life can never be
enjoyed; it can only be endured. K149

Too much liberty weakens whatever it touches. K150

Unqualified freedom in any area of human life is
deadly. In government it is anarchy, in domestic life free
love, and in religion antinomianism. K150

A healthy society requires that its members accept a
limited freedom. Each must curtail his own liberty that all
may be free, and this law runs throughout all the
created universe, including the kingdom of God. K150

The ideal Christian is one who knows he is free to do
as he will and *wills* to be a servant. K152

F R I E N D

God, being perfect, has capacity for perfect
friendship. G120

The highest privilege granted to man on earth is to be
admitted into the circle of the friends of God. G120

The true friend of God may sit in His presence for
long periods in silence. Complete trust needs no word of
assurance. G121

God is not satisfied until there exists between Him
and His people a relaxed informality that requires no
artificial stimulation. G121

True friends trust each other. G121

To seek to be friends with those who will not be the
friends of Christ is to be a traitor to our Lord. H168

G

GIFTS AND GIVING

God's gifts now take the place of God, and the whole course of nature is upset by the monstrous substitution. A22

Our gifts and talents should also be turned over to Him. They should be recognized for what they are, God's loan to us, and should never be considered in any sense our own. A28

That eternal life which was with the Father is now the possession of believing men, and that life is not God's gift only, but His very Self. B27

There is a place in the religious experience where we love God for Himself alone, with never a thought of His benefits. C149

The Just died for the unjust; and because He did, the unjust may now live with the Just in complete moral congruity. Thanks be to God for His unspeakable gift. D49

"For Thy sake" will rescue the little, empty things from vanity and give them eternal meaning. D70

To God there are no small offerings if they are made in the name of His Son. D71

Any talent may be used for evil as well as for good, but every talent comes from God nevertheless. D93

God's gifts in nature have their limitations. They are finite because they have been created, but the gift of eternal life in Christ Jesus is as limitless as God. F47

The God who gave all *to* us will continue to give all *through* us as we come to know Him better. F116

God giveth to all men liberally, but it would be absurd to think that God's liberality will make a man more godly than he wants to be. G63

No man gives anything acceptable to God until he has first given himself in love and sacrifice. G105

No man gives at all until he has given all. G105

Not by its size is my gift judged, but by how much of me there is in it. G105

It is the nature of God to share. His mighty acts of creation and redemption were done for His good pleasure, but His pleasure extends to all created things. H59

Four considerations should govern our Christian giving. They are: (1) That we give systematically; (2) that we give from a right motive; (3) that we give enough in proportion to what we possess, and (4) that we give to the right place or places. K146

My giving will be rewarded not by how much I gave but by how much I had left. K147

G L O R Y

God's glory is and must forever remain the Christian's true point of departure. Anything that begins anywhere else, whatever it is, is certainly not New Testament Christianity. D23

Everything God does is praiseworthy and deserves
our deepest admiration. Whether He is making or
redeeming a world, He is perfect in all His doings and
glorious in all His goings forth. E119

God acts only for His glory and whatever comes from
Him must be to His own high honor. Any doctrine, any
experience that serves to magnify Him is likely to be
inspired by Him. Conversely, anything that veils His
glory or makes Him appear less wonderful is sure to be
of the flesh or the devil. H122

G O D

God is a Person and in the deep of His mighty nature
He thinks, wills, enjoys, feels, loves, desires and suffers as
any other person may. In making Himself known to
us He stays by the familiar pattern of personality. A13

The modern scientist has lost God amid the wonders
of this world; we Christians are in real danger of losing
God amid the wonders of His Word! A13

God is a Person and, as such, can be cultivated as any
person can. A13

The world is perishing for lack of the knowledge of
God and the church is famishing for want of His
presence. A38

What a broad world to roam in, what a sea to swim in
is this God and Father of our Lord Jesus Christ. A39

God is so vastly wonderful, so utterly and completely
delightful that He can, without anything other than
Himself, meet and overflow the deepest demands of
our total nature, mysterious and deep as that nature is. A42

God has objective existence independent of and apart
from any notions which we may have concerning
Him. A55

God is real. He is real in the absolute and final sense
that nothing else is. A55

Back of all, above all, before all is God; first in
sequential order, above in rank and station, exalted in
dignity and honor. A101

God was our original habitat and our hearts cannot
but feel at home when they enter again that ancient and
beautiful abode. A104

Nothing will or can restore order till our hearts make
the great decision; God shall be exalted above. A105

For all things God is the great Antecedent. Because He
is, we are and everything else is. He is that "dread,
unbeginning One," self-caused, self-contained and
self-sufficient. B20

Begin where we will. God is there first. B20

We cannot think rightly of God until we begin to
think of Him as always being *there,* and *there first.* B20

God hates artificiality and pretense. B33

God in His essential Being is unique in the only sense
that word will bear. That is, there is nothing like Him in
the universe. What He is cannot be conceived by the
mind because He is "altogether other" than anything with
which we have had experience before. B95

No man has ever entertained a thought which can be
said to describe God in any but the vaguest and most
imperfect sense. Where God is known at all it must be
otherwise than by our creature-reason. B95

Just because God cannot tell us *what He is* He very
often tells us *what He is like.* B96

We have as much of God as we actually want. B124

He is not hard to please, though He may be hard to satisfy. C15

God is the most winsome of all beings and His service one of unspeakable pleasure. C15

God is the sum of all patience and the essence of kindly good will. C16

For each of us the time is surely coming when we shall have nothing but God. C50

To God quality is vastly important and size matters little. When set in opposition to size, quality is everything and size nothing. D26

God is spirit and His universe is basically spiritual. D26

God simply is without qualification. "I AM THAT I AM" is how He in condescending patience accounts to created intelligence for His uncreated Being. D72

God has no size, for the obvious reason that none of the attributes of matter apply to Him and size is an attribute of matter. D72

To attribute size to God is to make Him subject to degrees, which He can never be, seeing that the very idea of degree relates to created things only. D72

That which is infinite cannot be greater or less, larger or smaller, and God is infinite. D72

In God there is motion, but never wasted motion; He always works toward a predetermined end. D101

God contains past and future in His own all-encompassing Being. To Him every event has already occurred, or perhaps it would be more accurate to say it is occurring. With Him there can never be a memory of things past nor an expectation of things to come, but only a knowledge of all things past and future as instantaneously present before His mind. D115

In God there is no *was* or *will be,* but a continuous and unbroken *is.* In Him history and prophecy are one and the same. D115

Everything that God is accords with all else that He is. Every thought He entertains is one with every other thought. His attitude toward sin and righteousness and life and death and human misery has not changed but remains exactly what it has been from the dark beginnings of precreation times before mankind had emerged into the stream of history. D116

God is not contained: He contains. D120

God is the essence of all beauty, the fountain of all spiritual sweetness that can be known or desired by moral beings. D124

Always God must be first. E110

God is not like anything; that is, He is not *exactly* like anything or anybody. F6

To admit that there is One who lies beyond us, who exists outside of all our categories, who will not be dismissed with a name, who will not appear before the bar of our reason, nor submit to our curious inquiries: this requires a great deal of humility, more than most of us possess, so we save face by thinking God down to our level, or at least down to where we can manage Him. Yet how He eludes us! For He is everywhere while He is nowhere, for "where" has to do with matter and

space, and God is independent of both. He is
unaffected by time or motion, is wholly self-dependent
and owes nothing to the worlds His hands have
made. F26

God cannot be elevated. Nothing is above Him,
nothing beyond Him. Any motion in His direction is
elevation for the creature; away from Him, descent.
He holds His position out of Himself and by leave of
none. As no one can promote Him, so no one can
degrade Him. F33

God needs no defenders. He is the eternal
Undefended. F34

In His love and pity God came to us as Christ. F35

The God of Abraham has withdrawn His conscious
Presence from us, and another god whom our fathers
knew not is making himself at home among us. This
god we have made and because we have made him we
can understand him; because we have created him he
can never surprise us, never overwhelm us, nor astonish
us, nor transcend us. F43

Whatever God is and all that God is, He is without
limit. F45

God never hurries. There are no deadlines against
which He must work. F47

We benefit eternally by God's being just what He
is. F93

We must take refuge from God in God. F107

God always acts like Himself. G42

God is uncreated, self-existent, infinite, sovereign,
eternal; these attributes are His alone and by their very

definition cannot be shared with another. G120

God being who He is must always be sought for
Himself, never as a means toward something else. H56

Whoever seeks God as a means toward desired ends
will not find God. The mighty God, the maker of heaven
and earth, will not be one of many treasures, not even
the chief of all treasures. He will be all in all or He will be
nothing. God will not be used. His mercy and grace
are infinite and His patient understanding is beyond
measure, but He will not aid men in their selfish
striving after personal gain. He will not help men to attain
ends which, when attained, usurp the place He by
every right should hold in their interest and affection. H57

God's primary reason for everything is His own good
pleasure. H58

Some things are not debatable; there is no other side to
them. There is only God's side. H114

God is a just and holy Being who will not trifle with
men nor allow them to trifle with Him. K40

In God every moment is new and nothing ever gets
old. K106

GOD AND MAN

You and I are in little (our sins excepted) what God is
in large. Being made in His image we have within us the
capacity to know Him. A14

God is spirit and only the spirit of man can know Him
really. A40

Every soul belongs to God and exists by His pleasure.
God being who and what He is, and we being who and
what we are, the only thinkable relation between us is

one of full Lordship on His part and complete submission on ours. A102

A man by his sin may waste himself, which is to waste that which on earth is most like God. This is man's greatest tragedy, God's heaviest grief. C99

Nothing, no one, can hinder God or a good man! C128

Man has no say about the time or the place of his birth; God determines that without consulting the man himself. C158

Man in the plan of God has been permitted considerable say; but never is he permitted to utter the first word nor the last. That is the prerogative of the Deity, and one which He will never surrender to His creatures. C158

God reserves the right to take up at the last where He began at the first, and you are in the hands of God whether you will or not. C159

Until a man has gotten into trouble with his heart he is not likely to get out of trouble with God. C159

To know man we must begin with God. D20

We try to climb up to high position when God has ordained that we go down. D51

God made man in His own image and gave him intellect, emotion and will along with moral perception and the ability to know and worship his Creator. D73

It is dissimilarity that creates the sense of remoteness between creatures and between men and God. D121

God is not greater for our being, nor would He be less if we did not exist. That we do exist is altogether of God's free determination, not by our desert nor by divine necessity. F34

When Jesus walked on earth He was a man acting like God; but equally wonderful is it that He was also God acting like Himself in man and in a man. G39

God does not dwell passively in His people; He *wills* and *works* in them. G42

God and man exist for each other and neither is satisfied without the other. G83

The greatest need of the human personality is to experience God Himself. This is because of who God is and who and what man is. G83

The image of God currently popular is that of a distracted Father, struggling in heartbroken desperation to get people to accept a Saviour of whom they feel no need and in whom they have very little interest. To persuade these self-sufficient souls to respond to His generous offers God will do almost anything, even using salesmanship methods and talking down to them in the chummiest way imaginable. This view of things is, of course, a kind of religious romanticism which, while it often uses flattering and sometimes embarrassing terms in praise of God, manages nevertheless to make man the star of the show. H27

God is Himself the end for which man was created. H58

To be right with God has often meant to be in trouble with men. H114

To bring ourselves into a place where God will be eternally pleased with us should be the first responsible act of every man. K38

That God should be glorified in us is so critically important that it stands in lonely grandeur, a moral imperative more compelling than any other which the human heart can acknowledge. K38

Seeing who God is and who we are, a right relationship between God and us is of vital importance. K38

God desires that all men should become Christlike, for in so doing they present larger and more perfect objects for the reception of His outpoured love. L45

No man is ever the same after God has laid His hand upon him. L143

GOODNESS OF GOD

The fellowship of God is delightful beyond all telling. He communes with His redeemed ones in an easy, uninhibited fellowship that is restful and healing to the soul. He is not sensitive nor selfish nor temperamental. C15

God is the sum of all patience and the essence of kindly good will. We please Him most, not by frantically trying to make ourselves good, but by throwing ourselves into His arms with all our imperfections, and believing that He understands everything and loves us still. C15

How good it would be if we could learn that God is easy to live with. He remembers our frame and knows that we are dust. C16

The goodness of God is the drive behind all the blessings He daily bestows upon us. God created us because He felt good in His heart and He redeemed us for the same reason. [F82]

To allow that God could be other than good is to deny the validity of all thought and end in the negation of every moral judgment. [F82]

If God is not good, then there can be no distinction between kindness and cruelty, and heaven can be hell and hell, heaven. [F82]

Divine goodness, as one of God's attributes, is self-caused, infinite, perfect, and eternal. Since God is immutable He never varies in the intensity of His loving-kindness. He has never been kinder than He now is, nor will He ever be less kind. [F83]

Always God's goodness is the ground of our expectation. [F83]

Though the kindness of God is an infinite, overflowing fountain of cordiality, God will not force His attention upon us. [F84]

To the frightened He is friendly, to the poor in spirit He is forgiving, to the ignorant, considerate; to the weak, gentle; to the stranger, hospitable. [F84]

The greatness of God rouses fear within us, but His goodness encourages us not to be afraid of Him. To fear and not be afraid—that is the paradox of faith. [F84]

As mercy is God's goodness confronting human misery and guilt, so grace is His goodness directed toward human debt and demerit. [F93]

G O S P E L

At the heart of the Christian message is God Himself
waiting for His redeemed children to push in to conscious
awareness of His Presence. A37

If we would know the power of the Christian message
our nature must be invaded by an Object from beyond it;
that That which is external must become internal; that
the objective Reality which is God must cross the
threshold of our personality and take residence
within. B-Preface

The gospel is not good news only, but a judgment as
well upon everyone that hears it. B35

The message of the Cross is good news indeed for the
penitent, but to those who "obey not the gospel" it
carries an overtone of warning. B35

There is about the gospel an urgency, a finality which
will not be heard or felt except by the enabling of the
Spirit. B35

For sinners who want to cease being willful sinners
and become obedient children of God the gospel message
is one of unqualified peace, but it is by its very nature
also an arbiter of the future destinies of men. B35

The God who by the *word* of the gospel *proclaims* men
free, by the *power* of the gospel *actually makes them free*.
To accept less than this is to know the gospel in word
only, without its power. B39

The gospel has power to deliver men from the
tyranny of social approval and make them free to do the
will of God. B42

The message of the gospel . . . is the message of a
new creation in the midst of an old, the message of the

invasion of our human nature by the eternal life of God and the displacing of the old by the new. B42

The message of Christ lays hold upon a man with the intention to alter him, to mold him again after another image and make of him something altogether different from what he had been before. C57

The Gospel not only furnishes transforming power to remold the human heart; it provides also a model after which the new life is to be fashioned, and that model is Christ Himself. C59

The gospel in its scriptural context puts the glory of God first and the salvation of man second. D23

The gospel is light but only the Spirit can give sight. D63

The glory of the gospel is its freedom. E73

The gospel message embodies three distinct elements: an announcement, a command, and a call. It announces the good news of redemption accomplished in mercy; it commands all men everywhere to repent and it calls all men to surrender to the terms of grace by believing on Jesus Christ as Lord and Saviour. F112

The witness of the church is most effective when she declares rather than explains, for the gospel is addressed not to reason but to faith. G11

The teachings of Christ reveal Him to be a realist in the finest meaning of that word. Nowhere in the Gospels do we find anything visionary or overoptimistic. He told His hearers the whole truth and let them make up their minds. He might grieve over the retreating form of an inquirer who could not face up to the truth, but He

never ran after him to try to win him with rosy
promises. He would have men follow Him, knowing the
cost, or He would let them go their ways. G116

One of the glories of the Christian gospel is its ability
not only to deliver a man from sin but to orient him, to
place him on a peak from which he can see yesterday
and today in their relation to tomorrow. H94

The Christian gospel is a message of freedom through
grace and we must stand fast in the liberty wherewith
Christ has made us free. H160

The gospel is the official proclamation that Christ died
for us and is risen again, with the added announcement
that everyone who will believe, and as a result of that
belief will cast in his lot with Christ in full and final
committal, shall be saved eternally. K39

The gospel message declares that the wronged God
took the wrong upon Himself in order that the one who
committed the wrong might be saved. L19

The gospel message includes the idea of amendment,
of separation from the world, of cross-carrying and
loyalty to the kingdom of God even unto death. L19

The Christian message has ceased to be a
pronouncement and has become a proposition. L55

The gospel is a divine thing. It receives no virtue from
any of man's religions or philosophies. It came down to
us out of heaven. M46

GOVERNMENT

Any form of human government, however lofty,
deals with the citizen only as long as he lives. At the
graveside it bids him adieu. It may have made his
journey a little easier, and, if so, all lovers of the human

race will thank God for that. But in the cool earth,
slaves and free men lie down together. M46

G R A C E

No one can know the true grace of God who has not
first known the fear of God. C38

Abounding sin is the terror of the world, but
abounding grace is the hope of mankind. F47

It is by His grace that God imputes merit where none
previously existed and declares no debt to be where one
had been before. F93

Grace is the good pleasure of God that inclines Him to
bestow benefits upon the undeserving. F93

Grace takes its rise far back in the heart of God, in the
awful and incomprehensible abyss of His holy being; but
the channel through which it flows out to men is Jesus
Christ, crucified and risen. F93

God will always be Himself, and grace is an attribute
of His holy being. He can no more hide His grace than
the sun can hide its brightness. F94

In olden times men looked forward to Christ's
redeeming work; in later times they gaze back upon it,
but always they came and they come by grace,
through faith. F95

The grace of God is infinite and eternal. As it had no
beginning, so it can have no end, and being an attribute of
God, it is as boundless as infinitude. F95

No one was ever saved other than by grace, from
Abel to the present moment. F95

All thanks be to God for grace abounding. F96

Grace in its true New Testament meaning is foreign
to human reason, not because it is contrary to reason but
because it lies beyond it. The doctrine of grace had to
be revealed; it could not have been discovered. G98

Grace will save a man but it will not save him and his
idol. H90

The operations of grace within the heart of a believing
man will turn that heart away from sin and toward
holiness. H132

G R A T I T U D E

Thanksgiving has great curative power. C123

A thankful heart cannot be cynical. C123

We cannot be too grateful, for it would be like loving
too much or being too kind. L162

Gratitude is an offering precious in the sight of God,
and it is one that the poorest of us can make and be not
poorer but richer for having made it. L162

Gratitude felt and expressed becomes a healing, life-
building force in the soul. L162

G R E A T N E S S

The way to spiritual greatness has always been
through much suffering and inward pain. B124

True greatness lies in character, not in ability or
position. D50

The greatness that men seem to have is as the
greatness of moonlight, which is but the glory of the sun
reflected. Man's glory is borrowed. H116

HAPPINESS
(see also JOY)

The true Christian ideal is not to be happy but to be holy. B100

God being a God of infinite goodness must by the necessity of His nature will for each of His creatures the fullest measure of happiness consistent with its capacities and with the happiness of all other creatures. D135

A selfish desire for happiness is as sinful as any other selfish desire because its root is in the flesh which can never have any standing before God! E43

The whole hectic scramble after happiness is an evil as certainly as is the scramble after money or fame or success. It springs out of a vast misunderstanding of ourselves and of our true moral state. E44

The doctrine of man's inalienable right to happiness is anti-God and anti-Christ. E45

The man who really knows himself can never believe in his right to be happy. E45

No man should desire to be happy who is not at the same time holy. E46

God has charged Himself with full responsibility for our eternal happiness and stands ready to take over the management of our lives the moment we turn in faith to Him. F63

I do not believe that it is the will of God that we should seek to be happy, but rather that we should seek to be holy and useful. H104

There is an ignoble pursuit of irresponsible happiness among us. H104

There are times when it's sinful to be happy. H104

Things cannot bring happiness; they can only add more weight to the already overburdened heart. L131

In this day of universal apprehension when men's hearts are failing them for fear of those things that are coming upon the earth, we Christians are strategically placed to display a happiness that is not of this world and to exhibit a tranquillity that will be a little bit of heaven here below. M52

H E A R T
(see also INNER MAN, SPIRIT, SPIRITUALITY)

God made us for Himself: that is the only explanation that satisfies the heart of a thinking man, whatever his wild reason may say. A33

The holy heart alone can be the habitation of the Holy Ghost. B100

Until a man has gotten into trouble with his heart he is not likely to get out of trouble with God. C39

The human heart lives by its sympathies and affections. C67

The human heart cannot exist in a vacuum. If men do not have joy in their hearts they will seek it somewhere else. C68

The widest thing in the universe is not space; it is the potential capacity of the human heart. C112

Only God can work in the heart. C114

If we surrender our hearts to God we may expect a wondrous enlargement. C115

Keep your heart with all diligence and God will look after the universe! D67

God is more concerned with the state of people's hearts than with the state of their feelings. E45

To the pure in heart nothing really bad can happen. E133

The human heart is heretical by nature. Popular religious beliefs should be checked carefully against the Word of God, for they are almost certain to be wrong. G98

Make your heart a vacuum and the Spirit will rush in to fill it. H41

The human heart is heretical by nature and runs to error as naturally as a garden to weeds. H162

HEAVEN AND HELL

The most godly Christian is the one who knows himself best, and no one who knows himself will believe that he deserves anything better than hell. D136

We inhabit a world suspended halfway between heaven and hell, alienated from one and not yet abandoned to the other. D140

Hell is a place of no pleasure because there is no love there. F101

The man who is seriously convinced that he deserves to go to hell is not likely to go there, while the man who

believes that he is worthy of heaven will certainly
never enter that blessed place. H15

H I S T O R Y

History is little more than the story of man's sin, and
the daily newspaper a running commentary on it. D124

H O L I N E S S

If we would do holy deeds we must be holy men,
every day and all the days that God grants us here
below. C107

Go to God and have an understanding. Tell Him that
it is your desire to be holy at any cost and then ask Him
never to give you more happiness than holiness. E46

We have learned to live with unholiness and have
come to look upon it as the natural and expected
thing. F103

We cannot grasp the true meaning of the divine
holiness by thinking of someone or something very pure
and then raising the concept to the highest degree we
are capable of. God's holiness is not simply the best we
know infinitely bettered. F104

We know nothing like the divine holiness. It stands
apart, unique, unapproachable, incomprehensible and
unattainable. The natural man is blind to it. He may
fear God's power and admire His wisdom, but His
holiness he cannot even imagine. F104

Holy is the way God is. To be holy He does not
conform to a standard. He is that standard. He is
absolutely holy with an infinite, incomprehensible
fullness of purity that is incapable of being other than it
is. F105

God is holy and He has made holiness the moral
condition necessary to the health of His universe. Sin's

temporary presence in the world only accents this. F106

Whatever is holy is healthy; evil is a moral sickness that must end ultimately in death. F106

The holiness of God, the wrath of God, and the health of the creation are inseparably united. God's wrath is His utter intolerance of whatever degrades and destroys. F106

Holiness God can and does impart to His children. He shares it with them by imputation and by impartation, and because He has made it available to them through the blood of the Lamb, He requires it of them. F106

We must take refuge from God in God. Above all we must believe that God sees us perfect in His Son while He disciplines and chastens and purges us that we may be partakers of His holiness. F106

Before the uncreated fire of God's holiness angels veil their faces. F106

We must hide our unholiness in the wounds of Christ. F107

Watchfulness, prayer, self-discipline and acquiescence in the purposes of God are indispensable to any real progress in holiness. G54

There are many who wish they were holy or victorious or joyful but are not willing to meet God's conditions to obtain. G64

Every man is as holy as he really wants to be. But the want must be all-compelling. H40

The holy man will be the useful man and he's likely to be a happy man too; but if he seeks happiness and forgets holiness and usefulness, he's a carnal man. H104

Wherever the holiness of God confronts unholiness there is conflict. This conflict arises from the irreconcilable natures of holiness and sin. H110

God's first concern for His universe is its moral health, that is, its holiness, whatever is contrary to this is necessarily under His eternal displeasure. H110

HOLY SPIRIT

It is time for us to seek again the leadership of the Holy Ghost. Man's lordship has cost us too much. B47

The idea of the Spirit held by the average church member is so vague as to be nearly nonexistent. B66

One quality belonging to the Holy Spirit, of great interest and importance to every seeking heart, is penetrability. He can penetrate matter, such as the human body; He can penetrate mind; He can penetrate another spirit, such as the human spirit. He can achieve complete penetration of and actual intermingling with the human spirit. He can invade the human heart and make room for Himself without expelling anything essentially human. The integrity of the human personality remains unimpaired. Only moral evil is forced to withdraw. B69

There can be no doubt that the need above all other needs in the Church of God at this moment is the power of the Holy Spirit. B92

Only the Spirit can save us from the numbing unreality of Spiritless Christianity. B93

For our deep trouble there is no cure apart from a visitation, yes, an *invasion* of power from above. Only the Spirit Himself can show us what is wrong with us and only the Spirit can prescribe the cure. B93

Only the inworking of the Spirit's power can discover to us the solemn majesty and the heart ravishing mystery of the Triune God. B93

The Holy Spirit is first of all *a moral flame.* B99

The Holy Spirit is a living Person and should be treated as a person. B126

For multitudes of professed Christians today the Holy Spirit is not a necessity. They have learned to cheer their hearts and warm their hands at other fires. C69

The inward operation of the Holy Spirit is necessary to saving faith. D63

When the Spirit presents Christ to our inner vision it has an exhilarating effect on the soul much as wine has on the body. E9

God has given us the Holy Spirit to illuminate our minds. He is eyes and understanding to us. We dare not try to get on without Him. G52

The work of the Spirit in the human heart is not an unconscious or automatic thing. Human will and intelligence must yield to and cooperate with the benign intentions of God. G54

There are two spirits abroad in the earth: the spirit that works in the children of disobedience and the Spirit of God. These two can never be reconciled in time or in eternity. The spirit that dwells in the once-born is forever opposed to the Spirit that inhabits the heart of the twice-born. H21

The Spirit is an imperative necessity. Only the Eternal Spirit can do eternal deeds. H66

The man who has been taught by the Holy Spirit will be a seer rather than a scholar. The difference is that the scholar sees and the seer sees through; and that is a mighty difference indeed. H150

God does His work by the operation of the Spirit, while Christian leaders attempt to do theirs by the power of trained and devoted intellect. Bright personality has taken the place of the divine afflatus. K93

The Holy Spirit never differs from Himself, and wherever He touches a human mind His sure marks are always present so plainly that there can be no mistaking them. M103

The Holy Spirit teaches the same thing to everyone; however different the subjects may be from each other, the fine touch of the Spirit's hand may be detected on each one. M103

H O N O R

Our great honor lies in being just what Jesus was and is. To be accepted by those who accept Him, rejected by all who reject Him, loved by those who love Him and hated by everyone that hates Him. What greater glory could come to any man? D59

To be called to follow Christ is a high honor; higher indeed than any honor men can bestow upon each other. H11

Before God and the angels it is a great honor to follow Christ, but before men it is not so. The Christ the world pretends now to honor was once rejected and crucified by that same world. The great saint is honored only after he is dead. H14

H U M I L I T Y

For the Christian, humility is absolutely indispensable.
Without it there can be no self-knowledge, no repentance,
no faith and no salvation. K138

[There are] two classes of Christians: the proud who
imagine they are humble and the humble who are afraid
they are proud. There should be another class: the self-
forgetful who leave the whole thing in the hands of Christ
and refuse to waste any time trying to make
themselves good. They will reach the goal far ahead of
the rest. K141

I

IDOLATRY

Among the sins to which the human heart is prone, hardly any other is more hateful to God than idolatry, for idolatry is at bottom a libel on His character. F3

The idolatrous heart assumes that God is other than He is—in itself a monstrous sin—and substitutes for the true God one made after its own likeness. F3

The essence of idolatry is the entertainment of thoughts about God that are unworthy of Him. F3

IMAGE OF GOD

God has made us in His likeness, and one mark of that likeness is our free will. B49

Everything that God does in His ransomed children has as its long range purpose the final restoration of the divine image in human nature. Everything looks forward to the consummation. C60

The widest thing in the universe is not space; it is the potential capacity of the human heart. Being made in the image of God, it is capable of almost unlimited extension in all directions. C112

God never abandoned the creatures made in His image. D29

One soul made in the image of God is more precious to Him than all the starry universe. Astronomy deals with space and matter and motion; theology deals with life and personality and the mystery of being. D75

We tend by a secret law of the soul to move toward our mental image of God. [F1]

When the Scripture states that man was made in the image of God, we dare not add to that statement an idea from our own head and make it mean "in the *exact* image." To do so is to make man a replica of God, and that is to lose the unicity of God and end with no God at all. [F7]

The sovereign God has permitted us to have a measure of conditional sovereignty, a mark of the divine image once given at the Creation and partially lost by the Fall. [M86]

IMMUTABILITY OF GOD

God cannot change for the better. Since He is perfectly holy, He has never been less holy than He is now and can never be holier than He is and has always been. Neither can God change for the worse. [F49]

One who can suffer any slightest degree of change is neither self-existent, self-sufficient, nor eternal, and so is not God. [F50]

God is self-existent, He is not composed. There are in Him no parts to be altered. [F50]

The law of mutation belongs to a fallen world, but God is immutable, and in Him men of faith find at last eternal permanence. [F51]

God never changes moods or cools off in His affections or loses enthusiasm. [F53]

Nothing has entered the being of God from eternity, nothing has been removed, and nothing has been changed. [F87]

INCARNATION

In His love and pity God came to us as Christ. F35

The man who walked among us was a demonstration, not of unveiled deity but of perfect humanity. The awful majesty of the Godhead was mercifully sheathed in the soft envelope of human nature to protect mankind. F35

We know how God would act if He were in our place—*He has been in our place*. It is the mystery of godliness that God was manifest in human flesh. G39

We know how God acts in heaven because we saw Him act on earth. G39

God did not visit the race to rescue it; in Christ He took human nature unto Himself, and now He is one of us. L151

INDIVIDUALITY

A community of believers must be composed of persons who have each one met God in individual experience. D113

Any forward step in the Church must begin with the individual. F114

The church in any locality is what its individual members are, no better and no worse. L154

We will find that we have within us a secret garden where no one can enter except ourself and God. Not only does no one else enter, no one else *can* enter. M104

This secret inner chamber is the sacred trysting place for Christ and the believing soul; no one among all our dearest friends has the open sesame that will permit him to enter there. M104

I N F I N I T U D E

When we say that God is infinite we mean that He knows *no bounds.* F45

God's infinitude belongs to us and is made known to us for our everlasting profit. F46

The Christian man possesses God's own life and shares His infinitude with Him. F47

Only the Infinite can know the infinite. F57

We do not say "more unique" or "very infinite." Before infinitude we stand silent. F59

I N F L U E N C E

We fashion ourselves by exposing our lives to the molding influences, good or bad, that lie around us:

> —*Friends,*
> —*Literature,*
> —*Music,*
> —*Pleasures,*
> —*Ambitions,*
> —*Thoughts.* D128

The Scriptures, critical self-discipline, honesty of heart and increased trust in the inward operations of the Holy Spirit will save us from being too greatly influenced by temperament. H84

I N N E R   M A N
(see also HEART, SPIRIT, SPIRITUALITY)

Let us beware of tinkering with our inner life, hoping ourselves to rend the veil. God must do everything for us. Our part is to yield and trust. A47

A spiritual kingdom lies all about us, enclosing us, embracing us, altogether within reach of our inner selves, waiting for us to recognize it. A52

Being has ceased to have much appeal for people and
doing engages almost everyone's attention. C75

Modern Christians lack symmetry. They know
almost nothing about the inner life. C75

It is the inner world that matters, because that is the
only world over which we have control and the only one
for which we shall be held responsible. The inner
world consists of our thoughts and emotions, presided
over by our will. D65

Deep inside every man there is a private sanctum
where dwells the mysterious essence of his being. H9

Inward assurance comes out of the stillness. We must
be still to know. K15

It is enough to believe the Scriptures, and they make it
very clear that a human being is essentially a spirit clothed
in a body, and that the inner life is the key to all the rest
of the life. M82

The whole Bible magnifies the inner and eternal part
of man and lays correspondingly lighter emphasis upon
the external and temporal. M82

The solution to life's problems is spiritual because the
essence of life is spiritual. It is astonishing how many
difficulties clear up without any effort when the inner
life gets straightened out. M83

Church difficulties are spiritual also and admit of a
spiritual answer. Whatever may be wrong in the life of
any church may be cleared up by recognizing the
quality of the trouble and dealing with it at the root. M83

J

J O Y
(see also HAPPINESS)

In God there is life enough for all and time enough to enjoy it. F47

True Christian joy is the heart's harmonious response to the Lord's song of love. F102

The Christian owes it to the world to be supernaturally joyful. M52

The "keep smiling" school of applied psychology is not even remotely related to the true faith of Christ. M52

True joy cannot be artificially induced. M52

The fountain of Christian joy flows out from the throne of God, pure, refreshing and sweet everlastingly. M52–53

J U D G M E N T

Neither science nor learning can quench the fires of judgment in that day, but a Christian can steal a quick look at Calvary and know that his judgment is past. D111

We have not been able to bring earth to the judgment of heaven so we have brought heaven to the judgment of the earth. Pity us, Lord, for we know not what we do! H56

Christ stands before no man to be judged, but every man stands before Him. L88

J U S T I C E

Justice, when used of God, is a name we give to the
way God is, nothing more; and when God acts justly He
is not doing so to conform to an independent criterion,
but simply acting like Himself in a given situation. F87

God's compassion flows out of His goodness, and
goodness without justice is not goodness. God spares us
because He is good, but He could not be good if He
were not just. F88

Through the work of Christ in atonement, justice is
not violated but satisfied when God spares a sinner. F88

Redemptive theology teaches that mercy does not
become effective toward a man until justice has done its
work. F88

Justice discharged and mercy operative is more than a
pleasant theological theory; it announces a fact made
necessary by our deep human need. F89

Because of our sin we are all under sentence of death,
a judgment which resulted when justice confronted our
moral situation. F89

God's justice stands forever against the sinner in utter
severity. The vague and tenuous hope that God is too
kind to punish the ungodly has become a deadly opiate
for the consciences of millions. It hushes their fears and
allows them to practice all pleasant forms of iniquity
while death draws every day nearer and the command to
repent goes unregarded. As responsible moral beings
we dare not so trifle with our eternal future. F89

KNOWLEDGE

The way to deeper knowledge of God is through the lonely valleys of soul poverty and abnegation of all things. A23

The man who would know God must give time to Him. B22

Knowledge by acquaintance is always better than mere knowledge by description, and the first does not presuppose the second nor require it. B67

A man can die of starvation knowing all about bread, and a man can remain spiritually dead while knowing all the historic facts of Christianity. B68

The Christian is strong or weak depending upon how closely he has cultivated the knowledge of God. C11

God can be known satisfactorily only as we devote time to Him. C12

God will respond to our efforts to know Him. C13

The yearning to know What cannot be known, to comprehend the Incomprehensible, to touch and taste the Unapproachable, arises from the image of God in the nature of man. F9

We can never know who or what we are till we know at least something of what God is. F28

The God we must learn to know is the Majesty in the heavens, God the Father Almighty, Maker of heaven and earth, the only wise God our Saviour. F114

To know God is at once the easiest and the most difficult thing in the world. F115

To know God it is necessary that we be like God to some degree, for things wholly dissimilar cannot agree and beings wholly unlike can never have communion with each other. G84

To know God well he [the Christian] must think on Him unceasingly. G135

All of God is accessible to you through Christ. Cultivate His knowledge above everything else on earth. H40

Knowledge to be our own must be digested by thinking. H147

In the Scriptures knowledge is a kind of experience and wisdom has a moral content. Knowledge without humility is vanity. K122

In the Christian life we know most when we know that we do not know, and we understand best when we know that we understand little and that there is much that we will never understand. K122

We cannot know God by thinking, but that we must do a lot of thinking if we would know Him well. L47

For those who know not and know they know not, there may in the mercy of God be hope: for those who think they know there can only be increasing darkness. L106

L

L A W

The way to deal with a law of God is to work along with it. M87

By faith and obedience we can put every divine law to work for us. And the law of sowing and reaping may be brought to our service and made to toil for our everlasting good. So kind is God and so thoughtful of His creatures. M87

L E A D E R S H I P
(see also MINISTRY, PREACHING, PROPHET)

The lick-spittle attitude of popular Christian leaders toward the world's celebrities would make such men as Elijah or George Fox sick to the stomach. M21

Whatever is getting the attention from our spiritual leaders is what we finally come to accept as orthodoxy in any given period of history. And right now we are definitely not hearing much about the loveliness of Jesus. M58

More and more, our religious leaders are coming to place confidence in shadows and are teaching others to do the same. And just so far as shadows are accepted as real, the one great Reality is ignored. It is hard to think how a greater tragedy could possibly come upon us. M89

L E G A L I S M

The effort to be forgiven by works is one that can never be completed because no one knows or can know how much is enough to cancel out the offense. G95

The essence of legalism is self-atonement. The seeker tries to make himself acceptable to God by some act of restitution, or by self-punishment or the feeling of regret. G98

Legalism is natural to the human heart. G98

Long after we have learned from the Scriptures that we cannot by fasting, or the wearing of a hair shirt or the making of many prayers, atone for the sins of the soul, we still tend by a kind of pernicious natural heresy to feel that we can please God and purify our souls by the penance of perpetual regret. G98

L I F E

Not to us has it been given to have life in ourselves. For life we are wholly and continually dependent upon God, the Source and Fountain of life. B54

The life that halts short of the cross is but a fugitive and condemned thing, doomed at last to be lost beyond recovery. B62

To be saved appears to be the highest ambition of most Christians today. To have eternal life and know it is the highest aspiration of many. Here they begin and here they end. C112

Whatever God is, and all that God is, He is in Himself. All life is in and from God, whether it be the lowest form of unconscious life or the highly self-conscious, intelligent life of a seraph. No creature has life in itself; all life is a gift from God. F32

Life is a short and fevered rehearsal for a concert we cannot stay to give. F46

Whatever is possessed of natural life runs through its cycle from birth to death and ceases to be, but the life of God returns upon itself and ceases never. F47

Back of every wasted life is a bad philosophy, an erroneous conception of life's worth and purpose. H94

Human life has its central core where lie the things men live by. These things are constant. They change not from age to age, but are the same among all races throughout the world always. H115

The most important thing about a life is its direction. L29

No one has any true right to claim my life except the One who gave His own life for my redemption. L57

In almost everything touching our common life on earth God is pleased when we are pleased. L77

LIFE AND DEATH

Whether we admit it or not the stroke of death is upon us, and it will be saving wisdom for us to learn to trust not in ourselves but in Him that raiseth the dead. B55

Before all who wish to follow Christ the way lies clear. It is the way of death unto life. Always life stands just beyond death and beckons the man who is sick of himself to come and know the life more abundant. But to reach the new life he must pass through the valley of the shadow of death, and . . . at the sound of those words many will turn back and follow Christ no more. But to whom shall we go? "Thou hast the words of eternal life." C61

God offers life, but not an improved old life. The life He offers is life out of death. H44

LIFE ETERNAL

When God infuses eternal life into the spirit of a man, the man becomes a member of a new and higher order of being. F52

L I G H T

The only safe light for our path is the light which is reflected from Christ, the Light of the World. B18

If He who called Himself the Light of the World was only a flickering torch, then the darkness that enshrouds the earth is here to stay. B65

The man who has met God is not looking for something—he has found it; he is not searching for light—upon him the Light has already shined. C157

To find the way we need more than light; we need also sight. D59

Forever God stands apart, in light unapproachable. F70

It is sin against light that destroys men, not the rejection of Christ, though that rejection leaves the sinner desolate in his sin and shuts him out forever from the forgiving love of God. K14

We are accountable not only for the light we have but also for the light we might have if we were willing to obey it. L100

Behind all our failure to find light is an unconfessed and possibly an unconscious love of darkness. L100

L O N E L I N E S S

Everyone of us has had experiences which we have not been able to explain: a sudden sense of loneliness, or a feeling of wonder or awe in the face of the universal vastness. A78

We are lonely with an ancient and cosmic loneliness. B23

Most of the world's great souls have been lonely. Loneliness seems to be one price the saint must pay for his saintliness. H168

The pain of loneliness arises from the constitution of our nature. God made us for each other. H172

If God is shut out, then there can be only everlasting loneliness and numb despair. M104

Where God is not known in the inner shrine, the individual must try to compensate for his sense of aloneness in whatever way he can. Most persons rush away to the world to find companionship and surround themselves with every kind of diversionary activity. All devices for killing time, every shallow scheme for entertainment, are born out of this inner loneliness. M104

L O S T N E S S

The man who dies out of Christ is said to be lost, and hardly a word in the English tongue expresses his condition with greater accuracy. He has squandered a rare fortune and at the last he stands for a fleeting moment and looks around, a moral fool, a wastrel who has lost in one overwhelming and irrecoverable loss, his soul, his life, his peace, his total, mysterious personality, his dear and everlasting all. C99

Men are lost but not abandoned; that is what the Holy Scriptures teach and that is what the Church is commissioned to declare. G30

The man who does not know where he is is lost; the man who does not know why he was born is worse lost; the man who cannot find an object worthy of his true devotion is lost utterly; and by this description the human race is lost, and it is a part of our lostness that we do not know how lost we are. H93

L O V E

We cannot love by fiat. Love is too gentle, too frail a creature to spring up at the command of another. C142

Love that can offer reasons is a rational thing and has not attained to a state of complete purity. It is not perfect love. C148

Perfect love knows no *because*. C149

Love wills the good of all and never wills harm or evil to any. F98

To know that love is of God and to enter into the secret place leaning upon the arm of the Beloved—this and only this can cast out fear. F99

Acts of self-sacrifice are common to love. F100

It is of the nature of love that it cannot lie quiescent. It is active, creative and benign. F102

The final test of love is obedience. Not sweet emotions, not willingness to sacrifice, not zeal, but obedience to the commandments of Christ. G134

No law has ever been passed that can compel one moral being to love another, for by the very nature of it love must be voluntary. No one can be coerced or frightened into loving anyone. H35

If we love God we will love His children. All true Christian experience will deepen our love for other Christians. H130

Loving wrong objects is fatal to spiritual growth; it twists and deforms the life and makes impossible the appearing of the image of Christ in the soul. It is only as we love right objects that we become right, and only as we go on loving them that we continue to experience a slow but continuous transmutation toward the objects of our purified affection. K157

What we love is therefore not a small matter to be lightly shrugged off; rather it is of present, critical and everlasting importance. It is prophetic of our future. It tells us what we shall be, and so predicts accurately our eternal destiny. K157

We are to a large degree the sum of our loves and we will of moral necessity grow into the image of what we love most; for love is among other things a creative affinity; it changes and molds and shapes and transforms. It is without doubt the most powerful agent affecting human nature next to the direct action of the Holy Spirit of God within the soul. K157

Not only are we all in process of becoming; *we are becoming what we love.* K157

Love is within our power of choice, otherwise we would not be commanded to love God nor be held accountable for not loving Him. K159

We are not responsible to *feel* but we *are* responsible to love, and true spiritual love begins in the will. K160

God is love, and is for that reason the source of all the love there is. L45

L O V E   F O R   G O D

Once the seeking heart finds God in personal experience there will be no further problem about loving Him. To know Him is to love Him and to know Him better is to love Him more. C143

The phrase "the love of God," when used by Christians, almost always refers to God's love for us. We must remember that it can also mean our love for God. C147

It is a strange and beautiful eccentricity of the free God that He has allowed His heart to be emotionally identified with men. Self-sufficient as He is, He wants our love and will not be satisfied till He gets it. Free as He is, He has let His heart be bound to us forever. F100

In the love which any intelligent creature feels for God there must always be a measure of mystery. G126

The gravest question any of us face is whether we do or do not love the Lord. G132

Love for Christ is a love of willing as well as a love of feeling, and it is psychologically impossible to love Him adequately unless we will to obey His words. G134

The first and greatest commandment is to love God with every power of our entire being. Where love like that exists there can be no place for a second object. H58

God wills that we should love Him for Himself alone with no hidden reasons, trusting Him to be to us all our natures require. H59

The taking over of the romantic love ideal into our relation to God has been extremely injurious to our Christian lives. The idea that we should "fall in love" with God is ignoble, unscriptural, unworthy of us and certainly does no honor to the Most High God. We do not come to love God by a sudden emotional visitation. Love for God results from repentance, amendment of life and a fixed determination to love Him. As God moves more perfectly into the focus of our hearts our love for Him may indeed rise and swell within us till like a flood it sweeps everything before it. K159

L O V E   O F   G O D

The highest love of God is not intellectual, it is spiritual. A40

The deep, deep love of God is the fountain out of which flows our future beatitude, and the grace of God in Christ is the channel by which it reaches us. D137

Since love cannot desire for its object anything less than the fullest possible measure of enjoyment for the longest possible time, it is virtually beyond our power to conceive of a future as consistently delightful as that which Christ is preparing for us. D138

Love . . . is not something God has and which may grow or diminish or cease to be. His love is the way God is, and when He loves He is simply being Himself. F16

His love is measureless. It is more: it is boundless. It has no bounds because it is not a thing but a facet of the essential nature of God. His love is something He *is*, and because He is infinite that love can enfold the whole created world in itself and have room for ten thousand times ten thousand worlds beside. F47

Whatever may befall us, God knows and cares as no one else can. F57

The words "God is love" mean that love is an essential attribute of God. Love is something true of God but it is not God. It expresses the way God is in His unitary being, as do the words holiness, justice, faithfulness and truth. F98

God is self-existent, His love had no beginning; because He is eternal, His love can have no end; because He is infinite, it has no limit; because He is holy, it is the quintessence of all spotless purity; because He is immense, His love is an incomprehensibly vast, bottomless, shoreless sea before which we kneel in joyful silence and from which the loftiest eloquence retreats confused and abashed. F98

God is love and God is sovereign. His love disposes Him to desire our everlasting welfare and His sovereignty enables Him to secure it. F99

God's love tells us that He is friendly and His Word assures us that He is our friend and wants us to be His friends. F99

The love of God is one of the great realities of the universe, a pillar upon which the hope of the world rests. F102

God does not love populations, He loves people. He loves not masses, but men. He loves us all with a mighty love that has no beginning and can have no end. F102

God is Himself the only being whom He can love directly; all else that He loves is for His own sake and because He finds some reflection of Himself there. L44

God being who and what He is must love Himself with pure and perfect love. L44

It is hard for a sinful man to believe that God loves Him. His own accusing conscience tells him it could not be so. L45

God is love, so His loving is not something He may do nor not do at His will. Loving us is not an intermittent act or series of acts which God does in between other acts. His love flows steadily out upon the whole human race in an unbroken and continuous fullness. M97

There is not a time, not a fraction of time, when God's love is not active toward us. It is as constant as the being of God, for it *is* the being of God in unforced, normal expression. M97

God does not love us because we are hard or easy to love; He loves us because He is God, not because we are good or bad or more attractive or less so. M97

God's love is not drawn out of Him by its object; it flows out from God in a steady stream because He is love. M97

"God so loved the world," not because the world was lovable but because God is love. Christ did not die for us that God might love us; He died for us because God already loved us from everlasting. M97

Love is not the result of redemption; it is the cause of it. M97

M

MAN

The burden borne by mankind is a heavy and a crushing thing. A111

There is hardly a man or woman who dares to be just what he or she is without doctoring up the impression. A114

We are created beings, and as such are derived, not self-existent. Not to us has it been given to have life in ourselves. B54

We must never underestimate the ability of human beings to get themselves tangled up. C83

One thing seems to be quite forgotten: the world moves and times change but people remain the same always. C155

Every human being is in a state of becoming, of passing from what he was to what he is to be. And this is as true of the Christian as of every other person. D127

Think God away and man has no ground of existence. F28

Nothing can hurt a good man. F99

What a man *is* comes first in the sight of God. What he does is determined by what he is, so *is* is of first importance always. G36

The race of Adam is under death sentence. There is no commutation and no escape. H44

We have but to become acquainted with, or even listen to, the big names of our times to discover how wretchedly inferior most of them are. H96

There is a notion abroad that to win a man we must agree with him. Actually the exact opposite is true. H114

It is now quite possible to talk for hours with civilized men and women and gain absolutely nothing from it. Conversation today is almost wholly sterile. H144

As we draw nearer to the ancient Source of our being we find that we are no longer learned or ignorant, modern or old-fashioned, crude or cultured, white or colored; in that awesome Presence we are just *men*. Artificial distinctions fade away. Thousands of years of education disappear in a moment and we stand again where Adam and Eve stood after the Fall, where Cain stood, and Abel, outside the Garden, frightened and undone and fugitive from the terror of the broken law. K17

We are all in process of becoming. We have already moved from what we were to what we are, and we are now moving toward what we shall be. K156

The human race is one. L50

Man's nature indicates that he was created for three things: To think, to worship and to work. L58

MATERIALISM
(see also POSSESSIONS)

Secularism, materialism, and the intrusive presence of *things* have put out the light in our souls and turned us into a generation of zombies. We cover our deep ignorance with words, but we are ashamed to wonder, we are afraid to whisper "mystery." F18

M E R C Y

Mercy is an attribute of God, an infinite and inexhaustible energy within the divine nature which disposes God to be actively compassionate. F90

God is merciful as well as just. He has always dealt in mercy with mankind and will always deal in justice when His mercy is despised. F91

Nothing that has occurred or will occur in heaven or earth or hell can change the tender mercies of our God. Forever His mercy stands, a boundless, overwhelming immensity of divine pity and compassion. F91

It is human misery and sin that call forth the divine mercy. F91

Mercy never began to be, but from eternity was; so it will never cease to be. F91

To receive mercy we must first know that God is merciful. F92

We must believe that God's mercy is boundless, free and, through Jesus Christ our Lord, available to us now in our present situation. F92

M I N D
(see also THOUGHT)

Whatever men may think of human reason God takes a low view of it. B78

When God Himself appears before the mind, awesome, vast and incomprehensible, then the mind sinks into silence and the heart cries out "O Lord God!" D86

The imagination, since it is a faculty of the natural mind, must necessarily suffer both from its intrinsic limitations and from an inherent bent toward evil. D94

What comes into our minds when we think about God is the most important thing about us. F1

The mightiest thought the mind can entertain is the thought of God, and the weightiest word in any language is its word for God. F2

The human mind, being created, has an understandable uneasiness about the Uncreated. F26

Self-conscious intellectualism is offensive to man and, I am convinced, to God also but it is significant that every major revelation in the Scriptures was made to a man of superior intellect. G52

A guileless mind is a great treasure; it is worth any price. H91

Our intellectual activities in the order of their importance may be graded this way: first, cogitation; second, observation; third, reading. H144

Knowledge is the raw material out of which that finest of all machines, the mind, creates its amazing world. H146

The mind should be an eye to see with rather than a bin to store facts in. H150

Perception of ideas rather than the storing of them should be the aim of education. H150

There is scarcely anything on earth more beautiful than a Spirit-filled mind, certainly nothing more wonderful than an alert and eager mind made incandescent by the presence of the indwelling Christ. H150

Our Lord has little good to say of the unilluminated mind, but He revels in the mind that has been renewed and enlightened by grace. H150

The human intellect even in its fallen state is an awesome work of God, but it lies in darkness until it has been illuminated by the Holy Spirit. H150

Man is a worshiper and only in the spirit of worship does he find release for all the powers of his amazing intellect. K102

When the mind attempts to find out God it is confronted by obscurity. It is surrounded with mystery and blinded by the light no man can approach unto. L47

We cannot withhold our intellects from the blazing altar and still hope to preserve the true faith of Christ. L68

Sin has its seat deep within the mind where it pollutes the emotions (desires), the intellect (imaginations) and the will (purposes). L71

When the Bible speaks of the mind it does not refer to the intellect alone. The whole personality is included in the concept; the bent of the will, the moral responses, the sympathies and antipathies are there also, as well as the intellect. L71

It will probably be found at last that there is no sin except sin of the mind. L71

All our acts are born out of our minds and will be what the mind is at last. L73

MINISTRY
(see also LEADERSHIP, PREACHING, PROPHET)
By gift and calling the minister is a man apart. E24

The church is God's witness to each generation, and her ministers are her voice. Through them she becomes vocal. E24

The ministry is one of the most perilous of professions. K76

An ineffective, half-alive minister is a better advertisement for hell than a good man dead. K76

An effective, Christlike minister is a constant embarrassment to the devil, a threat to his dominion, a rebuttal of his best arguments and a dogged reminder of his coming overthrow. K76

The devil hates the Spirit-filled minister with an intensity second only to that which he feels for Christ Himself. K76

M O O D
(see also FEELINGS)

Faith is at the foundation of all Christian living, and because faith has to do with the character of God, it is safe from all vacillations of mood. M51

The relation of faith to mood may be stated by means of a number of metaphors: if faith is the tree, mood is the blossom; if faith is the flower, mood is the fragrance; if faith is the instrument, mood is the melody. And who will deny the vital place of the blossom, the fragrance and the music in human life? M51

M O R A L I T Y

The cause of all our human miseries is a radical dislocation, an upset in our relation to God and to each other. A99

The moral state of the penitent when he comes to Christ does not affect the result, for the work of Christ sweeps away both his good and his evil and turns him into another man. B27

God is always glorified when He wins a moral victory over us, and we are always benefited, immeasurably and gloriously benefited. C118

Within the last century man has leaped ahead in scientific achievement but has lagged behind morally, with the result that he is now technically capable of destroying the world and morally incapable of restraining himself from doing so. E89

The New Testament knows nothing of the working of the Spirit in us apart from our own moral responses. G54

Moral power has always accompanied definitive beliefs. H164

That we Christians modify the moral teachings of Christ at our convenience to avoid the stigma of being thought different is a proof of our backsliding, and the shame of it will not be removed until we have repented and brought our lives completely under the discipline of Christ. K43

There are moral situations where it is immoral to say nothing and basely immoral to do nothing. K142

MOTIVE

The man of God set his heart to exalt God above all; God accepted his intention as fact and acted accordingly. Not perfection, but holy intention made the difference. A106

It is not what a man does that determines whether his work is sacred or secular, it is why he does it. The motive is everything. A127

Let a man sanctify the Lord God in his heart and he can thereafter do no common act. A127

The test by which all conduct must finally be judged is motive. C89

As water cannot rise higher than its source, so the moral quality in an act can never be higher than the motive that inspires it. C89

Christians, and especially very active ones, should take time out frequently to search their souls to be sure of their motives. C90

Religious acts done out of low motives are twice evil, evil in themselves and evil because they are done in the name of God. C90

In the sight of God we are judged not so much by what we do as by our reasons for doing it. C91

N

NEW BIRTH
(see also REDEMPTION, REGENERATION, SALVATION)

A Christian is what he is not by ecclesiastical manipulation but by the new birth. He is a Christian because of a Spirit which dwells in him. B111

Men do not become Christians by associating with church people, nor by religious contact, nor by religious education; they become Christians only by an invasion of their nature by the Spirit of God in the New Birth. B113

The spirit that dwells in the once-born is forever opposed to the Spirit that inhabits the heart of the twice-born. This hostility began somewhere in the remote past before the creation of man and continues to this day. The modern effort to bring peace between these two spirits is not only futile but contrary to the moral laws of the universe. D21

Whoever is born of God is one with everyone else who is born of God. D74

Every redeemed soul is born out of the same spiritual life as every other redeemed soul and partakes of the divine nature in exactly the same manner. D75

The new birth makes us partakers of the divine nature. There the work of undoing the dissimilarity between us and God begins. D122

The new birth makes us partakers of the divine nature. D122

The new birth does not produce the finished product. The new thing that is born of God is as far from completeness as the new baby born an hour ago. [D137]

The genuinely renewed man will have a new life center. [H63]

The ethics of Jesus cannot be obeyed or even understood until the life of God has come to the heart of a man in the miracle of the new birth. [L103]

O

OBEDIENCE AND
DISOBEDIENCE

Obedience to the word of Christ will bring an inward revelation of the Godhead. A58

God being who He is must have obedience from His creatures. Man being who he is must render that obedience. C143

The Christian can hope for no manifestation of God while he lives in a state of disobedience. D102

Let a man refuse to obey God on some clear point, let him set his will stubbornly to resist any commandment of Christ, and the rest of his religious activities will be wasted. D102

If we would have God's blessing upon us we must begin to obey. E53

God will not accept praying in lieu of obeying. We only deceive ourselves when we try to make the substitution. E53

Prayer will become effective when we stop using it as a substitute for obedience. E53

The final test of love is obedience, not sweet emotions, not willingness to sacrifice, not zeal, but obedience to the commandments of Christ. G134

Love for Christ is a love of willing as well as a love of feeling, and it is psychologically impossible to love Him adequately unless we will to obey His words. G134

The man that believes will obey; failure to obey is convincing proof that there is not true faith present. H33

To attempt the impossible God must give faith or there will be none, and He gives faith to the obedient heart only. H33

We must be willing to obey if we would know the true inner meaning of the teachings of Christ and the apostles. H93

Obedience will strengthen faith and faith will increase knowledge. L46

Obedience is the big problem: and unwillingness to obey is the cause of continued darkness. L100

OLD AND NEW

Nothing that matters is new. D88

Nothing is new that matters and nothing that matters can be modernized. D88

Nothing new can save my soul; neither can saving grace be modernized. D90

The old way is the true way and there is no new way. The Lamb of God was slain "before the foundation of the world." D90

We must each come as Abel came, by atoning blood and faith demonstrated in repentance. No new way has been discovered. D90

OMNIPOTENCE

Sovereignty and omnipotence must go together. One cannot exist without the other. F65

God possesses what no creature can: an incomprehensible plenitude of power, a potency that is absolute. F65

God has delegated power to His creatures, but being self-sufficient, He cannot relinquish anything of His perfections and, power being one of them, He has never surrendered the least iota of His power. He gives but He does not give away. All that He gives remains His own and returns to Him again. Forever He must remain what He has forever been, the Lord God omnipotent. F66

Omnipotence is not a name given to the sum of all power, but an attribute of a personal God whom we Christians believe to be the Father of our Lord Jesus Christ and of all who believe on Him to life eternal. F67

Since He has at His command all the power in the universe, the Lord God omnipotent can do anything as easily as anything else. All His acts are done without effort. He expends no energy that must be replenished. His self-sufficiency makes it unnecessary for Him to look outside of Himself for a renewal of strength. All the power required to do all that He wills to do lies in undiminished fullness in His own infinite being. F67

OMNIPRESENCE
(see also PRESENCE OF GOD)

God is everywhere here, close to everything, next to everyone. F74

The doctrine of the divine omnipresence personalizes man's relation to the universe in which he finds himself. This great central truth gives meaning to all other truths and imparts supreme value to all his little life. God is present, near him, next to him, and this God sees him and knows him through and through. F75

He is there as He is here and everywhere, not confined to tree or stone, but free in the universe, near to everything, next to everyone, and through Jesus Christ immediately accessible to every loving heart. [F76]

The certainty that God is always near us, present in all parts of His world, closer to us than our thoughts, should maintain us in a state of high moral happiness most of the time. [F76]

O M N I S C I E N C E

God knows instantly and effortlessly all matter and all matters, all mind and every mind, all spirit and all spirits, all being and every being, all creaturehood and all creatures, every plurality and all pluralities, all law and every law, all relations, all causes, all thoughts, all mysteries, all enigmas, all feeling, all desires, every unuttered secret, all thrones and dominions, all personalities, all things visible and invisible in heaven and in earth, motion, space, time, life, death, good, evil, heaven, and hell. [F56]

Because God knows all things perfectly, He knows no thing better than any other thing, but all things equally well. He never discovers anything. He is never surprised, never amazed. [F56]

In the divine omniscience we see set forth against each other the terror and fascination of the Godhead. That God knows each person through and through can be a cause of shaking fear to the man that has something to hide— some unforsaken sin, some secret crime committed against man or God. The unblessed soul may well tremble that God knows the flimsiness of every pretext and never accepts the poor excuses given for sinful conduct, since He knows perfectly the real reason for it. "Thou hast set our iniquities before thee, our secret sins in the light of thy countenance." [F57]

How unutterably sweet is the knowledge that our
Heavenly Father knows us completely. No talebearer can
inform on us, no enemy can make an accusation stick;
no forgotten skeleton can come tumbling out of some
hidden closet to abash us and expose our past; no
unsuspected weakness in our characters can come to light
to turn God away from us, since He knew us utterly
before we knew Him and called us to Himself in the full
knowledge of everything that was against us. [F57]

OPTIMISM AND PESSIMISM

The cross-carrying Christian . . . is both a confirmed
pessimist and an optimist the like of which is to be found
nowhere else on earth. [G13]

Faith is not optimism, though it may breed optimism;
it is not cheerfulness, though the man of faith is likely to
be reasonably cheerful; it is not a vague sense of well-
being or a tender appreciation for the beauty of human
togetherness. Faith is confidence in God's self-
revelation as found in the Holy Scriptures. [G51]

Strange as it may be, the holiest souls who have ever
lived have earned the reputation for being pessimistic. [H98]

The unknown saints are not pessimists, nor are they
misanthropes or joy-killers. They are by virtue of their
godly faith the world's only true optimists. [H98]

ORIGIN

Origin is a word that can apply only to things created.
When we think of anything that has origin we are not
thinking of God. God is self-existent, while all created
things necessarily originated somewhere at some time.
Aside from God, nothing is self-caused. [F25]

P

PAST, PRESENT, AND FUTURE
(see also TIME AND ETERNITY)

We habitually stand in our *now* and look back by faith to see the past filled with God. We look forward and see Him inhabiting our future; but our *now* is uninhabited except for ourselves. B23

For each of us the time is surely coming when we shall have nothing but God. Health and wealth and friends and hiding places will all be swept away and we shall have only God. To the man of pseudo faith that is a terrifying thought, but to real faith it is one of the most comforting thoughts the heart can entertain. C50

We look forward to events predicted and backward to events that have occurred; but God contains past and future in His own all-encompassing Being. D115

Toward the world to come we are all headed. E130

We must face today as children of tomorrow. We must meet the uncertainties of this world with the certainty of the world to come. E131

Because God lives in an everlasting now, He has no past and no future. F39

All that God is He has always been, and all that He has been and is He will ever be. F50

Regret for a sinful past will remain until we truly believe that for us in Christ that sinful past no longer exists. G100

No living thing can subsist for long on its
yesterdays. K100

Every man holds his future in his hand. L40

Our today is bound to all our yesterdays, and our
tomorrow will be the sum of our present and our
past. M86

The first gift of life is not by works, but by faith in the
work of a sufficient Redeemer; but after the miracle of the
new birth has been accomplished, the Christian to a
large extent carries his future in his hands. M87

P E A C E

One of the greatest hindrances to internal peace which
the Christian encounters is the common habit of dividing
our lives into two areas—the sacred and the
secular. A117

What wicked men do should not disturb the good
man's tranquillity. D65

The world talks of peace, and by peace it means the
absence of war. What it overlooks is that there is another
meaning of the word, namely, tranquillity of heart,
and without that kind of peace the peace of the world will
continue to be but an unattainable dream. D109

Peace has fled the halls of learning and if found at all is
found now among the lowly. D109

In spite of all the books lately published, inward
tranquillity cannot be found on the earth. D109

Not the educators nor the legislators nor the scientists
can bring us tranquillity of heart, and without tranquillity
whatever else they give us is useless at last. D110

True peace is a gift of God and today it is found only in the minds of innocent children and in the hearts of trustful Christians. D110

Harmony within our own hearts depends mostly upon our getting into harmony with God. Morning comes not by our pushing out the darkness but by waiting for the coming of the sun. M83

PERFECTION

The Word of God well understood and religiously obeyed is the shortest route to spiritual perfection. E67

Man, being imperfect, can never quite know perfection in anything, least of all in his relation to the incomprehensible Godhead. G120

PERSONALITY

A loving Personality dominates the Bible, walking among the trees of the garden and breathing fragrance over every scene. A50

Always a living Person is present, speaking, pleading, loving, working, and manifesting Himself whenever and wherever His people have the receptivity necessary to receive the manifestation. A50

Human personality is dear to God because it is of all created things the nearest to being like Himself. C98

A good personality and a shrewd knowledge of human nature is all that any man needs to be a success in religious circles today. D59

In this day when shimmering personalities carry on the Lord's work after the methods of the entertainment world it is refreshing to associate for a moment even in the pages of a book with a sincere and humble man who keeps his own personality out of sight and places the emphasis upon the inworking of God. E18

POSSESSIONS
(see also MATERIALISM)

The man who has God for his treasure has all things in One. A20

The blessed ones who possess the Kingdom are they who have repudiated every external thing and have rooted from their hearts all sense of possessing. A23

The way to deeper knowledge of God is through the lonely valleys of soul poverty and abnegation of all things. A23

This possessive clinging to things is one of the most harmful habits in the life. A28

The very smell of the currency we pass around indicates where it has been. It smells of itself—as though it could tell its own story of crime and violence and immorality. B90

In the kingdom of God the surest way to lose something is to try to protect it, and the best way to keep it is to let it go. D96

It is better to throw our little all to the four winds than to get old and sour defending it. D96

It is better to be cheated a few times than to develop a constant suspicion that someone is trying to cheat us. D99

It is better to have the house burglarized than to spend the rest of our days and nights sitting with a rifle across our knees watching over it. D99

Give it up, and keep it. Defend it, and lose it. That is a law of the kingdom and it applies to every regenerated soul. D99

A real Christian need not defend his possession nor his position. God will take care of both. Let go of your treasures and the Lord will keep them for you unto life

eternal. Hang onto them and they will bring you
nothing but trouble and misery to the end of your
days. D99

Any temporal possession can be turned into
everlasting wealth. Whatever is given to Christ is
immediately touched with immortality. D107

The miser keeps his gold, the poor man suffers on in
his poverty and the whole course of nature is upset. G49

P O W E R

It is hard for us sons of the Machine Age to remember
that there is no power apart from God. Whether physical,
intellectual, moral or spiritual, power is contained in
God, flows out from Him and returns to Him again. D24

The power of God . . . is not something God has; it is
something God is. Power is something that is true of God
as wisdom and love are true of Him. D25

Whatever God is He is infinitely. In Him lies all the
power there is; any power at work anywhere is His. Even
the power to do evil must first have come from Him
since there is no other source from which it could
come. D26

The power of God is one with God's will, and works
only as He wills that it should. D26

The boundless power of our infinite God is all around
us, enfolding us, preserving us in being and keeping us
unto salvation ready to be revealed. D27

If we miss seeing God in His works we deprive
ourselves of the sight of a royal display of wisdom and
power so elevating, so ennobling, so awe-inspiring as
to make all attempts at description futile. E119

The only power God recognizes in His church is the power of His Spirit, whereas the only power actually recognized today by the majority of evangelicals is the power of man. K93

P R A I S E

"Gospel" boogie singing now furnishes for many persons the only religious joy they know. C69

As we go on into God we shall see the excellency of the life of constant communion where all thoughts and acts are prayers, and the entire life becomes one holy sacrifice of praise and worship. C82

A great deal of praise in conservative circles is perfunctory and forced, where it is not downright insincere. G129

Many of our popular songs and choruses in praise of Christ are hollow and unconvincing. G129

P R A Y E R

Prayer at its best is the expression of the total life. C81

All things else being equal, our prayers are only as powerful as our lives. In the long pull we pray only as well as we live. C81

Some prayers are like a fire escape, used only in times of critical emergency—never very enjoyable, but used as a way of terrified escape from disaster. C81

To pray effectively it is required of us that there be no unblessed areas in our lives, no parts of the mind or soul that are not inhabited by the Spirit, no impure desires allowed to live within us, no disparity between our prayers and our conduct. C82

It requires a serious mind and a determined heart to pray past the ordinary into the unusual. D10

We pour out millions of words and never notice that the prayers are not answered. D34

If one-tenth of one percent of the prayers made in the churches of any ordinary American village on one Sunday were answered the country would be transformed overnight. D34

We not only do not expect our prayers to be answered but would be embarrassed or even disappointed if they were. D34

Many a wordy brother would withdraw his request quickly enough if he had any intimation that God was taking it seriously. D34

While the prayer of faith enables us to lay hold of the omnipotence of God and bring about many wonderful changes here below, there are some things that not even prayer can change. D66

When we become too glib in prayer we are most surely talking to ourselves. D66

In the average church we hear the same prayers repeated each Sunday year in and year out with, one would suspect, not the remotest expectation that they will be answered. D100

The familiar phrase, the religious tone, the emotionally loaded words have their superficial and temporary effect, but the worshiper is no nearer to God, no better morally and no surer of heaven than he was before. D100

We ask Him to come when He is already present and waiting for us to recognize Him. D102

We plead for Him to speak when He has already spoken and is at that very moment speaking. D102

In our private prayers and in our public services we are forever asking God to do things that He either has already done or cannot do because of our unbelief. D102

When we are praying for something we have every right to look for the answer. Never should we fear to look at the facts. Either God answered or He did not, and there is no point in shutting our eyes and refusing to admit it when it is plain that no answer has been received. E12

Prayer is never an acceptable substitute for obedience. E52

Retire from the world each day to some private spot, even if it be only the bedroom. . . . Stay in the secret place till the surrounding noises begin to fade out of your heart and a sense of God's presence envelops you. Deliberately tune out the unpleasant sounds and come out of your closet determined not to hear them. Listen for the inward Voice till you learn to recognize it. Stop trying to compete with others. Give yourself to God and then be what and who you are without regard to what others think. Reduce your interests to a few. Don't try to know what will be of no service to you. Avoid the digest type of mind—short bits or unrelated facts, cute stories and bright sayings. Learn to pray inwardly every moment. After a while you can do this even while you work. Practice candor, childlike honesty, humility. Pray for a single eye. Read less, but read more of what is important to your inner life. Never let your mind remain scattered for very long. Call home your roving thoughts. Gaze on Christ with the eyes of your soul. Practice spiritual concentration. E106

We cannot help things by claiming He has answered when He has not. E123

Prayer is not in itself meritorious. It lays God under no obligation nor puts Him in debt to any. He hears prayer because He is good, and for no other reason. F83

Prayer is not a sure fire protection against error for the reason that there are many kinds of prayer and some of them are worse than useless. G50

All things else being equal, the praying man is less likely to think wrong than the man who neglects to pray. G51

In spite of the difficulties we encounter when we pray, prayer is a powerful and effective way to get right, stay right and stay free from error. G51

Prayer at stated times is good and right; we will never outgrow the need of it while we remain on earth. But this kind of prayer must be supported and perfected by the habit of constant, unspoken prayer. G67

Prayer that takes its value from the number of times certain words are repeated is pagan, not Christian. G88

Piqued prayers can be dangerous. G93

Oft-repeated prayers become vain when they have lost their urgency. G109

We should examine our prayers every now and again to discover how much sincerity and spontaneity they possess. We should insist on keeping them simple, candid, fresh and original. And above all we should never seek to induce holy emotions. G109

To pray with confidence the petitioner must be certain that his request falls within the broad will of God for His people. H86

It is futile to beg God to act contrary to His revealed purposes. H86

God wants us to pray and He wants to answer our prayers, but He makes our use of prayer as a privilege to commingle with His use of prayer as a discipline. H86

To receive answers to prayer we must meet God's terms. H86

The truth is that God always answers the prayer that accords with His will as revealed in the Scriptures, provided the one who prays is obedient and trustful. H87

A man may engage in a great deal of humble talk before God and get no response because unknown to himself he is using prayer to disguise disobedience. H90

We still pray for revival, with no awareness of our dark betrayal and no intention to repent. All such prayers are vain. K25

Prayer cannot be taught; it can only be done. K61

Praying itself must be the work of the individual. K61

Everyone must pray as if he alone could pray, and his approach must be individual and independent; independent, that is, of everyone but the Holy Ghost. K61

True prayer cannot be imitated nor can it be learned from someone else. K61

Prayer will increase in power and reality as we repudiate all pretense and learn to be utterly honest before God as well as before men. K64

All prayer is comfortable when the heart is having fellowship with God and the inner eyes are looking upon His blessed face. K107

The highest kind of prayer is never the making of requests. L14

Faith is only genuine as it eventuates into prayer. L32

Men may, and often do, pray without faith (though this is not true prayer), but it is not thinkable that men should have faith and not pray. L32

If, however, the desired object is legitimate and innocent, then there are three possible ways by which it may be obtained: one is to work for it, another is to pray for it and a third is to work and pray for it. M110

Some things are altogether out of the sphere of possibility for us, and yet altogether within God's gracious will for us. What to do? Prayer is the immediate answer. M110

It is useless to ask God for something we could obtain with a bit of effort properly directed. M110

No instructed Christian will waste his time praying for things that are within his own power to obtain. To do so is to deceive ourselves and make a farce of the whole concept of prayer. If work will get it for us, then work it is or we can go without it. M110–111

God will not contribute to our delinquency by supplying us with gifts which we could get for ourselves but have done nothing to obtain. M111

Whether it be a desire to open a closed field, win a hostile tribe, obtain a better job, build a new church, have a successful meeting, rear a family, get through school or do any one of an almost infinite number of legitimate things, the method is likely to be the twofold one of work and prayer. M111

P R E A C H I N G
(see also LEADERSHIP, MINISTRY, PROPHET)

Good hearers are as important as good preachers. C22

To speak to God on behalf of men is probably the highest service any of us can render. The next is to speak to men in the name of God. Either is a privilege possible to us only through the grace of our Lord Jesus Christ. D–FOREWORD

To be effective the preacher's message must be alive; it must alarm, arouse, challenge; it must be God's present voice to a particular people. Then, and not till then, is it the prophetic word and the man himself a prophet. E24

To preach the truth it is often necessary that the man of God know the people's hearts better than they themselves do. E25

The man who preaches truth and applies it to the lives of his hearers will feel the nails and the thorns. He will lead a hard life—but a glorious one. E29

We are not diplomats but prophets, and our message is not a compromise but an ultimatum. H44

We who preach the gospel must not think of ourselves as public relations agents sent to establish good will between Christ and the world. H44

In a very real sense no man can teach another; he can only aid him to teach himself. H149

To pray successfully is the first lesson the preacher
must learn if he is to preach fruitfully; yet prayer is the
hardest thing he will ever be called upon to do and,
being human, it is the one act he will be tempted to do
less frequently than any other. He must set his heart to
conquer by prayer, and that will mean that he must first
conquer his own flesh, for it is the flesh that hinders
prayer always. K60

Prayer should be continuous, preaching but
intermittent. K61

No man should stand before an audience who has not
first stood before God. K61

It is a dubious compliment to a preacher to say that he
is original. K72

The true messenger of God is not always successful as
men judge success. K73

The true minister is one not by his own choice but by
the sovereign commission of God. K73

The true preacher is a man of God speaking to men;
he is a man of heaven giving God's witness on earth. K73

The preacher is a servant of the Lord and of the
people. He is in great moral peril when he forgets this. K73

The clergyman meets religious people almost
exclusively. People are on their guard when they are with
him. K78

It is easy for the minister to be turned into a privileged
idler, a social parasite with an open palm and an expectant
look. K79

The minister should voluntarily impose upon himself a life of labor as arduous as that of a farmer, a serious student or a scientist. K79

God's Word is ever the same, but what it will do at any time in any place depends largely upon the moral purity, wisdom and spiritual power of those who preach it. L155

PRESENCE OF GOD
(see also OMNIPRESENCE)

At the heart of the Christian message is God Himself waiting for His redeemed children to push in to conscious awareness of His Presence. A37

The presence of God is the central fact of Christianity. A37

The instant cure of most of our religious ills would be to enter the Presence in spiritual experience, to become suddenly aware that we are in God and that God is in us. A38

The world is perishing for lack of the knowledge of God and the Church is famishing for want of His Presence. A38

God Himself is here waiting our response to His Presence. This eternal world will come alive to us the moment we begin to reckon upon its reality. A52

A spiritual kingdom lies all about us, enclosing us, embracing us, altogether within reach of our inner selves, waiting for us to recognize it. A52

God is here. No point is nearer to God than any other point. It is exactly as near to God from any place as it is from any other place. No one is in mere distance any further from or any nearer to God than any other person. A62

Wherever we are, God is here. There is no place, there can be no place, where He is not. A62

Adam sinned and, in his panic, frantically tried to do the impossible: he tried to hide from the presence of God. A63

We need never shout across the spaces to an absent God. He is nearer than our own soul, closer than our most secret thoughts. A66

The Universal Presence is a fact. God is here. The whole universe is alive with His life. A71

They who worship the God who is present may ignore the objections of unbelieving men. B25

Nothing can take the place of the *touch* of God in the soul and the sense of Someone there. B25

God is altogether present wherever He is present at all. B73

The truth is that He is nearer to us than we are to ourselves. D121

The knowledge that we are never alone calms the troubled sea of our lives and speaks peace to our souls. F76

The immanence of God in His universe makes possible the enjoyment of the "real Presence" by the saints of God in heaven and on earth simultaneously. Wherever they may be, He is present to them in the fullness of His Godhead. H78

Let God hide His face and nothing thereafter is worth the effort. H117

Most Christians speak of God in the manner usually reserved for a departed loved one, rarely as of one present; but they do not often speak to Him. K65

A convinced atheist is more logical than a Christian who tries to worship an Absentee God. K66

Men need God above everything else, yet are uncomfortable in His presence. K66

One advantage gained from thinking of God as being absent is that we may assume that He is pleased with whatever we may be trying to do, as long as it is not downright wicked. K67

The average Christian thinks of God as being at a safe distance looking the other way. K67

Since Protestants have no pope to keep them in line and since God is too far away to be consulted, the only limit to our modern religious folly is the amount the people will stand; and present indications are that they will stand plenty and pay for it, too. K67

P R O G R E S S

Progress in the Christian life is exactly equal to the growing knowledge we gain of the Triune God in personal experience. C11

More spiritual progress can be made in one short moment of speechless silence in the awesome presence of God than in years of mere study. C146

No responsible person will deny that some changes made by the race over the years have been improvements, and so may have represented progress and advance, though just what we are supposed to be advancing toward has not been made very clear by our leaders. C155

Any movement toward Christ is ascent, and any
direction away from Him is down. H14

It will cost something to walk slow in the parade of
the ages while excited men of time rush about confusing
motion with progress. M10

P R O M I S E S

Fallen men, though they cannot fulfill their promises,
are always able to make good on their threats. D110

God will always do what He has promised to do
when His conditions are met. G28

The man who believes the promises of God expects to
see them fulfilled. Where there is no expectation there is
no faith. K135

God's promises conform to reality, and whoever
trusts them enters a world not of fiction but of fact. K135

Christian expectation in the average church follows
the program, not the promises. K137

A promise is never better or worse than the character
of the one who makes it. L38

P R O P H E T
(see also LEADERSHIP, MINISTRY, PREACHING)

Between the scribe who has read and the prophet who
has seen there is a difference as wide as the sea. A4

A prophet is one who knows his times and what God
is trying to say to the people of his times. E20

Scholars can interpret the past; it takes prophets to
interpret the present. E22

Nothing God has yet done for us can compare with all
that is written in the sure word of prophecy. E126

The prophet must hear the message clearly and deliver it faithfully, and that is indeed a grave responsibility; but it is to God alone, not to men. K72

The differences between the orator and the prophet are many and radical, the chief being that the orator speaks for himself while the prophet speaks for God. K72

The orator originates his message and is responsible to himself for its content. The prophet originates nothing but delivers the message he has received from God who alone is responsible for it, the prophet being responsible to God for its delivery only. K72

PURSUIT OF GOD

We pursue God because, and only because, He has first put an urge within us that spurs us to the pursuit. A11

The impulse to pursue God originates with God, but the outworking of that impulse is our following hard after Him. A12

If we would find God amid all the religious externals we must first determine to find Him, and then proceed in the way of simplicity. A18

We need not fear that in seeking God only we may narrow our lives or restrict the motions of our expanding hearts. The opposite is true. We can well afford to make God our All, to concentrate, to sacrifice the many for the One. A18

Our pursuit of God is successful just because He is forever seeking to manifest Himself to us. A65

Much of our difficulty as seeking Christians stems from our unwillingness to take God as He is and adjust our lives accordingly. We insist upon trying to modify Him and to bring Him nearer to our own image. A101

The man who has met God is not looking for something—he has found it; he is not searching for light—upon.him the Light has already shined. C157

We are called to an everlasting preoccupation with God. G46

God is never found accidentally. H56

The man that has the most of God is the man who is seeking the most ardently for more of God. H106

Only engrossment with God can maintain perpetual spiritual enthusiasm because only God can supply everlasting novelty. K106

R E A L I T Y

The great Reality is God, the Author of that lower
and dependent reality which makes up the sum of created
things, including ourselves. A55

God is real. He is real in the absolute and final sense
that nothing else is. All other reality is contingent upon
this. A55

Imagination projects unreal images out of the mind
and seeks to attach reality to them. Faith creates nothing;
it simply reckons upon that which is already there. A55

God and the spiritual world are real. We can reckon
upon them with as much assurance as we reckon upon the
familiar world around us. A55

At the root of the Christian life lies belief in the
invisible. The object of the Christian's faith is unseen
reality. A56

The presence of God is not imaginary, neither is
prayer the indulgence of a delightful fancy. D93

The most realistic book in the world is the Bible. God
is real, men are real and so is sin and so are death and hell,
toward which sin inevitably leads. D93

Faith engages God, the one great Reality, who gave
and gives existence to all things. K135

God is the only absolute Reality; all other reality is
relative and contingent. M88

While the things we know and experience day by day are real, they are not real in themselves, but only as God gives them existence. They could not continue to be should God withdraw His constant word of creation and leave them to themselves for even one short moment. M88

All things are but shadows cast by the great Reality, God, and if we were to gain the whole world and miss God, we should have no more than a handful of shadows. M88–89

REDEMPTION
(see also NEW BIRTH, REGENERATION, SALVATION)

Man who moved out of the heart of God by sin now moves back into the heart of God by redemption. B27

Redemption is not a strange work which God for a moment turned aside to do; rather it is His same work performed in a new field, the field of human catastrophe. B27

The whole purpose of God in redemption is to make us holy and to restore us to the image of God. C25

The first announcement of God's redemptive intention toward mankind was made to a man and a woman hiding in mortal fear from the presence of the Lord. D38

The work of Christ in redemption will achieve ultimately the expulsion of sin, the only divisive agent in the universe, and the unification of all things. D117

The primary work of Christ in redemption is to justify, sanctify and ultimately to glorify a company of persons salvaged from the ruin of the human race. D139

Redemption became necessary not because of what men were doing only, but because of what they were. G36

Seen from our human standpoint redemption must rank first among all the acts of God. No other achievement of the Godhead required such vast and precise knowledge, such perfection of wisdom or such fullness of moral power. G83

The purpose of Christ's redeeming work was to make it possible for bad men to become good—deeply, radically and finally. H64

Every redeemed soul is born out of the same spiritual life as every other redeemed soul and partakes of the divine nature in exactly the same manner. H75

The supreme work of Christ in redemption is not to save us from hell but to restore us to Godlikeness again. K158

REGENERATION
(see also NEW BIRTH, REDEMPTION, SALVATION)

The offer of pardon on the part of God is conditioned upon intention to reform on the part of man. C42

There can be no spiritual regeneration till there has been a moral reformation. C42

The converted man is both reformed and regenerated. C43

Unless the sinner is willing to reform his way of living he will never know the inward experience of regeneration. C43

Baptism, confirmation, the receiving of the sacraments, church membership—these mean nothing unless the supreme act of God in regeneration also takes place. D11

The mysterious operation of God in regenerating grace and His further work of the Spirit's anointing are transactions so highly personal that no third party can know or understand what is taking place. D112

The primary work of the Holy Spirit is to restore the lost soul to intimate fellowship with God through the washing of regeneration. G37

The truly regenerated man is a new creature; he belongs to another order of being; he has another kind of life, another origin, another destiny. L103

R E G R E T

Regret is a kind of frustrated repentance that has not been quite consummated. Once the soul has turned from all sin and committed itself wholly to God there is no longer any legitimate place for regret. G99

Regret may be no more than a form of self-love. G100

Regret for a sinful past will remain until we truly believe that for us in Christ that sinful past no longer exists. G100

R E L A T I O N S H I P   T O   G O D

The temptation to make our relation to God judicial instead of personal is very strong. C11

My personal relation to God matters. That takes priority over everything else. D90

Seeing who God is and who we are, a right relationship between God and us is of vital importance. That God should be glorified in us is so critically important that it stands in lonely grandeur, a moral imperative more compelling than any other which the human heart can acknowledge. To bring ourselves into a place where God will be eternally pleased with us should be the first responsible act of every man. K38

To become like God is and must be the supreme goal
of all moral creatures. K158

We all come into the world with one tremendous
question facing us, the question of our relation to the God
from whose hand we came. M65

R E L I G I O N
(see also SCIENCE AND RELIGION)

Religion, so far as it is genuine, is in essence the
response of created personalities to the creating
personality, God. A13

When religion has said its last word, there is little that
we need other than God Himself. A18

Religion has accepted the monstrous heresy that noise,
size, activity and bluster make a man dear to God. A80

To the absence of the spirit may be traced that vague
sense of unreality which almost everywhere invests
religion in our times. B90

It was religion that put Christ on the cross, religion
without the indwelling Spirit. B103

Our notion of God must always determine the quality
of our religion. C14

The deadening effect of religious make-believe on the
human mind is beyond all describing. C53

We fear extremes and shy away from too much ardor
in religion as if it were possible to have too much love or
too much faith or too much holiness. C56

The one thing that religious persons want most is to
be changed, to be made over from what they are into
something they desire to be. C57

Religion correctly assumes the fluidity of human nature. It assumes that the human character is in flux and can be directed into prechosen channels leading to desired ends. C57

The whole religious machine has become a noisemaker. C75

Powerless religion may put a man through many surface changes and leave him exactly what he was before. C75

Religious extroversion has been carried to such an extreme in evangelical circles that hardly anyone has the desire, to say nothing of the courage, to question the soundness of it. Externalism has taken over. C75

The pitiable attempt of churchmen to explain everything for the smiling unbeliever has had an effect exactly opposite to that which was intended. It has reduced worship to the level of the intellect and introduced the rationalistic spirit into the wonders of religion. C79

If true religion consisted in outward practices, then it could be destroyed by laws forbidding those practices. C129

Religion is disengaged from practical life and retired to the airy region of fancy where dwell the sweet insubstantial nothings which everyone knows do not exist but which they nevertheless lack the courage to repudiate publicly. D33

We settle for words in religion because deeds are too costly. D34

There is probably not another field of human activity where there is so much waste as in the field of religion. D100

True religion leads to moral action. E56

The essence of true religion is spontaneity, the sovereign movings of the Holy Spirit upon and in the free spirit of redeemed man. E70

The low state of religion in our day is largely due to the lack of public confidence in religious people. E76

Of all work done under the sun religious work should be the most open to examination. E122

True religion confronts earth with heaven and brings eternity to bear upon time. F–Preface

Religion is interested primarily in the One who is the source of all things, the master of every phenomenon. F67

To stay free from religious ennui we should be careful not to get into a rut, not even a good rut. G109

True religion is removed from diet and days, from garments and ceremonies, and placed where it belongs— in the union of the spirit of man with the Spirit of God. H10

Religious externals may have a meaning for the God- inhabited soul; for any others they are not only useless but may actually become snares, deceiving them into a false and perilous sense of security. H11

That religion may be very precious to some persons is admitted, but never important enough to cause division or risk hurting anyone's feelings. H113

In this dim world of pious sentiment all religions are equal and any man who insists that salvation is by Jesus Christ alone is a bigot and a boor. H113

One mark of the low state of affairs among us is religious boredom. H134

We are paying a frightful price for our religious boredom. And that at the moment of the world's mortal peril. H136

The way to escape religion as a front is to make it a fount. See to it that we pray more than we preach. K96

The religious snob is devoid of truth. Snobbery and truth are irreconcilable. K127

That religion lies in the will is an axiom of theology. L11

Religion without the Son of God is worldly religion. L135

REPENTANCE

The truest and most acceptable repentance is to reverse the acts and attitudes of which we repent. B75

The teaching of salvation without repentance has lowered the moral standards of the Church and produced a multitude of deceived religious professors who erroneously believe themselves to be saved when they are still in the gall of bitterness and the bond of iniquity. C44

The promise of pardon and cleansing is always associated in the Scriptures with the command to repent. C44

We must be careful that our repentance is not simply a change of location. D82

To move across from one sort of person to another is
the essence of repentance: the liar becomes truthful, the
thief honest, the lewd pure, the proud humble. The
whole moral texture of the life is altered. F52

Repentance, though necessary, is not meritorious but
a condition for receiving the gracious gift of pardon
which God gives of His goodness. F83

God will take nine steps toward us, but He will not
take the tenth. He will *incline* us to repent, but He cannot
do our repenting for us. G30

It is of the essence of repentance that it can only be
done by the one who committed the act to be repented
of. G30

Where real repentance is, there is obedience; for
repentance is not only sorrow for past failures and sins, it
is a determination to begin now to do the will of God
as He reveals it to us. H33

Repentance is primarily a change of moral purpose, a
sudden and often violent reversal of the soul's
direction. H36

No man has truly repented until his sin has wounded
him near to death, until the wound has broken him and
defeated him and taken all the fight and self-assurance
out of him and he sees himself as the one who nailed his
Saviour on the tree. H102

Every call to repentance is a call to negative as well as
to positive moral action. "Cease to do evil; learn to do
well." L76

Repentance is among other things a sincere apology to
God for distrusting Him so long, and faith is throwing
oneself upon Christ in complete confidence. L124

R E P R O O F

When reproved pay no attention to the source. Do not ask whether it is a friend or an enemy that reproves you. An enemy is often of greater value to you than a friend because he is not influenced by sympathy. C30

Keep your heart open to the correction of the Lord and be ready to receive His chastisement regardless of who holds the whip. C30

R I G H T E O U S N E S S
(see also VIRTUE)

Self-rightousness is an effective bar to God's favor because it throws the sinner back upon his own merits and shuts him out from the imputed righteousness of Christ. B36

Too many Christians want to enjoy the thrill of feeling right but are not willing to endure the inconvenience of being right. C52

It is more important that we retain a right spirit toward others than that we bring them to our way of thinking, even if our way is right. E92

The cross is always in the way of righteousness. G115

When God *declares* a man righteous He instantly sets about to *make* him righteous. H65

The wicked will always have the money and the talent and the publicity and the numbers, while the righteous will be few and poor and unknown. H69

To be right with God has often meant to be in trouble with men. H114

S

SAINT

However deep the mystery, however many the paradoxes involved, it is still true that men become saints not at their own whim but by sovereign calling. B48

It is not possible that the afflicted saint should feel a stab of pain to which Christ is a stranger. C132

We must insist on New Testament sainthood for our converts, nothing less; and we must lead them into a state of heart purity, fiery love, separation from the world and poured-out devotion to the Person of Christ. E13

The average so-called Bible Christian in our times is but a wretched parody on true sainthood. E13

Unsaintly saints are the tragedy of Christianity. E75

The Lord takes peculiar pleasure in His saints. F1(X)

The secret of saintliness is not the destruction of the will but the submergence of it in the will of God. G31

The saints of the Most High will be serious-minded, thoughtful persons. G52

The true Christian is a saint in embryo. G53

SALVATION
(see also NEW BIRTH, REDEMPTION, REGENERATION)

God never made salvation depend upon new moons or holy days or sabbaths. A94

Essentially salvation is the restoration of a right
relation between man and his Creator, a bringing back to
normal of the Creator-creature relation. A99

In saving men God is but doing again (or rather
continuing to do) the same creative work as at the
beginning of the world. To Him each ransomed soul is
a world wherein He performs again His pleasant work as
of old. B29

Salvation must include a judicial change of status, but
what is overlooked by most teachers is that *it also includes
an actual change in the life of the individual*. B37

Salvation is from our side a choice, from the divine
side it is a seizing upon, an apprehending, a conquest by
the Most High God. B49

God rescues us by breaking us, by shattering our
strength and wiping out our resistance. Then He invades
our natures with that ancient and eternal life which is
from the beginning. So He conquers us and by that
benign conquest saves us for Himself. B57

We might well pray for God to invade and conquer
us, for until He does, we remain in peril from a thousand
foes. B57

They who follow a merely human Saviour follow no
Saviour at all, but an ideal only, and one furthermore that
can do no more than mock their weaknesses and
sins. B64

It is altogether doubtful whether any man can be saved
who comes to Christ for His help but with no intention
to obey Him. C85

The wise man will note that the things we cannot
understand have nothing to do with our salvation. We are
saved by the truth we know. D27

The inward operation of the Holy Spirit is necessary
to saving faith. D63

The work of Christ as Saviour is twofold: to "save his
people from their sins" and to reunite them forever with
the God from whom sin had alienated them. D80

Our Lord called men to follow Him but He never
made the way look easy. Indeed one gets the distinct
impression that He made it appear extremely hard.
Sometimes He said things to disciples or prospective
disciples that we today discreetly avoid repeating when
we are trying to win men to Him. G75

Our Lord recognizes no classes, high or low, rich or
poor, old or young, man or woman: all are human and all
are alike to Him. His invitation is to all mankind. H12

In the divine scheme of salvation the doctrine of faith
is central. God addresses His words to faith, and where
no faith is no true revelation is possible. "Without faith
it is impossible to please him." H29

God salvages the individual by liquidating him and
then raising him again to newness of life. H44

Christ can and will save a man who *has been*
dishonest, but He cannot save him *while* he is
dishonest. H90

In this dim world of pious sentiment all religions are
equal and any man who insists that salvation is by Jesus
Christ alone is a bigot and a boor. H113

Salvation comes not by "accepting the finished work"
or "deciding for Christ." It comes by believing on the
Lord Jesus Christ, the whole, living, victorious Lord
who, as God and man, fought our fight and won it,
accepted our debt as His own and paid it, took our

sins, and died under them and rose again to set us free. This is the true Christ, and nothing less will do. H142

Now I would hasten to disclaim all sympathy with the popular salvation-by-willpower cult. I am in radical disagreement with all forms of quasi-Christianity that depends upon the "latent power within us" or trust to "creative thinking" instead of to the power of God. All these paper-thin religious philosophies break down at the same place—in the erroneous assumption that the stream of human nature can be made to run backward up over the falls. This it can never do. "Salvation is of the Lord." K160

To be saved a lost man must be picked up bodily by the power of God and raised to a higher level. There must be an impartation of divine life in the wonder of the second birth. K160

S A T A N

The devil is declared in the Scriptures to be an enemy of God and of all good men. He is said to be a liar, a deceiver and a murderer who achieves his ends by guile and trickery. D41

Satan hates God for His own sake, and everything that is dear to God he hates for the very reason that God loves it. D41

S C I E N C E   A N D   R E L I G I O N
(see also RELIGION)

The modern scientist has lost God amid the wonders of His world; we Christians are in real danger of losing God amid the wonders of His Word. A13

Science, the sweet talking goddess which but a short time ago smilingly disposed of the Bible as a trustworthy guide and took the world by the hand to lead it into a man-made millennium, has turned out to be a dragon capable of destroying the same world with a flick of her fiery tail. D108

The modern vogue of bringing science to the support of Christianity proves not the truth of the Christian faith but the gnawing uncertainty in the hearts of those who must look to science to give respectability to their belief. E113

We must have faith; and let us not apologize for it, for faith is an organ of knowledge and can tell us more about ultimate reality than all the findings of science. E118

Philosophy and science have not always been friendly toward the idea of God, the reason being that they are dedicated to the task of accounting for things and are impatient with anything that refuses to give an account of itself. F26

The philosopher and the scientist will admit that there is much that they do not know; but that is quite another thing from admitting that there is something which they can *never* know, which indeed they have not technique for discovering. F26

The trustworthiness of God's behavior in His world is the foundation of all scientific truth. F66

SCRIPTURES
(see also *BIBLE, VOICE OF GOD*)

The Holy Scriptures tell us what we could never learn in any other way: They tell us who we are and what we are, how we got here, why we are here and what we are required to do while we remain here. They trace our history from the beginning down to the present time and on into the centuries and millenniums ahead. They track us into the atomic age, through the space age and on into the golden age. They reveal that at an appropriate time direction of the world will be taken away from men and placed in the hands of the Man who alone has the wisdom and power to rule it. E30

The Scriptures not only teach truth, they show also its uses for mankind. F80

Let me accept anything else instead of the Scriptures and I have been cheated and robbed to my eternal confusion. G82

Cast of mind may easily determine our views when the Scriptures are not clear. H82

We naturally tend to interpret Scripture in the light (or shadow) of our own temperament and let our peculiar mental cast decide the degree of importance we attach to various religious doctrines and practices. H83

The Scriptures are in print what Christ is in person. H127

Thoughts are things, and the thoughts of the Holy Scriptures form a lofty temple for the dwelling place of God. H127

In whatever language they appear the Scriptures continue century after century to say the same thing to everyone. K42

Apart from the Scriptures we have no sure philosophy; apart from Jesus Christ we have no true knowledge of God; apart from the inliving Spirit we have no ability to live lives morally pleasing to God. L108

To study the Scriptures for their literary beauty alone is to miss the whole purpose for which they were written. L165

SECOND ADVENT OF CHRIST

If the tender yearning is gone from the advent hope today there must be a reason for it; and I think I know what it is, or what they are, for there are a number of them. One is simply that popular fundamentalist theology has emphasized the utility of the cross rather than the beauty of the One who died on it. The saved man's relation to Christ has been made contractual instead of personal. The "work" of Christ has been stressed until it has eclipsed the person of Christ. Substitution has been allowed to supersede identification. What He did for me seems to be more important than what He is to me. D133

We must love someone very much to stay awake and long for his coming, and that may explain the absence of power in the advent hope even among those who still believe in it. D133

Another reason for the absence of real yearning for Christ's return is that Christians are so comfortable in this world that they have little desire to leave it. D133

Possibly nothing short of a world catastrophe that will destroy every false trust and turn our eyes once more upon the Man Christ Jesus will bring back the glorious hope to a generation that has lost it. H157

It should be noted that there is a vast difference between the doctrine of Christ's coming and the *hope* of His coming. The first we may hold without feeling a trace of the second. Indeed there are multitudes of Christians today who hold the doctrine of the second coming. H157

SECULARISM

We are today suffering from a secularized mentality. Where the sacred writers saw God, we see the laws of nature. Their world was fully populated; ours is all but

empty. Their world was alive and personal; ours is
impersonal and dead. God ruled their world; ours is ruled
by the laws of nature and we are always once removed
from the presence of God. F66

S E L F

Self can live unrebuked at the very altar. A45

The self-sins are self-righteousness, self-pity, self-
confidence, self-sufficiency, self-admiration, self-love and
a host of others like them. They dwell too deep within
us and are too much a part of our natures to come to our
attention till the light of God is focused upon them. A45

Self is the opaque veil that hides the Face of God from
us. A46

The world of sense intrudes upon our attention day
and night for the whole of our lifetime. It is clamorous,
insistent and self-demonstrating. It does not appeal to
our faith; it is here, assaulting our five senses, demanding
to be accepted as real and final. But sin has so clouded
the lenses of our hearts that we cannot see that other
reality, the City of God, shining around us. The world
of sense triumphs. The visible becomes the enemy of the
invisible; the temporal, of the eternal. A56

It is easy to learn the doctrine of personal revival and
victorious living; it is quite another thing to take our cross
and plod on to the dark and bitter hill of self-
renunciation. D9

The desire to be held in esteem by our fellow men is
universal and as natural to us as is the instinct for self-
preservation. D52

Accept yourself. Apart from sin, which you have
forsaken and which you mean to practice no more, there
is nothing about yourself of which you need be
ashamed. D67

In God, self is not sin but the quintessence of all possible goodness, holiness and truth. F29

So subtle is self that scarcely anyone is conscious of its presence. F29

The desire to be pleasing to God is commendable certainly, but the effort to please God by self-effort is not, for it assumes that sin once done may be undone, an assumption wholly false. G98

Hardly anything else reveals so well the fear and uncertainty among men as the length to which they will go to hide their true selves from each other and even from their own eyes. G101

Self-knowledge is so critically important to us in our pursuit of God and His righteousness that we lie under heavy obligation to do immediately whatever is necessary to remove the disguise and permit our real selves to be known. G101

RULES FOR SELF-DISCOVERY
1. *What we want most.*
2. *What we think about most.*
3. *How we use our money.*
4. *What we do with our leisure time.*
5. *The company we enjoy.*
6. *Whom and what we admire.*
7. *What we laugh at.* G102

Boasting is an evidence that we are pleased with self; belittling, that we are disappointed in it. Either way we reveal that we have a high opinion of ourselves. H71

Self-derogation is bad for the reason that self must be there to derogate. Self, whether swaggering or groveling, can never be anything but hateful to God. H71

Self is one of the toughest plants that grows in the garden of life. It is, in fact, indestructible by any human means. Just when we are sure it is dead it turns up somewhere as robust as ever to trouble our peace and poison the fruit of our lives. H72

Christ never intended that we should rest in a mere theory of self-denial. H73

The healthy soul is the victorious soul and victory never comes while self is permitted to remain unjudged and uncrucified. H73

Of all forms of deception self-deception is the most deadly, and of all deceived persons the self-deceived are the least likely to discover the fraud. H88

It is the "himself" which has enslaved and corrupted the man. Deliverance comes only by denial of that self. L42

SEPARATION
(see also COMMITMENT, CONSECRATION)

Whether or not the Christian should separate himself from the world is not open to debate. M34

Christ taught the necessity of separation from the world and of complete consecration to God as the only way to escape the shadows and obtain those riches that cannot pass away. M89

The modern Christian who insists upon separation as a condition of true spirituality is not the old-fashioned narrow person he is currently declared to be. His religious philosophy is altogether sound and wholly in accord with the total sum of things in heaven and earth. God being who and what He is and things being what they are, complete consecration is the only way to peace for any of us. M89

SERVICE

No one can long worship God in spirit and in truth before the obligation to holy service becomes too strong to resist. D126

Fellowship with God leads straight to obedience and good works. That is the divine order and it can never be reversed. D126

It is inconceivable that a sovereign and holy God should be so hard up for workers that He would press into service anyone who had been empowered regardless of his moral qualifications. G37

Gifts and power for service the Spirit surely desires to impart; but holiness and spiritual worship come first. G37

Before there can be acceptable service there must be an acceptable life. G106

Christian service, like every other phase of religion, can become a very hollow affair. M69

The church has marked out certain work and approved it as service acceptable to God, and for the most part the church has been right. But it should be kept in mind that it is not the kind or quantity of work that makes it true service—it is the *quality*. M69

If we are wise we will give attention now to the quality of our service; it is obvious that it will be too late to do anything about it when the service is ended and the account rendered up. M69

In Christian service *motive* is everything, for it is motive that gives to every moral act its final quality. M70

SIN

We must of necessity be servant to someone, either to God or to sin. A104

The abuse of a harmless thing is the essence of sin. C32

Sin has many sides and many ramifications. It is like a disease with numberless complications, any one of which can kill the patient. It is lawlessness, it is a missing of the mark, it is rebellion, it is perversion, it is transgression; but it is also waste—a frightful, tragic waste of the most precious of all treasures. C99

We do God no honor and ourselves no good by assuming that we have sinned if we have not. C127

Nature itself, the brute creation, the earth and even the astronomical universe, have all felt the shock of man's sin and have been adversely affected by it. D29

Human nature tends to excesses by a kind of evil magnetic attraction. D40

We Christians must look sharp that our Christianity does not simply refine our sins without removing them. D80

God's holy character requires that He refuse to admit sin into His fellowship. D80

The will of God is that sin should be removed, not merely refined. D83

Sin has many manifestations but its essence is one. A moral being, created to worship before the throne of God, sits on the throne of his own selfhood and from that elevated position declares, "I AM." That is sin in its concentrated essence; yet because it is natural it appears to be good. F29–30

"The essence of sin is to will one thing," for to set our will against the will of God is to dethrone God and make ourselves supreme in the little kingdom of Mansoul. F30

Sins are because sin is. [F30]

Against our deep creature-sickness stands God's infinite ability to cure. [F47]

Sin has made us timid and self-conscious. [F83]

The just penalty for sin was exacted when Christ our Substitute died for us on the cross. [F88]

God hates sin and can never look with pleasure upon iniquity, but where men seek to do God's will He responds in genuine affection. [F101]

Sin has done frightful things to us and its effect upon us is all the more deadly because we were born in it and are scarcely aware of what is happening to us. [G14]

Sin is so frightful, so destructive to the soul that no human thought or act can in any degree diminish its lethal effects. Only God can deal with it successfully; only the blood of Christ can cleanse it from the pores of the spirit. [G99]

Sin sees only today, or at most tomorrow; never the day after tomorrow, next month or next year. [H47]

To commit a sin a man must for the moment believe that things are different from what they really are; he must confound values; he must see the moral universe out of focus; he must accept a lie as truth and see truth as a lie; he must ignore the signs on the highway and drive with his eyes shut; he must act as if he had no soul and was not accountable for his moral choices. [H47]

Sin is never a thing to be proud of. No act is wise that ignores remote consequences, and sin always does. [H47]

Sin is basically an act of moral folly, and the greater the folly the greater the fool. [H48]

The idea that sin is modern is false. There has not been a new sin invented since the beginning of recorded history. H48

The man who hates his sins too much will get into trouble with those who do not hate sin enough. H62

Not only is it right for God to display anger against sin, but I find it impossible to understand how He could do otherwise. H111

In spite of all our smooth talk sin continues to ride the race of man. H118

Sin has done a pretty complete job of ruining us and the process of restoration is long and slow. K111

Sin is at bottom the abuse of things in themselves innocent, an illegitimate use of legitimate gifts. K111

Human sin began with loss of faith in God. L123

The Christian mourns over his sin and is comforted. The worldling shrugs off his sin and continues in it. L135

Sin has its pleasures and the vast majority of human beings have a whale of a time living. L143

In spite of every effort of the pseudo-learned world to dispose of the sin question, it remains still, a perennial heartache to the sons and daughters of Adam and Eve. It is one of those persistent pains that lies deep in the soul and never quite stops hurting. M66

Sin is still the world's first problem. M66

If we but come to Jesus with our sin upon us and without any hope except His mercy, we shall surely be delivered from the ancient curse. M66

Sin demands an answer. It won't just go away. It must be carried away by redeeming blood, and redeeming blood was never shed by any other lamb except the Lamb of God. M66

S I N N E R

Before a sinful man can think a right thought of God, there must have been a work of enlightenment done within him. A11

A sinner cannot enter the kingdom of God. B36

A man by his sin may waste himself, which is to waste that which on earth is most like God. This is man's greatest tragedy, God's heaviest grief. C99

It is necessary to the moral health of the universe that God divide the light from the darkness and that He say at last to every sinner, "Depart from me, ye that work iniquity." D80

The sinner can never be quite himself. All his life he must pretend. He must act as if he were never going to die, and yet he knows too well that he is. He must act as if he had not sinned, when in his deep heart he knows very well that he has. He must act unconcerned about God and judgment and the future life, and all the time his heart is deeply disturbed about his precarious condition. He must keep up a front of nonchalance while shrinking from facts and wincing under the lash of conscience. All his adult life he must dodge and hide and conceal. E108

The natural man is a sinner because and only because he challenges God's selfhood in relation to his own. In all else he may willingly accept the sovereignty of God; in his own life he rejects it. For him, God's dominion ends where his begins. F29

The blood of Christ will shield the penitent sinner alone, but never the sinner and his idol. H90

Faith will justify the sinner, but it will never justify the sinner and his sin. H90

A sinful man *should* be afraid; he has plenty to be afraid of. The consequences of his sins, death, judgment and hell are all awaiting him and he cannot escape them by looking the other way. L86

S O U L

The soul has eyes with which to see and ears with which to hear. A58

Nothing twists and deforms the soul more than a low or unworthy conception of God. C13

Where there is a divine act within the soul there will always be a corresponding awareness. D14

The life of God in the soul of a man is wholly independent of the social status of that man. K43

S O V E R E I G N T Y

To discuss the authority of Almighty God seems a bit meaningless, and to question it would be absurd. F109

The sovereignty of God is a fact well established in the Scriptures and declared aloud by the logic of truth. But admittedly it raises certain problems which have not to this time been satisfactorily solved. F109

God sovereignly decreed that man should be free to exercise moral choice, and man from the beginning has fulfilled that decree by making his choice between good and evil. When he chooses to do evil, he does not thereby countervail the sovereign will of God but fulfills it, inasmuch as the eternal decree decided not

which choice the man should make but that he should
be free to make it. F110

Man's will is free because God is sovereign. F111

A God less than sovereign could not bestow moral
freedom upon His creatures. He would be afraid to do
so. F111

We know that God will fulfill every promise made to
the prophets; we know that sinners will some day be
cleansed out of the earth; we know that a ransomed
company will enter into the joy of God and that the
righteous will shine forth in the kingdom of their
Father; we know that God's perfections will yet receive
universal acclamation, that all created intelligences will
own Jesus Christ Lord to the glory of God the Father,
that the present imperfect order will be done away,
and a new heaven and a new earth will be established
forever. F111

In the moral conflict now raging around us whoever is
on God's side is on the winning side and cannot lose;
whoever is on the other side is on the losing side and
cannot win. Here there is not chance, no gamble. There is
freedom to choose which side we shall be on but no
freedom to negotiate the results of the choice once it is
made. By the mercy of God we may repent a wrong
choice and alter the consequences by making a new and
right choice. Beyond that we cannot go. F112

S P A C E

We should never think of God as being spatially near
or remote, for He is not here or there but carries here and
there in His heart. Space is not infinite, as some have
thought; only God is infinite and in His infinitude He
swallows up all space. D119

Space has to do with matter and spirit is independent
of it. D119

SPIRIT
(see also HEART, INNER MAN, SPIRITUALITY)

It is spirit that gives significance to matter and apart from spirit nothing has any value at last. [F69]

The Spirit of God is the Spirit of truth. It is possible to have some truth in the mind without having the Spirit in the heart, but it is never possible to have the Spirit apart from truth. [F104]

All life is at root spiritual. God is spirit, and since He is the Cause and Origin of everything, it follows that everything originally came out of spirit. [M82]

Prayer, humility and a generous application of the Spirit of Christ will cure just about any disease in the body of believers. [M83]

Deeds done in the Spirit, in obedience to Christ and with the purpose of bringing honor to the Triune God, are seeds of endless blessedness. [M87]

"He that soweth to the Spirit shall of the Spirit reap life everlasting." There it is, and we have but to submit *to* it to gain *from* it an everlasting reward. [M87]

SPIRIT FULLNESS

Every Christian can have a copious outpouring of the Holy Spirit in a measure far beyond that received at conversion. [B121]

Before a man can be filled with the Spirit *he must be sure he wants to be.* [B122]

The degree of fullness in any life accords perfectly with the intensity of true desire. We have as much of God as we actually want. [B124]

Before we can be filled with the Spirit *the desire to be filled must be all-consuming.* [B124]

The filling with the Spirit . . . requires that we give
up our all, that we undergo an inward death, that we rid
our hearts of that centuries-old accumulation of
Adamic trash and open all rooms to the heavenly Guest.
B126

Every man is as holy and as full of the Spirit as he
wants to be. He may not be as full as he wishes he were,
but he is most certainly as full as he wants to be. D8

We beg the Holy Spirit to fill us while all the time we
are preventing Him by our doubts. D102

The Spirit-filled man may literally dwell in a state of
spiritual fervor amounting to a mild and pure
inebriation. E9

Every man is as close to God as he wants to be; he is
as holy and as full of the Spirit as he wills to be. G64

Nowhere in the Scriptures nor in Christian biography
was anyone ever filled with the Spirit who did not know
that he had been, and nowhere was anyone filled who
did not know when. And no one was ever filled
gradually. H41

SPIRITUALITY
(see also HEART, INNER MAN, SPIRIT)

A satisfactory spiritual life will begin with a complete
change in relation between God and the sinner; not a
judicial change merely, but a conscious and
experienced change affecting the sinner's whole
nature. A100

We have tried to secure spiritual pleasures by working
upon fleshly emotions and whipping up synthetic feeling
by means wholly carnal. B81

Religious contentment is the enemy of the spiritual life
always. B124

We may as well accept it: there is no short cut to sanctity. C12

The great need of the hour among persons spiritually hungry is twofold: First, to know the Scriptures, apart from which no saving truth will be vouchsafed by our Lord; the second, to be enlightened by the Spirit, apart from whom the Scriptures will not be understood. C37

Contentment with earthly goods is the mark of a saint; contentment with our spiritual state is a mark of inward blindness. C55

Every godly soul knows how much spiritual meditations have meant to the total success of his inward life. D130

We may as well face it: the whole level of spirituality among us is low. We have measured ourselves by ourselves until the incentive to seek higher plateaus in the things of the Spirit is all but gone. E12

The concept of spirituality varies among different Christian groups. In some circles the highly vocal person who talks religion continually is thought to be very spiritual; others accept noisy exuberance as a mark of spirituality, and in some churches the man who prays first, longest and loudest gets a reputation for being the most spiritual man in the assembly. G110

A vigorous testimony, frequent prayers and loud praise may be entirely consistent with spirituality, but it is important that we understand that they do not in themselves constitute it nor prove that it is present. G112

True spirituality manifests itself in certain dominant desires.
1. *First is the desire to be holy rather than happy.*
2. *A man may be considered spiritual when he wants to see the honor of God advanced through his life.*

3. *The spiritual man wants to carry his cross.*
4. *Again a Christian is spiritual when he sees everything from God's viewpoint.*
5. *Another desire of the spiritual man is to die right rather than to live wrong.*
6. *The desire to see others advance at his expense.*
7. *The spiritual man habitually makes eternity-judgments instead of time-judgments.* G113

Nothing that man has discovered about himself or God has revealed any shortcut to pure spirituality. It is still free, but tremendously costly. G135

History shows clearly enough that true spirituality has never at any time been the possession of the masses. M20

S U C C E S S

The man who reaches the pinnacle is seldom happy for very long. D57

This mania to succeed is a good thing perverted. D57

T

T E S T I M O N Y

Human speech, a very gift of God to mankind, can become consolation for the bereaved or hope for the disconsolate, and it can rise higher and break into prayer and praise to the Most High God. D107

Our concern is not to explain but to proclaim. F62

The Christian is not sent to argue or persuade, nor is he sent to prove or demonstrate; he is sent to declare "Thus saith the Lord." K38

The Christian's message to the world must . . . be one of sin, righteousness and judgment. He must not accept in any measure the world's moral code, but stand boldly to oppose it and warn of the consequences of following it. And this he must do loudly and persistently, meanwhile taking great care that he himself walk so circumspectly that no flaw may be found in his life to give the lie to his testimony. K39

The Christian witness includes the faithful warning that God is a just and holy Being who will not trifle with men nor allow them to trifle with Him. K40

If it is right to praise God it is wrong not to praise Him and for that reason the tongue that is silent is sinful. K142

The fear that keeps us quiet when faith and love and loyalty cry out for us to speak is surely evil and must be judged as evil before the bar of eternal justice. K142

The sinfulness of silence and inaction is more than academic; it is sharply practical and may impinge upon the soul of any one of us at anytime. K143

The testimony of the true follower of Christ might well be something like this: The world's pleasures and the world's treasures henceforth have no appeal for me. I reckon myself crucified to the world and the world crucified to me. But the multitudes that were so dear to Christ shall not be less dear to me. If I cannot prevent their moral suicide, I shall at least baptize them with my human tears. I want no blessing that I cannot share. I seek no spirituality that I must win at the cost of forgetting that men and women are lost and without hope. If in spite of all I can do they will sin against light and bring upon themselves the displeasure of a holy God, then I must not let them go their sad way unwept. I scorn a happiness that I must purchase with ignorance. I reject a heaven that I must enter by shutting my eyes to the sufferings of my fellow men. I choose a broken heart rather than any happiness that ignores the tragedy of human life and human death. Though I, through the grace of God in Christ, no longer lie under Adam's sin, I would still feel a bond of compassion for all of Adam's tragic race, and I am determined that I shall go down to the grave or up into God's heaven mourning for the lost and the perishing. M36

THEOLOGY
(see also DOCTRINE)

Theology has a tendency to run to modes just as does philosophy. D78

In theology there is no "Oh!" and this is significant if not an ominous thing. Theology seeks to reduce what may be known of God to intellectual terms, and as long as the intellect can comprehend, it can find words to express itself. D86

There is the difference between theological knowledge and spiritual experience, the difference between knowing God by hearsay and knowing Him by acquaintance. And the difference is not verbal merely; it is real and serious and vital. D87

Bible exposition without moral application raises no opposition. E27

Theological truth is useless until it is obeyed. E27

Theology itself may exist as a semiopaque veil behind which God, if seen at all, is seen only imperfectly. E110

Theology is precious because it is the study of God. And the very English word in its composition puts God where He belongs—first. E110

Because we are the handiwork of God, it follows that all our problems and their solutions are theological. F27

A man need not be godly to learn theology. G56

THOUGHT
(see also MIND)

God's thoughts belong to the world of spirit, man's to the world of intellect, and while spirit can embrace intellect, the human intellect can never comprehend spirit. B77

What we think about when we are free to think about what we will—that is what we are or will soon become. D44

The Bible has a great deal to say about our thoughts; current evangelicalism has practically nothing to say about them. D44

Thinking stirs feeling and triggers action. That is the way we are made and we may as well accept it. D45

If we are honest with ourselves we can discover not only what we are but what we are going to become. We'll soon be the sum of our voluntary thoughts. D46

While our thoughts stir our feelings, and thus strongly influence our wills, it is yet true that the will can be and should be master of our thoughts. D47

A man will finally be what his active thoughts make him. D130

There are few emotions so satisfying as the joy that comes from the act of recognition when we see and identify our own thoughts. D149

That writer does the most for us who brings to our attention thoughts that lay close to our minds waiting to be acknowledged as our own. D149

The best way to control our thoughts is to offer the mind to God in complete surrender. G47

The Scriptures simply take for granted that the saints of the Most High will be serious-minded, thoughtful persons. They never leave the impression that it is sinful to think. G52

It would be easy to marshall an imposing list of Biblical quotations exhorting us to think, but a more convincing argument is the whole drift of the Bible itself. G52

Our thoughts are the product of our thinking, and since these are of such vast importance to us it is imperative that we learn how to think rightly. G95

Thinking is a kind of living. G95

Feats of thinking may create reputation, but habits of thinking create character. G95

God wills that we think His thoughts after Him. G96

To be heavenly-minded we must think heavenly thoughts. G97

When a true thought enters any man's mind, be he saint or sinner, it must of necessity be God's thought, for God is the origin of all true thoughts and things. That is why many real truths are spoken and written by persons other than Christians. H23

To do a wrong act a man must for the moment think wrong; he must exercise bad judgment. H46

Pure thinking will do more to educate a man than any other activity he can engage in. To afford sympathetic entertainment to abstract ideas, to let one idea beget another, and that another, till the mind teems with them; to compare one idea with others, to weigh, to consider, evaluate, approve, reject, correct, refine; to join thought with thought like an architect till a noble edifice has been created within the mind; to travel back in imagination to the beginning of the creation and then to leap swiftly forward to the end of time; to bound upward through illimitable space and downward into the nucleus of an atom; and all this without so much as moving from our chair or opening the eyes—this is to soar above all the lower creation and to come near to the angels of God. H145

Our spirits are vaster than our intellects and can penetrate behind the veil where our conscious thoughts cannot come. K134

We cannot know God by thinking, but that we must do a lot of thinking if we would know Him well. L47

Thinking carries a moral imperative. The searcher for truth must be ready to obey truth without reservation or it will elude him. L66

Great thoughts require a grave attitude toward life and mankind and God. L66

It is easier to follow degenerate public taste than to think for oneself. L68

It is doubtful whether any sin is ever committed until it first incubates in the thoughts long enough to stir the feelings and predispose the will toward it favorably. L72

A will firmly engaged with God can swing the intellectual powers around to think on holy things. L73

It is something of a happy paradox that while the thoughts deeply affect the will and go far to determine its choices, the will on the other hand has the power to control the thoughts. L73

TIME AND ETERNITY
(see also PAST, PRESENT, AND FUTURE)

We habitually stand in our *now* and look back by faith to see the past filled with God. We look forward and see Him inhabiting our future; but our *now* is uninhabited except for ourselves. B23

With God Abram's day and this day are the same. B28

Our preoccupation with . . . time is sad evidence of our basic want of faith. C76

Eternity is silent; time is noisy. C76

God is always first, and God will surely be last.
　　To say this is not to draw God downward into the stream of time and involve Him in the flux and flow of the world. He stands above His own creation and outside of time; but for the convenience of His creatures, who are children of time, He makes free use of time words when referring to Himself. So He says that He is

Alpha and Omega, the beginning and the ending, the first and the last. C158

Since God is uncreated, He is not Himself affected by that succession of consecutive changes we call time. F39

Began is a time word, and can have no personal meaning for the high and lofty One that inhabiteth eternity. F39

God dwells in eternity but time dwells in God. F39

Changes take place not all at once but in succession, one after the other, and it is the relation of "after" to "before" that gives us our idea of time. F39

We wait for the sun to move from east to west or for the hour hand to move around the face of the clock, but God is not compelled so to wait. For Him everything that will happen has already happened. F40

We are made for eternity as certainly as we are made for time, and as responsible moral beings we must deal with both. F41

To be made for eternity and forced to dwell in time is for mankind a tragedy of huge proportions. F41

How completely satisfying to turn from our limitations to a God who has none. Eternal years lie in His heart. For Him time does not pass, it remains; and those who are in Christ share with Him all the riches of limitless time and endless years. F47

For those out of Christ, time is a devouring beast. F47

Time is short, and eternity is long. H38

Everything that men do in their own strength and by means of their own abilities is done for time alone; the quality of eternity is not in it. Only what is done through the Eternal Spirit will abide eternally; all else is wood, hay, stubble. K93

God has set eternity in our hearts and we have chosen time instead. He is trying to interest us in a glorious tomorrow and we are settling for an inglorious today. L93

TOLERANCE AND INTOLERANCE

A new Decalogue has been adopted by the neo-Christians of our day, the first word of which reads "Thou shalt not disagree"; and a new set of Beatitudes too, which begins, "Blessed are they that tolerate everything, for they shall not be made accountable for anything." H67

In all our discussions there must never be any trace of intolerance; but we obviously forget that the most fervent devotees of tolerance are invariably intolerant of everyone who speaks about God with certainty. H113

TREASURE

The man who has God for his treasure has all things in One. A19

Treasure . . . may be discovered by this fourfold test: (1) It is what we value most. (2) It is what we would hate most to lose. (3) It is what our thoughts turn to most frequently when we are free to think of what we will. (4) It is what affords us the greatest pleasure. D106

So rich a treasure is this inward knowledge of God that every other treasure is as nothing compared with it. G84

TRINITY
(see also UNITY OF GOD)

There is in the awful and mysterious depths of the Triune God neither limit nor end. A14

The Christian doctrine of the Trinity boldly declares the equality of the Three Persons and the right of the Holy Spirit to be worshiped and glorified. B65

God is a Trinity in Unity. D25

The doctrine of the divine unity means not only that there is but one God; it means that the Triune God is one with Himself, of a single substance, without parts. D25

Some persons who reject all they cannot explain have denied that God is a Trinity. Subjecting the Most High to their cold, level-eyed scrutiny, they conclude that it is impossible that He could be both One and Three. These forget that their whole life is enshrouded in mystery. They fail to consider that any real explanation of even the simplest phenomenon in nature lies hidden in obscurity and can no more be explained than can the mystery of the Godhead. F17

The doctrine of the Trinity is truth for the heart. F20

T R U S T

The stroke of death is upon us, and it will be saving wisdom for us to learn to trust not in ourselves but in Him that raiseth the dead. B55

What we need very badly these days is a company of Christians who are prepared to trust God as completely now as they know they must do at the last day. C50

We can afford to trust God; but we can't afford not to. D99

Trust God in the dark till the light returns. D122

God constantly encourages us to trust Him in the dark. F63

If our faith is to have a firm foundation we must be convinced beyond any possible doubt that God is altogether worthy of our trust. G26

True faith is not the intellectual ability to visualize unseen things to the satisfaction of our imperfect minds; it is rather the moral power to trust Christ. G70

Nothing can hinder the heart that is fully surrendered and quietly trusting, because nothing can hinder God. G130

T R U T H

Divine truth is of the nature of spirit and for that reason can be received only by spiritual revelation. B76

Before there can be true inward understanding of divine truth there must be a moral preparation. C20

Truth that is not experienced is no better than error, and may be fully as dangerous. C55

The uncomprehending mind is unaffected by truth. D59

Truth is so vast and mighty that no one is capable of taking it all in and . . . it requires the whole company of ransomed souls properly to reflect the whole body of revealed truth. D76

Truth cannot enter a passive mind. It must be received into the mind by an active mental response, and the act of receiving it tends to alter it to a greater or less degree. D77

We should not assume that we have all the truth and that we are mistaken in nothing. Rather we should kneel in adoration before the pierced feet of Him who is the Truth and honor Him by humble obedience to His words. D79

Theological truth is useless until it is obeyed. The purpose behind all doctrine is to secure moral action. E27

Truth engages the citadel of the human heart and is not satisfied until it has conquered everything there. E27

Truth as set forth in the Christian Scriptures is a moral thing; it is not addressed to the intellect only, but to the will also. E27

Truth is a glorious but hard mistress. She never consults, bargains or compromises. E39

No man has any right to pick and choose among revealed truths. God has spoken. E56

The truth is self-validating and self-renewing; its whole psychology is that of attack. Its own vigorous attack is all the defense it needs. E97

Most of us go through life praying a little, planning a little, jockeying for position, hoping but never being quite certain of anything, and always secretly afraid that we will miss the way. This is a tragic waste of truth and never gives rest to the heart. F63

We can hold a correct view of truth only by daring to believe everything God has said about Himself. F79–80

Faith wakes at the voice of truth but responds to no other sound. F104

Truth is one but truths are many. Scriptural truths are interlocking and interdependent. G36

God intended that truth should move us to moral action. G48

Unused truth becomes as useless as an unused muscle. G59

Many of the doctrinal divisions among the churches
are the result of a blind and stubborn insistence that truth
has but one wing. G59

The essence of my belief is that there is a difference, a
vast difference, between fact and truth. Truth in the
Scriptures is more than a fact. A fact may be detached,
impersonal, cold and totally disassociated from life. Truth
on the other hand, is warm, living and spiritual. G92

A theological fact may be held in the mind for a
lifetime without its having any positive effect upon the
moral character; but truth is creative, saving,
transforming, and it always changes the one who receives
it into a humbler and holier man. G92

Truth, to be understood, must be lived; . . . Bible
doctrine is wholly ineffective until it has been digested
and assimilated by the total life. G92

An unblessed soul filled with the letter of truth may
actually be worse off than a pagan kneeling before a
fetish. G103

Should an atheist . . . state that two times two equals
four, he would be stating a truth and thinking God's
thought after Him, even though he might deny that
God exists at all. H23

Not facts, not scientific knowledge, but eternal Truth
delivers men, and that eternal Truth became flesh to dwell
among us. H25

Not only does God address His words of truth to
those who are able to receive them, He actually conceals
their meaning from those who are not. H28

What are the axiomatic truths upon which all human
life may rest with confidence? Fortunately they are not
many. Here are the chief ones:

1. *Only God is great.*
2. *Only God is wise.*
3. *Apart from God nothing matters.*
4. *Only what we do in God will remain to us at last.*
5. *Human sin is real.*
6. *With God there is forgiveness.*
7. *Only what God protects is safe.* H116

When men deal with things earthly and temporal they demand truth; when they come to the consideration of things heavenly and eternal they hedge and hesitate as if either could not be discovered or didn't matter anyway. H162

God's truth is the same wherever it is found and if the church conforms to the truth it will be the same church in doctrine and in practice throughout the entire world. K42

Among the purest gifts we have received from God is truth. Another gift, almost as precious, and without which the first would be meaningless, is our ability to grasp truth and appreciate it. K120

We may believe all that God has revealed, however self-contradictory it may appear to be, because all truths meet and harmonize in the truth, and the truth makes free. K134

The searcher for truth must be ready to obey truth without reservation or it will elude him. L66

Our response to truth should be eager and instant. We dare not dally with it; we dare not treat it as something we can obey or not obey, at our pleasure. It is a glorious friend, but it is nevertheless a hard master, exacting unquestioning obedience. L69

Apart from truth our human lives would lose all their value, and we ourselves become no better than the beasts that perish. L69

To know the truth is the greatest privilege any man can enjoy in this life, as truth itself is without doubt the richest treasure anyone can possess. L69

Truth is such a royal patron that we should embrace it without regard to cost. L70

We Christians above all people should value truth, for we profess to belong to the One who is the Truth. L70

It was Christ who capitalized truth and revealed that it was not an "it" at all but a Being with all the attributes of personality. "I am the Truth," He said, and followed truth straight to the cross. L97

Truth is a glorious but hard master. It makes moral demands upon us. It claims the sovereign right to control us, to strip us, even to slay us as it chooses. L97

Truth will never stoop to be a servant but requires that all men serve it. It never flatters men and never compromises with them. It demands all or nothing and refuses to be used or patronized. It will be all in all or it will withdraw into silence. L97

Truth is not a thing for which we must search, but a Person to whom we must hearken. L99

It is not the difficulty of discovering truth but the unwillingness to obey it that makes it so rare among men. L99

Truth is sovereign and will not allow itself to be trifled with. And it is easy to find for it is trying to find us. L100

To stand by the truth of God against the current religious vogue is always unpopular and may be downright dangerous. M20

U

UNITY OF GOD
(see also TRINITY)

The doctrine of the divine unity means not only that there is but one God; it means also that God is simple, uncomplex, one with Himself. The harmony of His being is the result not of a perfect balance of parts but of the absence of parts. F15

There is no conflict among the divine attributes. God's being is unitary. F80

V

VALUES

Nothing new can save my soul; neither can saving grace be modernized. We must each come as Abel came, by atoning blood and faith demonstrated in repentance. No new way has been discovered. The old way is the true way and there is no new way. The Lamb of God was slain "before the foundation of the world."

A few other things matter to be sure, but they begin there, go out from there and return there again. They are that we trust Christ completely, carry our cross daily, love God and our fellow men, walk in the light as God gives us to understand it; that we love mercy, and walk uprightly; that we fulfill our commission as ambassadors of Christ among men; that we grow in grace and in the knowledge of God and come at last to our end like a ripe shock of corn at harvest time. D90

One of the glories of the Christian religion is that faith and love can transmute lower values into higher ones. Earthly possessions can be turned into heavenly treasures. D106

Life as we know it in our painfully intricate civilization can be deadly unless we learn to distinguish the things that matter from those that do not. M11

A serious discourse calling for repentance, humbleness of mind and holiness of life is impatiently dismissed as old-fashioned, dull and lacking in "audience appeal." Yet these things are just the ones that rank highest on the list of things we need to hear, and by them we shall all be judged in that great day of Christ. M13

Before the judgment seat of Christ, very little will be heard of numbers or size; moral quality is about all that will matter then. M69

The careless song, the sermon preached for no higher reason than because it is Sunday again, the tithe tossed into the plate, the testimony given because it seems the thing to do—not one of these will stand up under the searching eyes of God. M70

Everything of lasting value in the Christian life is unseen and eternal. M82–83

V I C T O R Y

The degree of blessing enjoyed by any man will correspond exactly with the completeness of God's victory over him. B53

God is always glorified when He wins a moral victory over us, and we are always benefited, immeasurably and gloriously benefited. The glory of God and the everlasting welfare of His people are always bound up together. C117

V I R T U E
(see also RIGHTEOUSNESS)

There is no moral beauty but what Christ is the source of it. Every trait of lovely character we see in any believing man or woman is but an imperfect demonstration of how wonderful Jesus is. Even those moral beauties that appear to be "natural" to some people have their source in Him. For human goodness cannot exist apart from Christ. M58

Some good Christians are afraid to give notice to any lovely virtues which may appear here and there among God's people lest they detract from the glory of Christ. M59

If we know to begin with that all goodness is from
Christ, that all sweetness, all holiness, all loveliness are
out of Him and from Him and in Him, we will not
hesitate to recognize moral excellence wherever it may
occur on this dark planet. M59

V O I C E   O F   G O D
(see also BIBLE, SCRIPTURES)

God is speaking. Not God spoke, but *God is speaking*.
He is, by His nature, continuously articulate. He fills the
world with His speaking voice. A73

God's word in the Bible can have power only because
it corresponds to God's word in the universe. A74

It is the present Voice which makes the written Word
all-powerful. Otherwise it would lie locked in slumber
within the covers of a book. A74

The voice of God is the most powerful force in
nature, indeed the only force in nature, for all energy is
here only because the power-filled Word is being
spoken. A74

God is here and He is speaking. A75

That God is here and that He is speaking—these truths
are back of all other Bible truths; without them there
could be no revelation at all. A75

God did not write a book and send it by messenger to
be read at a distance by unaided minds. He spoke a Book
and lives in His spoken words, constantly speaking His
words and causing the power of them to persist across the
years. A75

The order and life of the world depend upon that
Voice, but men are mostly too busy or too stubborn to
give attention. A78

Whoever will listen will hear the speaking Heaven. A80

The Voice of God is a friendly Voice. No one need fear to listen to it unless he has already made up his mind to resist it. A80

True moral wisdom must always be an echo of God's voice. C18

God is not silent and has never been silent, but is speaking in His universe. K13

It is the still voice of God in the heart of every human being that renders everyone culpable before the bar of God's judgment and convicts of sin even those who have never been exposed to the written Word. K14

That the creative voice of God is constantly sounding throughout the creation is a truth forgotten by modern Christianity. Yet it was by His word that He called the world into being and it is by His word that all things are held together. K14

The written Word is effective because, and only because, the Living Word is speaking in heaven and the Living Voice is sounding in the earth. K14

If the living voice of God were not speaking in the world and in the hearts of men the written Word could have no real meaning for us. Because God is speaking in His world we are able to hear Him speak in His Word. K15

Until we find God through Christ, that inner "ground" will remain a kind of eternal thirst inside of us, and its voice, where that voice is recognized, will be a plea, an accusation, a thin plaintive cry deep within us asking for eternal life and restoration and God. M104

WILL

The will of God is the same for all. He has no
favorites within His household. All He has ever done for
any of His children He will do for all of His children.
The difference lies not with God but with us. A66

There are two worlds, set over against each other,
dominated by two wills, the will of man and the will of
God, respectively. B44

How deeply do men err who conceive of God as
subject to our human will or as standing respectfully to
wait upon our human pleasure. B50

To will the will of God is to do more than give
unprotesting consent to it; it is rather to choose God's will
with positive determination. B105

Let a man set his heart only on doing the will of God
and he is instantly free. C129

The dead church holds to the shell of truth without
surrendering the will to it, while the church that wills to
do God's will is immediately blessed with a visitation
of spiritual powers. G93

The root of all evil in human nature is the corruption
of the will. The thoughts and intents of the heart are
wrong and as a consequence the whole life is
wrong. H36

To love God with all our heart we must first of all will
to do so. H36

The will, not the feelings, determines moral direction. H36

The will is the automatic pilot that keeps the soul on course. H36

The important thing about a man is not where he goes when he is compelled to go, but where he goes when he is free to go where he will. H158

The highest expression of the will of God in this age is the church which He purchased with His own blood. K26

We need revival! We need a revival of consecration to death, a revival of happy abandonment to the will of God that will laugh at sacrifice and count it a privilege to bear the cross through the heat and burden of the day. K130

A will firmly engaged with God can swing the intellectual powers around to think on holy things. L73

God will not lead us except for His own glory and He cannot lead us if we resist His will. L75

Every desire should be brought to the test of God's will. If the desire is out of the will of God, it should be instantly dismissed as unworthy of us. M110

WISDOM

Let a man become enamored of Eternal Wisdom and set his heart to win her and he takes on himself a full-time, all-engaging pursuit. E39

God is wise in Himself, and all the shining wisdom of men or angels is but a reflection of that uncreated effulgence which streams from the throne of the Majesty in the heavens. F60

The idea of God as infinitely wise is at the root of all truth. F60

The whole history of the world is discovered to be but a contest between the wisdom of God and the cunning of Satan and fallen men. The outcome of the contest is not in doubt. F60

All God's acts are done in perfect wisdom, first for His own glory, and then for the highest good of the greatest number for the longest time. And all His acts are as pure as they are wise, and as good as they are wise and pure. F60

Without the creation, the wisdom of God would have remained forever locked in the boundless abyss of the divine nature. F61

The operation of the gospel, the new birth, the coming of the divine Spirit into human nature, the ultimate overthrow of evil, and the final establishment of Christ's righteous kingdom—all these have flowed and do flow out of God's infinite fullness of wisdom. F62

WONDER

It is a privilege to wonder, to stand in delighted silence before the Supreme Mystery and whisper, "O Lord God, thou knowest!" C79

So many wonders have been discovered or invented that nothing on earth is any longer wonderful. Everything is common and almost everything boring. D69

When God Himself appears before the mind, awesome, vast and incomprehensible, then the mind sinks into silence and the heart cries out "O Lord God!" D86

In theology there is no "Oh!" and this is a significant if not an ominous thing. D86

WORD AND DEED

The moral relation between words and deeds appears quite plainly in the life and teachings of Christ. He did before He spoke and the doing gave validity to the speaking. D32

We modern Christians are long on talk and short on conduct. We use the language of power but our deeds are the deeds of weakness. D32

It would be a convenient arrangement were we so constituted that we could not talk better than we live. D32

We settle for words in religion because deeds are too costly. It is easier to pray, "Lord, help me to carry my cross daily" than to pick up the cross and carry it. D34

How then shall we escape the snare of words without deeds?
It is simple, though not easy. First, let us say nothing we do not mean. Break the habit of conventional religious chatter. Speak only as we are ready to take the consequences. Believe God's promises and obey His commandments. Practice the truth and we may with propriety speak the truth. Deeds give body to words. As we do acts of power our words will take on authority and a new sense of reality will fill our hearts. D35

We are moral beings and as such we must accept the consequence of every deed done and every word spoken. E47

WORDS

It is not mere words that nourish the soul, but God Himself, and unless and until the hearers find God in personal experience they are not the better for having heard the truth. A-Preface

It is probably impossible to think without words, but if we permit ourselves to think with the wrong words, we shall soon be entertaining erroneous thoughts; for words, which are given us for the expression of thought, have a habit of going beyond their proper bounds and determining the content of thought. F14

Conversation today is almost wholly sterile. H144

Words are nòt truth, but caskets in which the gem of truth is carried. God will hold us responsible for meanings, not for texts only. K134

WORK

It is inconceivable that a sovereign and holy God should be so hard up for workers that He would press into service anyone who had been empowered regardless of his moral qualifications. G37

God wants worshipers before workers; indeed the only acceptable workers are those who have learned the lost art of worship. G37

The gospel of work, as someone has called it, has crowded out the gospel of Christ in many Christian churches. G136

No work, however sacrificial, will be permanent unless it is geared to eternity. Only what is done in a spirit of worship will last forever. L59

WORK OF GOD

"It is God which worketh in you." *He needs no one, but when faith is present He works through anyone.* F36

Everything that God does is done without effort or strain. He does all his acts with equal ease and tranquillity. M97

W O R L D

(see also COMPROMISE, FLESH)

Every man must choose his world. A57

If we truly want to follow God, we must seek to be other-worldly. A57

To be a friend of the world is to be a collaborator with evil and an enemy of God. B40

The world is whitewashed just enough to pass inspection by blind men posing as believers, and those same believers are everlastingly seeking to gain acceptance with the world. B111

By mutual concessions men who call themselves Christians manage to get on with men who have for the things of God nothing but quiet contempt. B111

Christianity is so entangled with the world that millions never guess how radically they have missed the New Testament pattern. Compromise is everywhere. B111

The world's spirit is strong, and it clings to us as close as the smell of smoke to our garments. B114

The world's press (which is always its real mouthpiece) will seldom give a child of God a fair deal. B115

Our warfare is not against mere worldly ways, but against the *spirit* of the world. B117

The world, in the New Testament meaning of the word, is simply unregenerate human nature wherever it is found, whether in a tavern or in a church. B117

Whatever springs out of, is built upon, or receives
support from fallen human nature is the world, whether it
is morally base or morally respectable. B117

We must have a new reformation. There must come a
violent break with that irresponsible, amusement-mad,
paganized pseudo religion which passes today for the
faith of Christ and which is being spread all over the
world by unspiritual men employing unscriptural
methods to achieve their ends. C110

To live in a world under siege is to live in constant
peril; to live there and be wholly unaware of the peril is to
increase it a hundredfold and to turn the world into a
paradise for fools. D42

It is time that we Christians awake to the fact that the
world cannot help us in anything that matters. D110

Worldliness is an accepted part of our way of life. Our
religious mood is social instead of spiritual. We have lost
the art of worship. We are not producing saints. E12

The whole world has been booby-trapped by the
devil, and the deadliest trap of all is the religious one.
Error never looks so innocent as when it is found in
the sanctuary. E84

If the spiritual view of the world is the correct one, as
Christianity boldly asserts that it is, then for every one of
us heaven is more important than earth and eternity
more important than time. E93

Any spirit that permits compromise with the world is
a false spirit. Any religious movement that imitates the
world in any of its manifestations is false to the cross of
Christ and on the side of the devil—and this regardless of
how much purring its leaders may do about "accepting
Christ" or "letting God run your business." E132

The weakness of so many modern Christians is that they feel too much at home in the world. E174

Since the Christian must deviate radically from the world he naturally comes in for the world's displeasure. G88

Our whole modern world is geared to destroy individual independence and bring all of us into conformity to all the rest of us. G88

The great majority of evangelical Christians, while kept somewhat in line by the pressure of group opinion, nevertheless have a boundless, if perforce secret, admiration for the world. G103

God is love and His kindness is unbounded, but He has no sympathy with the carnal mind. He remembers that we are dust, indeed, but He refuses to tolerate the doings of the flesh. G106

The church today is suffering from the secularization of the sacred. By accepting the world's values, thinking its thoughts and adopting its ways we have dimmed the glory that shines overhead. We have not been able to bring earth to the judgment of heaven so we have brought heaven to the judgment of the earth. Pity us, Lord, for we know not what we do! H56

That evangelism which draws friendly parallels between the ways of God and the ways of men is false to the Bible and cruel to the souls of its hearers. The faith of Christ does not parallel the world, it intersects it. H144

It is hard to focus attention upon a better world to come when a more comfortable one than this can hardly be imagined. H155

Almost everything the church is doing these days has been suggested to her by the world. H166

That world which our Saviour once refused to buy at the price of disobedience to God is now wooing His professed followers with every sly, deceptive artifice. K23

The glory which our Lord once rejected with cold scorn is now being admired and sought after by multitudes who make a loud profession of accepting the gospel. K23

In spite of the prophetic voices that are raised here and there among us, present-day believers are drawn to the world with irresistible force. K23

With the Bible open before us and a long tradition of truth behind us there would seem to be no reason for our present tragic failure to recognize the world's deceptive appeal and to stay clear of it. K23

The old trick which our Lord saw through so easily is charming His present-day followers into smiling acquiescence, corruption and decay. He knew its glory was but bait to catch foolish victims. He knew its bright promises were all lies. K23

Men think of the world, not as a battleground but as a playground. We are not here to fight, we are here to frolic. We are not in a foreign land, we are at home. We are not getting ready to live, we are already living, and the best we can do is to rid ourselves of our inhibitions and our frustrations and live this life to the full. K154

All conformity to the world is a negation of our Christian character and a surrender of our heavenly position. L36

Morally the world is like a bombed city. L59

This is a moral universe. At bottom it is not material, though it contains matter; it is not mathematical, though it involves numbers. The God who made the world is a moral being and He has filled His world with moral creatures. L121

The man of the world, despite his protestations to the contrary, actually accepts the sufficiency of this world and makes no provision for any other; he esteems earth above heaven, time above eternity, body above soul and men above God. He holds sin to be relatively harmless, believes pleasure to be an end in itself, accepts the rightness of the customary and trusts to the basic goodness of human nature. L135

The man of heaven lives for the kingdom within him; the man of earth lives for the world around him. The first is born of the Spirit; the other is born of the flesh and will perish with it. L136

Whatever promotes self, cheapens life, starves the soul, hopes without biblical grounds for hope, adopts current moral standards, follows the way of the majority whether it be right or wrong, indulges in the pleasures of the flesh to make bearable the secret thoughts of death and judgment—that is the world. L136

It takes a work of God in a man to sour him on the world and to turn him against himself; yet until this has happened to him he is psychologically unable to repent and believe. L144

W O R S H I P

Men who refuse to worship the true God now worship themselves with tender devotion. B52

Evangelistic and revival services in New Testament times were never divorced from worship. C94

The essence of spiritual worship is to love supremely, to trust confidently, to pray without ceasing and to seek to be Christlike and holy, doing all the good we can for Christ's sake. C130

The whole concept of ineffable worship has been lost to this generation of Christians. C145

God saves men to make them worshipers. D125

Worship is pure or base as the worshiper entertains high or low thoughts of God. F1

God wants worshipers before workers; indeed the only acceptable workers are those who have learned the lost art of worship. G37

It is quite impossible to worship God without loving Him. G126

Worship is elementary until it begins to take on the quality of admiration. G127

If Bible Christianity is to survive the present world upheaval, we shall need to recapture the spirit of worship. G131

The wise of the world who have not learned to worship are but demi-men, unformed and rudimentary. L59

Maintenance of the devotional mood is indispensable to success in the Christian life. L129

WRATH OF GOD

To understand God's wrath we must view it in the light of His holiness. God is holy and has made holiness to be the moral condition necessary to the health of His universe. H110

The holiness of God, the wrath of God and the health of the creation are inseparably united. Not only is it right for God to display anger against sin, but I find it impossible to understand how He could do otherwise. H111

A project, any project, no matter how small or large,
rarely comes to be by the hands of just one person.

To:

My clients, their families, and friends. Without you, this book
would not have been necessary, or even possible.

Ted, my editor, for your belief and faith in the book, your support,
and your gentle guidance.

Cathy A., for giving me insight, being patient with my mistakes,
and continuing to be my friend.

Doug G., for your "always there" professional encouragement
and support.

Gabriel McLellan, for your willingness to trace the source of
whatever "buried in forever" information I needed.

Joan Burton, for your time, advice, counsel, and support
to an "unknown."

Kevin, whose unconditional encouragement and faith is
always there.

Dave and Maureen, just 'cuz I know you're always there.

Bree, because you are in everything I do, and I love you.

Bob, for your love and support, for putting up with all the weird
hours, long hours "away," and picking up the slack, always with a
smile. For reading and suggesting and reading again. For being
there when the stress got too high and the energy too low.

Thanks, everybody!

Debb

Contents

*B*efore you begin reading this book, take a few minutes to complete this little quiz. Then forget about it.

At the end of the book, you'll see it again.

PERCEPTION OF HEARING LOSS

1. On a scale from one to ten (ten being *very*, five being *moderately*, and one being *not at all*), how disabling would you rate hearing loss? (Circle one number.)

1 - 2 - 3 - 4 - 5 - 6 - 7 - 8 - 9 - 10

As compared to blindness?

1 - 2 - 3 - 4 - 5 - 6 - 7 - 8 - 9 - 10

As compared to an amputated limb?

1 - 2 - 3 - 4 - 5 - 6 - 7 - 8 - 9 - 10

As compared to Alzheimer's disease?

1 - 2 - 3 - 4 - 5 - 6 - 7 - 8 - 9 - 10

2. What percentage of each age group do you think is affected by hearing loss?

- Newborns _____%
- Age 1 mo.–5 yrs. _____%
- Age 6–11 _____%
- Under 18 _____%
- Age 19–44 _____%
- Age 45–64 _____%
- Age 65–74 _____%
- Age 75 + _____%
- Total population _____%

Perception of Hearing Loss

3. Would you rather be hearing-impaired or blind? (Circle one.)

4. While conversing with a hearing-impaired person, I find that I will . . . (Circle your answers.)

- raise my voice   yes   no

- talk through another person, if present   yes   no

- overarticulate   yes   no

- get frustrated/discontinue the conversation   yes   no

- try to avoid communicating at all   yes   no

Preface

I know a lady who kept saying "There oughta be a book . . ."

As an audiologist, in many situations I often find myself explaining something for the umteenth time ("To him, you *do* mumble"), or answering a question that should have been addressed by someone else ("My doctor said I was deaf, but I can hear you"), or clarifying rumors ("My neighbor says XYZ hearing aid is the *only* one to buy!"). Each time, I'd remember Kathy muttering, "There oughta be a book . . ."

Hearing loss in the under-65 age group exists in much higher numbers than you might think. Of our five senses, hearing is often the one most taken for granted. What's disturbing is that so many people experience hearing loss and so few know how to deal with it.

"I hear the birds singing, and I say, 'Oh, listen. That is beautiful!' And she says, 'What? I cannot hear it.' And I feel sadness."

A young woman with a moderate hearing loss experiences difficulty with her boss who thinks she is "coming on to him" because she must get so close to hear him clearly. At night, when she is in her boyfriend's car, she never knows what he is saying because it is dark (and she cannot speech-read). She is afraid she might miss something, or say yes when she means no, and she is not comfortable about telling him she has a hearing loss.

Why do people take physical and emotional risks by hiding their hearing loss instead of just telling someone they are hearing-impaired? After reading this book, hopefully that question will be answered. You'll also learn how to cope with situations like these and many others.

1

- If you are the parent of a hearing-impaired child, you'll learn strategies for coping with education, communication, and how to separate behaviors that may be related to the hearing loss and those of just being a kid.

- If you are hearing-impaired, you will learn how to get maximum satisfaction from your hearing aids. You'll discover options and opportunities for involvement and information that you may never have known existed. You'll learn how to arrange environments to your best listening advantage and how to help others communicate most effectively with you.

- You will have a better understanding of the world of deafness, as well as the impact of hearing loss, only touched upon by this self-assessment done by a group of hearing-impaired adults.

  - 60 percent were often or always depressed by their hearing loss.

  - 55 percent felt their partner, friends, and/or families get irritated with them (because of their hearing loss).

  - 7 percent have ended a relationship with a close friend or lover because of their hearing loss. Three percent have at least contemplated the idea of divorce or separation, citing hearing loss as a major factor.

  - 79 percent avoid going to social events due to their hearing loss.

  - 52 percent do more leisure things alone.

  - 34 percent are often lonely.

  - 41 percent do not pursue educational goals due to difficulty hearing in class.

  - 17 percent find it difficult or impossible to discuss their hearing loss with their partner, family, friends.

  - 34 percent said that their hearing loss causes them problems at work.[1]

---

[1]From *Pillow Talk*, newsletter of the B.C. Chapter of the Canadian Hard-of-Hearing Association. April 1989.

People with normal hearing have expressed the following feelings toward those with a hearing loss:

- 100 percent were depressed or irritated by another's inability to hear and felt angry with that person for the way communication problems were handled.

- 80 percent felt guilty about feeling this way.[2]

Over the next 10 years, the number of people age 65 years and older will increase by 11 percent, and those 75 years and older by 26 percent.[3] Hearing loss is the most common, untreatable, non-life-threatening affliction experienced by this age group. Statistically, 27 to 45 percent of the 65 years and older population have a hearing loss.[4]

As our longevity increases, so does the number of hearing-impaired. Sooner or later, I'll be one of them, and so will you—and we will all encounter situations where appropriate, effective communication is necessary at best, helpful at least.

Reading this book will help you to better understand and communicate with your parents (or spouse, or neighbor), and it can teach your children to do the same for you. The problem of hearing loss may never disappear, but our attitude toward it can improve.

Between these covers is a handbook, a diary, and a consumer's guide. I have only one request: *Please* don't put it away on the shelf or in the drawer next to your discarded hearing aid.

And thanks, Kathy, for the thought.

---

[2]Ibid.

[3]*MONEY*, March 1990, p. 124.

[4]National Health Interview Survey, 1988. Statistics Canada Disability Database Program.

CHAPTER 1

The Invisible Handicap

As a clinical audiologist, I've often spoken with educators about hearing loss. This has led to a series of school presentations for kids from kindergarten through high school.

I often begin a presentation with the question "If a flying saucer landed in your back yard tonight, would you rush to school tomorrow and tell everyone about it?"

The little ones, kindergarten through about third grade, with typical unabashed enthusiasm proclaim, "Oh yes! I'd tell everyone!"

The older kids, though, are more hesitant about sharing such information. Until, as juniors and seniors in high school, few claim they would tell anyone, except *maybe* their best friend.

Why not? You believe in UFOs, don't you? If you're a Doubting Thomas, why? If you'd actually seen a UFO, you should be a believer now, shouldn't you? In fact, many people do not believe in the existence or presence of anything unless they see it for themselves. Some of us, though, even after we're supposed to know better, still clap when Tinker Bell is dying.

Others, the "older and wiser" ones, know that if you can't *see* something, it can't be real. Just *believing* isn't enough.

Guess what? They're wrong.

Hearing impairment is invisible, but it is very real. Sixty million baby boomers are expected to reach the age of 65, making up a healthy 20 percent of the population when they do. And approximately 30 percent of them will be hearing-impaired. Once they reach 75 years of age, that figure jumps to 40 percent or more.

Unfortunately, human nature being what it is, we tend to have

more tolerance and understanding for those things we can see, experience, and touch. You decide for yourself. Which of these scenes would arouse the most compassion in you?

1. A blind person making her way across a busy intersection

2. A woman trying to get directions from a busy gas station attendant and him having to repeat everything two or three times

There's no right or wrong here—just a personal choice as to which situation would inspire feelings of sympathy, maybe a desire to help. Most of you would want to help the "poor" blind person, but we'd sympathize with the gas station attendant who is visibly becoming more and more irritated. You don't know why the woman in the second example can't understand simple directions, but it is obvious what the first person's problem is.

Cocktail parties are a great place to play conversation games. You're being a good guest, mingling admirably, and trying to come up with topics that are deep, meaningful, profound. It's a game because most of us are anything *but* deep, meaningful, or profound when we've been drinking. We're only going to be there for a couple of hours anyway. But we try.

A good way to stimulate a round of party rhetoric is "Would you rather be deaf or blind?" You've answered this question already. (Remember the quiz you took at the beginning of the book?) So, which *would* you rather be? Now that you've made your choice, think about *why*. There are inherent and obvious, as well as very subtle, differences in the nature of the two impairments.

IS HEARING IMPAIRMENT A HANDICAP?

How we perceive our own personal limitations is directly related to (1) how deeply those limitations affect or alter our chosen life style, and (2) how willing we are to adapt. What one person considers a handicap may be another person's blessing.

Take my hair, for instance. Since I was in early grade school, I have truly despised my hair. In second grade, it all fell out—every last strand. When it grew back, which it did with a vengeance, it was much curlier and thicker than before. Where I once had beautiful

curls and waves I now had "clumps" that had a mind of their own and kinked into unreasonable shapes. The ends were my real nemesis—they *frizzed*! Now, instead of having a head of hair that Vidal Sassoon's models would kill for, I was crowned with something that made me look like an animated Boston Fern with feet. In my mind, I was handicapped.

As I grew older and wiser, I more often chose not to spend 45 minutes a day torturing my hair with all forms of heated curling rods and just let it do what it wanted. Other women would invariably praise the "beautiful perm" I had. "Thanks. It's natural," I'd mutter. With each compliment my face would contort in more pain. From their point of view, I was lucky, envied, even blessed. From my point of view, I was cursed. A matter of perception.

A friend and co-worker once told me, "A handicap is a label someone else gives you." It then becomes a judgment that you may or may not internalize. Funk and Wagnalls' *New Comprehensive International Dictionary of the English Language* defines *handicap* as "any disadvantage or hindrance making success in an undertaking more difficult." So, a handicap can be anything that gets in your way. The same Funk and Wagnalls dictionary explains *impairment* as "to diminish in quality, strength, or value; injure." It seems, then, that an impairment might be seen as a state of being, while a handicap is a state of mind. You can have one but not necessarily the other. It also seems that impairments *become* handicaps when one's environment demands interactions with others.

The World Health Organization defines a handicap as "a disadvantage experienced by the individual as a result of impairments and disabilities, *reflecting the individual's interaction with his or her environment.*"[1] (Italics are the author's.) This is the reference often cited in court when determining whether an individual's hearing loss is handicapping.

Bridging all age groups, approximately 1 out of every 10 North Americans is hearing-impaired. One in every 1500 newborns is hearing-impaired. By the age of five, as many as 8 percent of all children suffer from some degree of transient or permanent hearing loss. *Twenty-three million people in North America are hearing-impaired.*

---

[1]The Health and Activity Limitation Survey, Addendum to the Daily. Statistics Canada. May 31, 1988.

And you can't see it in one of them.

A hemiplegic can construct his home so that everything is within reach. There are no stairs, hallways are wide enough to accommodate the wheelchair, and counters are lower. In his home, he is impaired but not handicapped. When he goes downtown and does not have access to a public building because there is no ramp, then he is handicapped. His impairment gets in his way, preventing him from achieving his desired goal—mobility.

A blind person can arrange her home so that she knows where everything is, and she can memorize the number of steps to the bus stop. In her home and immediate environment, she is impaired, but she can accomplish goals and move around comfortably, doing generally as she wishes. This is no longer the case when she wants to read. Without Braille, her impairment becomes a handicap.

In each of these examples, the individuals were dependent on aid from *someone else* so their impairment did not become a handicap.

The fact that a wheelchair cannot go up stairs and a blind person cannot see to read is obvious to all. We can imagine how frustrating these hurdles can be, so we build ramps to public buildings and publish books in Braille. We sympathize, so we act. And we do so in a positive, supportive manner.

What is most basic to understanding hearing impairment is that there is nothing to *see*. Because we cannot see sound, it is difficult to imagine what life would be like without it. And because hearing loss is not visible, we tend to minimize its importance.

We can't hear what a hearing-impaired person hears. We can't relate. How many times have any of us had a conversation with someone and felt we weren't being understood? "Do I have to write it down for you?" "Read my lips!" We've probably all said that at one time or another. It is interesting that in both cases we refer to something concrete, something that can be *seen*. And in both cases, the action is generally *not* meant in a positive, supportive manner. It's hard to be sympathetic and supportive when you're frustrated or angry.

Hearing impairment generally elicits impatience from those with normal hearing. The need to repeat, the need to shout, the interrupted conversations are all unpleasant. (Incidentally, neither repetition nor shouting is necessary and, in some cases, not even helpful. More on this later.)

The World Health Organization defines a disability as "any restriction or lack (resulting from an impairment) of ability to perform an activity in the manner or within the range considered normal for a human being." The nature of a hearing disability is further defined by WHO as the "limited ability to hear what is being said in conversation with one other person or two or more persons, *even when wearing a hearing aid.*"[2] (Italics are the author's.)

Virtually everything we do in life is based, at one time or another, on verbal communication. If you don't believe me, try going through a typical day without uttering one word. How would you go about making yourself understood? Body language? Be careful. You're depending on people to correctly interpret your messages. If you are writing everything down, be prepared for others to get impatient at having to wait. So, will you just avoid any interaction? Get ready for a long, lonely day. Several experts in geriatrics believe that the senility of old age is really an emotional reaction to the breakdown in social communication and isolation in their acoustically fading world. You'll only begin to discover what it's like when your ability to communicate with another person is compromised by something beyond your control—the other person's willingness to communicate with you.

If there's a missing link, like it or not, you *need* the other person's help, tolerance, and patience to fill the gaps. The only alternative is to not communicate. Likewise, hearing people can learn the communication needs of hearing-impaired people and cultivate the patience "to accept those things I cannot change."

Hearing loss is a handicap because people make it that way.

> *"You know that the best part of me, my hearing, has become very weak . . . I lead a miserable life indeed.*
> *I have avoided all society, for I cannot talk with my fellow men. Often I have cursed my very existence."*
>
> Ludwig van Beethoven

---

[2] Ibid.

CHAPTER 2

Are You Deaf . . . or Just a Little Pregnant?

The Trouble with Generalizations

Generalizations and catch-all phrases are expressions that we all use from time to time. "I *never* do that!" "You *always* do this!" What ever happened to "sometimes," "often," and "maybe"?

Generalities get in the way of communication because they presume falsely. Phrases are used habitually, without regard to the real message they convey. I submit that none of us are such creatures of habit that we *always* or *never* do something, just as everyone that is hearing-impaired is not *deaf*, although this generalization is used frequently.

"Deaf and dumb" was first used to describe people who, because of their deafness, did not speak. But with all the subtle nuances of our language, as years passed we took this phrase a few steps further and dumb became synonymous with "stupid." Therein lies the root of a generalization that, for some, has become an attitude. *Deaf people are not stupid.* Part of the divergent transfer of meaning is understandable. Deaf people often *seem* to make stupid mistakes. Hearing-impaired people often *appear* unintelligent because of mis-understandings by people with normal hearing who are ignorant about the effects of hearing loss on communication. As a result of *our* ignorance, we give these people an unfounded and undeserving label. Cognitively, logically, we know that deaf and hearing-impaired

people are as smart as anyone. But on an emotional level, we still feel they are, well, not quite "with it."

DEAFNESS VS. HEARING IMPAIRMENT

The Funk and Wagnalls dictionary defines *deaf* as "adj. lacking or deficient in the sense of hearing." That's true, but they left out a critical component: *degree*.

Deafness can be total, with no auditory perception of sound (at the highest measurable levels). If loud enough, though, vibrations can be detected. That's why some deaf people are able to dance fairly well—if the music is loud enough.

Deafness also includes those who are "deficient in the sense of hearing" *so that the development of normal speech is severely impaired or not possible*. This includes the group of profoundly hearing-impaired people who cannot hear most sounds under 90 decibels—which is approximately equal to a table saw from a distance of three feet or less. And if they do, 90 decibels is only a whisper to them!

This is a very small (but significant) portion of those with hearing loss. All people with deficient hearing are hearing-impaired, but all hearing-impaired people are **not** deaf. You can't be "a little" deaf any more than you can be "a little" pregnant. The distinction is important, both in the way people relate to hearing loss and to the impact it has on one's life. Deaf is not just an adjective. Deafness is a state of being.

Some define those with a profound hearing loss as deaf only when they cannot use their hearing for the purpose of understanding speech. Others with the same degree of profound hearing loss (measurable hearing above 90 decibels) do rely on their hearing and speech for communication. The difference lies in the age of onset (was speech acquired before the hearing loss?), the nature of the hearing loss, and how much education was received prior to the hearing loss. The impact of deafness that results from mumps contracted at age 23 by a college graduate will be very different from that of the child left without hearing from mumps at age 4.

It is important to note that some deaf people retain their ability to articulate speech and be understood quite well. These people are exceptions and generally include only those whose deafness occurred *after* some speech and language was acquired.

HOW MUCH IS 50 PERCENT?

Percent hearing loss is another frequently used and often incorrect generalization. Many parents may have experienced this scenario: Mom takes Susie to the pediatrician and discovers she has a raging ear infection in both ears. Mom is given medication for Susie's ears, but precious little else. All too often, no information is offered about how this temporary infection may affect Susie's hearing, except, perhaps, to say, "She has a 60 percent hearing loss right now."

Mom is now concerned because—as she understands it—Susie can hear less than 50 percent of what's going on. Wow! That's a lot of hearing loss, or, conversely, that's only a little hearing. But how much is a little? How is mom to interpret this to augment, for the time being, communication with her child? Does this mean that Susie is hearing only the first 2/5 of each word? The last 2/5? Two out of every five words? What does the information mom received really mean?

There is actually a prescribed formula for figuring percent hearing loss that resulted from lawsuits involving people who lost their hearing. The courts needed a yardstick to measure the impact of this hearing loss on one's life and ability to communicate, and thereby determine the amount of money to which this person was entitled for compensation. I would have to look the formula up. It's not committed to memory because, in counselling for hearing loss, *it is not relevant*.

Used accurately, percent hearing loss refers to the amount of loss within a certain frequency range called the "speech frequencies." So called because they are critical for the understanding of speech, these frequencies generally include 2000 Hertz through 6000 Hertz. In court, a 60 percent hearing loss would have a much greater impact on one's ability to communicate than a 25 percent hearing loss. So the individual with a 60 percent hearing loss gets more money. *A courtroom is the only place where the use of percent hearing loss is appropriate.*

MEASURING HEARING LEVELS

It is important at this point to look at how hearing is measured, recorded, and the terms for various degrees of hearing loss.

**"Now you just relax and the Doctor will begin
your hearing test in just a moment."**

Reprinted with permission. Copyright 1988 by Patrick Hardin.

Hearing is measured and recorded on a chart called an *audiogram*. In a typical hearing test, the decibel or loudness level when a sound is just barely detected is being measured. The method of evaluating hearing is very exact, and the resultant hearing levels are referred to as "threshold levels." Remember, these are loudness levels at which a person *just barely* hears the sound.

Although the human ear is capable of perceiving sounds ranging from 20 Hertz to 20,000 Hertz, only those frequencies that are important to living successfully in our environment are typically measured—250 Hz through 8000 Hz. (The designation Hertz, abbreviated Hz, comes from the German physicist, Heinrich Rudolf Hertz, who was the first to produce, send, and measure electromagnetic waves and record them according to their physical properties as frequencies.)

Generally, the test includes absolute measurements of 250 Hz,

500 Hz, 1000 Hz, 2000 Hz, 4000 Hz, and 8000 Hz. For those of you familiar with music, you'll recognize these as octaves. The frequencies in between these octaves fall in line with the resulting slope of hearing levels. Sometimes hearing is measured at the inter-octave frequencies of 3000 Hz and 6000 Hz, particularly when looking at hearing loss from noise exposure.

The Audiogram

The following are audiograms for someone with normal hearing (Figure 2.1) and someone with a high-frequency hearing loss (Figure 2.2). For no profound reason, X is used to designate thresholds for the left ear, while O is used for the right ear. Each X is then connected with a line, as are all the Os, so that the overall level of hearing can

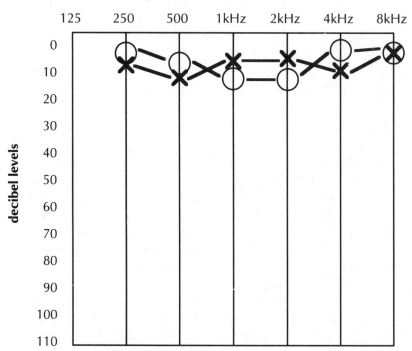

Figure 2.1 Normal Audiogram

TYPICAL HIGH-FREQUENCY HEARING LOSS
(Frequencies in Hertz/kHertz)

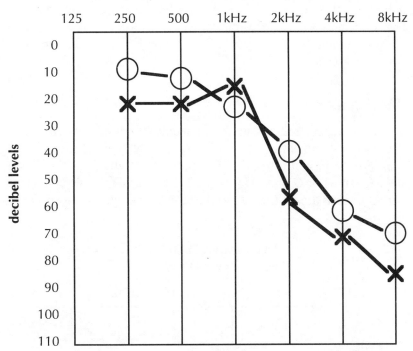

Figure 2.2 Typical High-Frequency Hearing Loss

be seen easily. The individual with the high-frequency hearing loss represented in Figure 2.2 would not be considered "deaf."

If you've never had your hearing tested, it's difficult to imagine a 20-decibel sound. It's like trying to imagine holding a briefcase with $20 million in it. Most of us can't. Figure 2.3 shows the same graph used to record an audiogram, but this one includes the loudness levels of speech and environmental sounds that we can relate to. I'll call it the "Speech and Environmental Chart."

In the S & E Chart, we can see that 20 decibels is about as loud as a whisper; 30 decibels is about as loud as a watch ticking (when held next to your ear); and 60 decibels is about as loud as a normal baby's crying. Your lawn mower is approximately 100 decibels loud. Most rock and roll bands play at a level between 110 and 140 decibels, just below the threshold of pain. (Some of us have higher pain thresh-

Frequency in Cycles per Second

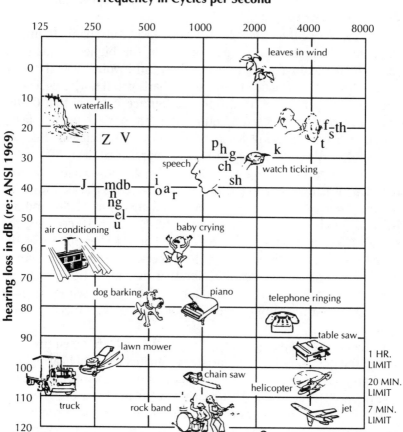

Figure 2.3 Speech and Environmental Chart

olds than others. No wonder you sometimes leave the pub or concert with a headache!)

Also superimposed on this chart are the loudness levels of the different vowels and consonants and what are called "blends" (/sh/, /ch/, /ng/, for example). Notice that over half of the consonant sounds appear on the right side of the chart, higher in pitch than 1000 Hz.

Vowels are "louder" and lower in pitch, so they appear on the left side of the chart.

Now, here's the Catch-22. We must hear consonants to understand speech. Most hearing loss occurs in the higher frequencies, above 1000 Hz. Just a mild hearing loss can involve several consonants. Down the left side of the S & E Chart, you'll notice decibel or loudness levels ranging from 0 to 120. Suffice it to say that 0 does not mean no hearing or no sound. It is simply a reference level. People can have hearing levels of −5 or −10 decibels. (Decibel, named after Alexander Graham Bell, is abbreviated dB.)

The important thing to understand regarding decibels is that they are measured on a logarithmic scale, which is a scale measured in 10s. Twenty dB has *10 times* the sound energy as 10 dB, and not twice as much, as you may have thought. For each 10 decibels, the sound energy increases by a factor of 10. Forty dB has 100 times the sound energy of 20 dB, and so on. For a person with a 40 dB hearing loss, the sound energy required for that person to hear is *10,000 times as great* as what is required for another person with very good hearing to hear the same sound. In a roundabout way, this correlates to loudness.

Referring to audiograms in Figures 2.4 and 2.5, down the right side of the graph are the appropriate designated levels of hearing loss. You'll notice there's not a percent figure among them! Audiologists counsel people regarding their hearing loss using these designations: mild, moderate, severe, and profound. As hearing loss progresses from one level to the next (mild to moderate, moderate to severe, and so on), the sound energy required for hearing increases approximately 10,000 to 15,000 times! The sound energy (or loosely, loudness) required for someone with a severe hearing loss of 70 dB would be 1,000,000 times as loud compared to someone with normal hearing!

HEARING LOSS AND UNDERSTANDING SPEECH

Now, let's superimpose the two previous audiograms onto the S & E Chart, and we'll see just how much the individual with the high-frequency hearing loss is missing (Figures 2.4 and 2.5 on pages 20, 21).

Remember, the line across the audiogram represents levels at which an individual just barely hears the sound, or the "threshold" level. Everything *below* the line is audible. Any sounds *above* the line

are not audible. In Audiogram A, this person's hearing is normal. All speech and environmental sounds are audible without a problem. In Audiogram B, this person cannot hear /p/, /h/, /g/, /k/, /t/, /f/, /s/, or /th/. /Ch/ and /sh/ are just barely audible. How do you think "the cat is on the front porch" would sound to this person?

Getting back to the mother with the sick child, the doctor would explain how the medicine was to be taken, that the child should get bed rest and fluids, but she *should* also inform the mother that the child's ability to understand speech is moderately, perhaps severely, compromised at this point.

Typically, doctors seem to take the threshold level of hearing and directly transcribe it to mean percent. In this example, the child is just barely hearing at 60 dB, and that is considered a severe hearing loss. The child may not respond as expected, may not respond at all when spoken to, and may appear to be "not listening." No wonder! She's not hearing any consonants and, we can assume, only a few vowels.

Ideally, the doctor would then offer some tips on how to help the child better understand what is being said so that frustration in communicating does not add to the miserable way the child feels physically. In lieu of this, our doctor's choice would be to defer counselling regarding degree of hearing loss to an audiologist.

For the hearing-impaired, understanding speech can be a real chore, depending on how severely their hearing is affected. Some environmental sounds may also disappear. Not being able to hear a whisper, for a child, could be devastating. How else can you share a secret with a friend? Your clock may suddenly be "broken" because you do not hear it ticking. If impaired severely enough, a new mother may not be able to hear her baby crying and, as a result, suffer extreme anxiety. The telephone may suddenly develop a "problem" with its ring, or cannot be heard at all.

The problems of deafness, however, are more complex.

WHAT IT REALLY MEANS TO BE DEAF

Going back to the S & E Chart, imagine not being able to hear anything softer than a table saw, or an 18-wheel truck, or the engine of a jet. Imagine these sounds as only a whisper. Imagine only being able to *feel* sound as a sort of rumbling vibration in your body.

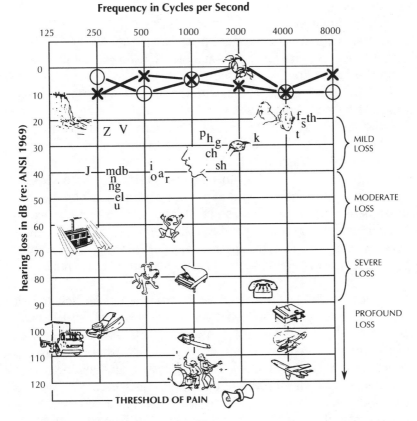

Figure 2.4 Audiogram A

Imagine these, and you can imagine deafness.

I said earlier that "deaf" was not only an adjective but also a state of being. Profound hearing loss, above 90 dB, alters one's life in a way only deaf people can truly know. They are uncoupled from the world in the most basic of ways, unable to use the acoustic feedback of their environment and the consort of friends that the rest of us take for granted.

Deaf people tend to live in their own close-knit communities— in their own world. They form their own clubs, have their own schools, and even their own language. In many ways, the deaf com-

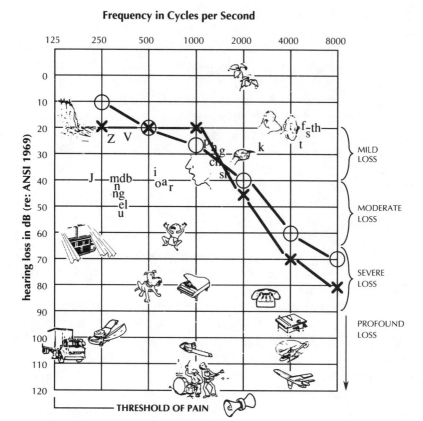

Figure 2.5 Audiogram B

munity more closely resembles a cultural minority than a group of handicapped people.

American Sign Language, or ASL, *is* the language of the deaf. A language all its own, ASL has its own set of rules governing grammar and syntax, use of idioms and accents, just like French, Spanish, or Russian. So much does it belong to deaf people that "hearing people" who learn and become fluent in ASL say that, when watching two deaf people talk, they have difficulty understanding all of what is being said.

Deaf people do not sign the same way with each other as they

do with a hearing person. The unbelievable speed and dexterity used in signing is, to most of us, amazing and very difficult to acquire as a second language. Any deaf person can recognize a hearing person just by watching them sign (assuming they are both fluent).

When I was trying to learn ASL, all of the manual dexterity I thought I had went right out the window. My fingers were like a group of bickering kindergartners fighting over space and refusing to do what they were told! One tiny shift in hand position can mean an entirely different word or phrase. And finger spelling? A deaf person can sign "Czechoslovakia" in two seconds or less. I can't even say it that fast with my voice!

Sentences are arranged differently, and ASL doesn't use a lot of the extraneous words in English, such as "a," "the," and "it." ASL is a very basic, concise, uncomplicated language—and also a very beautiful one. The hand and facial expressions are dramatic. There is something almost dance-like in watching two or more deaf people telling a joke or having an argument.

The effects of deafness on a child reach into every corner of his or her life, and also that of the family. Some congenitally deaf children learn to speak and are able to attend a regular school with the additional help of an aide. Many do not. Their families, if they want to communicate, must learn to sign. At a young age, and throughout life, their deafness will limit their communication circles. Special schools are often the only source of a quality education. A deaf child will probably never be able to appreciate music as you and I do. Beethoven's accomplishments were incredible but sad, for he could not hear performed much of the beautiful music that he had created.

Hearing aids, as an aid to understanding speech, are often useless to deaf people. They are, however, quite helpful for environmental feedback. Deafness does not mean a totally silent world. There are many sounds in our environment that can be heard by deaf people, especially when wearing hearing aids, that serve to alert them to a presence. A honking horn is one. The acoustic feedback of low rumbling lets deaf people know there is something going on around them.

In the deaf person's world, sound is a privilege, sometimes cloaked as a blessing and sometimes a curse. Some sounds are annoying to a deaf person because of the loudness or pitch or amount of distortion. This is sometimes difficult for a hearing person to understand. "You should be grateful you're hearing *something*," we

think. But we must remember that only a deaf person actually knows what it sounds like to them.

If you or I were to become deaf, we might say the sounds we miss most are the singing of the birds or the laughter of a child. Many deaf people say the two sounds they miss the most are not being able to hear music truly and not being able to hear running water! Seeing the water rush from the faucet without a sound drives them bananas!

If you have the need to communicate frequently over the phone with deaf people, or are deaf yourself, there is an agency that publishes an *international* telephone directory just for TDD numbers (Telecommunication Device for the Deaf). Subscribers pay a fee to be listed in the directory, which includes just about any type of service one could imagine—businesses, state agencies, doctors, dentists, interpreters —anyone who wishes to be listed and pays the fee! Write to or call:

Telecommunications for the Deaf, Inc. (TDI)
814 Thayer Avenue
Silver Spring, MD 20910
301-589-3786 (voice)
301-589-3006 (TDD)

Yes, there is a world of difference between being deaf and being hearing-impaired. To appreciate that, just sit quietly . . . and listen.

You Have To Be Deaf To Understand

What is it like to "hear" a hand?
You have to be deaf to understand!

What is it like to be a small child,
In a school, in a room void of sound—
With a teacher who talks and talks and talks,
And then when she does come around to you,
She expects you to know what she's said?
You have to be deaf to understand.

Or the teacher who thinks that to make you
*   smart,*
You must first learn how to talk with your
*   voice;*

So mumbo-jumbo with hands on your face
For hours and hours without patience or end,
Until out comes a faint resembling sound?
You have to be deaf to understand.

What is it like to be curious,
To thirst for knowledge you can call your own,
With an inner desire that's set on fire—
And you ask a brother, sister, or friend
Who looks in answer and says, "Never mind!"?
You have to be deaf to understand.

What is it like in a corner to stand,
Though there's nothing you've done really
*   wrong,*
Other than try to make use of your hand
To a silent peer to communicate
A thought that comes to your mind all at once?
You have to be deaf to understand.

What is it like to be shouted at
When one thinks that will help you to hear;
Or misunderstand that words of a friend
Who is trying to make a joke clear,
And you don't get the point because he's failed?
You have to be deaf to understand.

What is it like to be laughed in the face
When you try to repeat what is said;
Just to make sure that you've been understood,
And you find that the words were misread—
And you want to cry out, "Please help me,
*   friend!"?*
You have to be deaf to understand.

What is it like to have to depend
Upon one who can hear to phone a friend;
Or place a call to a business firm
And be forced to share what's personal, and

Then find that your message wasn't made clear?
You have to be deaf to understand.

What is it like to be deaf and alone
In the company of those who can hear—
And you only guess as you go along,
For no one's there with a helping hand,
As you try to keep up with words and song?
You have to be deaf to understand.

What is it like on the road of life
To meet with a stranger who opens his mouth—
And speaks out a line at a rapid pace;
And you can't understand the look in his face
Because it is new and you're lost in the race?
You have to be deaf to understand.

What is it like to comprehend
Some nimble fingers that paint the scene,
And make you smile and feel serene
With the "spoken word" of the moving hand
That makes you part of the world at large?
You have to be deaf to understand.

What is it like to "hear" a hand?
Yes, you have to be deaf to understand.

Willard J. Madsen

CHAPTER *3*

The Missing Link
Hearing Loss and Communication

*F*rom the moment we are born, we begin learning about our world using sound. Some studies have shown that babies react to sounds while they are still in the womb. Our mothers coo to us, and we learn to associate this with pleasure. We learn there are other people around us because voices sound different. We gradually learn to associate some sounds with happiness, some with curiosity, some with fear, and so on. Our environment develops more meaning and more definition by the variety of sounds we hear and understand.

Eventually, everything we do (well, almost) is dictated by the sounds we hear. We rise to the sound of the alarm clock. We answer the phone because it rings. We speak to one another, and we recognize that different tones of voice convey different meanings. As students, we knew class was over when the bell rang, and we knew we were late if we were not seated when the bell rang again! The dog barks, and we know someone is outside. We pet the cat. She purrs, and we know she is happy. Without our hearing, the world becomes a very confusing, frustrating, and sometimes scary place to be.

All that we hear is actually a series of sounds or frequencies strung together like a chain link fence. When one or two links are missing, the fence becomes weak. When several links in several places are missing, the fence will not stand up. If you have the type of hearing loss that is profound, and it began at or soon after birth, you did not begin to learn by using sounds. As a result, you do not depend on sound for learning. If you are born with hearing but lose it

before the age of five, you will experience extreme difficulty learning language and communicating with the "hearing" world. Neurological brain patterns for language use have not been firmly established and will be lost quickly with the passage of time. The auditory feedback required for controlling your voice level and tone will also be gone.

If you have the type of hearing loss that comes and goes with a cold or allergy, you will experience inconsistent auditory feedback— hearing your own voice and learning to adjust voice level, intonation, and to learn speech and language. The volume you felt was appropriate last week for listening to the radio is now not loud enough. Next week, you find it's too loud. Half the time, people seem to be whispering. The rest of the time, they seem to be shouting. You can hear your own voice just fine, yet you're accused of whispering. In school, what sounded perfectly normal one day sounds like something you've never heard the next. You lose your ability to rely on what you hear to correctly guide you.

If you have the type of hearing loss that begins in adulthood, you could be the last to realize it! You can't *know* you haven't heard something if you haven't heard it, but everyone else expects you to know! You don't answer the phone because you don't hear it ringing. "Where were you all day?" becomes an accusation. You ruined the tea because you didn't hear the kettle whistling. You got up late for an important appointment because you didn't hear the alarm clock.

And you're confused. "I never used to have these problems," you think to yourself. Life is injected with paranoia because now you're never really confident. Your hearing, all that you've relied on so totally in the past, is failing you. Just like the fence with the missing link. The fence falls over. The mosaic of communication comes unglued.

Hearing loss has many causes and, depending on the cause, few cures. Although the causes are many and varied, there are only two resultant effects on hearing. One is a reduction in loudness, the other a loss of clarity. Often there are both.

CONDUCTIVE HEARING LOSS

When you have a cold or your allergies flare up, and your ears feel like a field of cotton is growing in there, you are experiencing a "conductive" hearing loss, so named because sound cannot be prop-

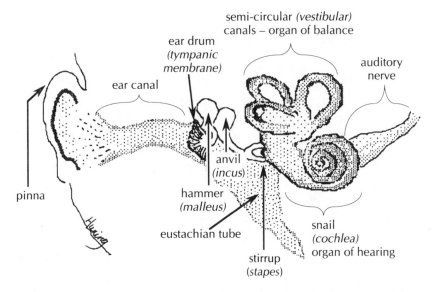

Figure 3.1 The ear is an incredibly complex system. Not only does it have the task of deciphering meaningful messages from unseen sound waves in the air, but it is also responsible for maintaining our balance. If any one portion of the ear is not healthy, often the other portions are also adversely affected.

erly "conducted" or transferred through the mechanical portion of the auditory system. There is nothing wrong with the pipe. There's just a plug in the flow.

You can have the same effect with a punctured eardrum. The hole prevents the eardrum from vibrating properly, which in turn prevents the complete transfer of sound through the auditory system. In addition to the hole impeding the transmission of sound, any water that can enter the middle ear through this hole severely restricts the bones of the middle ear system in their ability to vibrate. The middle ear is intended to remain a dry, air-filled cavity for this reason. If moisture gets in, the middle ear becomes a great environment for growing bacteria because it is dark and now very damp. So, if you have a punctured eardrum—either a temporary or permanent one— you should *never* expose your head to water without a plug in the ear with the punctured eardrum. Swim plugs work well and are available in just about any drugstore. If you or your child has tubes in one or both eardrums, the tube itself is creating a hole and the

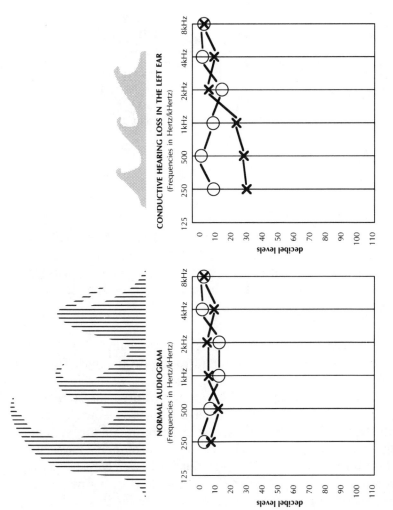

Figure 3.2

30

same precautions should be taken until the tubes are out *and* the holes left by the tubes have closed.

The effect of a conductive hearing loss is a general reduction in loudness. Think of sound as a wave. The wave is still there, but instead of being a tidal wave, it's just a little ripple (see Figure 3.2).

The first difference you might notice is the size of the "waves." The second and major consequence of a conductive hearing loss is impaired hearing in the lower frequency ranges, with the resultant effect being a muting of sound. This is quite different from most sensori-neural hearing loss, where hearing is impaired in the higher frequency ranges and consequently has a direct effect on the clarity of sound. The important thing to remember with a conductive hearing loss is that the full message is still there, as far as what you hear. The *integrity* of the message is the same. Basically, it sounds like everyone is whispering and the world has turned the volume down. You mean it literally when you say, "I can't hear you."

This is the easiest type of hearing loss to handle because everything you've come to recognize sounds the same—just softer. It also has the easiest solution: Turn everything up. This also has the unfortunate effect of turning everyone else off, because what is loud enough for your current hearing needs is too loud for everyone else's! For children, especially between the ages of 1 and 10 years when ear infections and allergies are prevalent, this type of hearing loss can have a devastating effect on their learning. More on this in Chapter 5.

With a conductive hearing loss, your hearing may fluctuate— it is fine for a couple of days, not so good for awhile, better again, and then worse. If you have, say, a perforated eardrum, your hearing probably won't change much as a result of the perforation (depending, of course, on the size). If you have allergies, your hearing will probably be very much on-again, off-again due to the accumulation and absorption cycle of fluid behind the eardrum.

The fluctuating nature of a conductive hearing loss can drive the one experiencing it right 'round the bend, and everyone else goes along for the ride. "I can't hear you" accompanies every attempt at conversation. Sometimes you hear, and sometimes you don't, never knowing exactly how something is going to sound. Everyone else is yelling at you (or so they feel). One day you can barely hear them. The next day, speech seems suddenly amplified to an almost painful level. You find yourself riding an acoustic roller coaster.

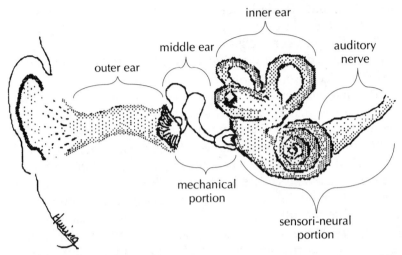

Figure 3.3 The ear is divided into three sections—the outer, middle, and inner ear. The mechanical section corresponds to the middle ear, while the sensory portion is contained within the inner ear. The neural portion of the system is the auditory nerve.

The portion of the auditory system affected by a conductive hearing loss is referred to as the "mechanical" portion (Figure 3.3). Sound vibrations hit the eardrum, the eardrum vibrates, and behind it, three tiny bones vibrate. This occurs in the outer- and middle-ear regions. Restriction of the mechanical portion is what causes a conductive hearing loss. At this point, the sensory and neural portions of the system are not involved, which is why a conductive hearing loss does not alter the clarity or integrity of sound.

The other two parts of the auditory system, referred to as the sensory and neural portions, are responsible for giving meaning to what comes through the mechanical portion. The sensory portion "perceives" sound, and the neural portion transmits those perceptions to the auditory cortex of the brain for interpretation.

SENSORI-NEURAL HEARING LOSS

When the sensory and/or neural parts of the system are involved, the problem is a sensori-neural hearing loss. This type of hearing loss results in a reduction of clarity, causing a breakdown in the integrity

of speech *as perceived by the listener*. Sometimes, this causes a perception of decreased volume. The bigger problem is that nothing sounds *clear*. This is the most common type of hearing loss in people over the age of 20. To understand why speech doesn't sound clear, we need to cover some additional anatomy and what happens when the system breaks down.

The sensori-neural portion of the auditory system has three areas, each devoted to a different function. (For clarity, refer back to Figures 3.1 and 3.3.) The first, located in the inner ear, is called the *cochlea* (*ko*-klee-a). Also in the inner ear are the semicircular canals, a series of three connected tubes, each one positioned on a different "plane" representing the vertical, horizontal, and oblique axes to the ground. Feedback from these canals tells us where we are in space— standing up, lying down, and when we're about to fall over! It is through this feedback mechanism that we are able to maintain our balance. Anyone that has had an infection of the inner ear (*not* the middle ear) can relate to the almost constant feeling of dizziness and disturbance of balance.

Both the cochlea and the semicircular canals are filled with fluid and thousands of tiny hairs. Movement of the fluid in the semicircular canals causes the tiny hairs to bend. This triggers nerves to fire a message to the brain that tells us whether we're standing on our feet, standing on our head, or lying on our side.

Next in the system is the auditory nerve. Not a part of the inner ear, the auditory nerve "connects" the cochlea to the auditory cortex in the brain.

Also known as the "snail" because of the way it wraps around itself in a coil, the cochlea can be likened to a musical instrument filled with fluid. Imagine the coils of the cochlea unwound so it looks like a flexible test tube. Running the length of this tube is a "rubber band" known as the basilar membrane, thick at one end and thin at the other. This membrane is also suspended in fluid and attached at both ends to the walls of the cochlea. If you could pluck the rubber band anywhere along its length, much like a guitar string, you would hear a tone. Pluck toward the thin end and the tones are higher pitched. Pluck toward the thick end and the tones are lower.

Imagine that the rubber band is covered with tiny hairs. Thousands of them. The base of each hair communicates with a tiny neuron that carries messages along the auditory nerve to the brain. The ability to recognize and appreciate what you hear, whether it is

speech, music, or environmental sounds, is *entirely* dependent on those hairs being complete and intact.

To understand how all this ties together, we must remember that sound is vibration—the movement of molecules through the air. When different vibrations enter the ear and strike the eardrum, it also vibrates. Then the tiny bones in the middle ear, the *hammer*, *anvil*, and *stirrup*, vibrate. (The three bones with their medical terms, the *malleus*, *incus*, and *stapes*, are shown in Figure 3.1.) Incidentally, these are the smallest bones in the body. All three could easily fit on the nail of your little finger! These vibrations continue to travel through the cochlea, along the rubber band, the same way that ripples spread in an ever-widening circle when you throw a pebble into a lake.

Remember that plucking the rubber band at different places generates different tones? This means that the rubber band is "tuned." When the vibrations enter the cochlea and travel along the rubber band, the band will vibrate the *hardest* at the same points that compare to the sounds coming in.

Let's say the tone middle C vibrates through the system and reaches the rubber band. The area on the band tuned to middle C will vibrate more than any other area. See Figure 3.4.

When an area of the band vibrates, so do the little hairs on that area. This vibration of the hairs stimulates the neurons to send a message along the auditory nerve, and your brain registers "Aha! Middle C!"

Most sounds that we hear, however, are not broken down so simply. They contain a multitude of frequencies, or "tones." The

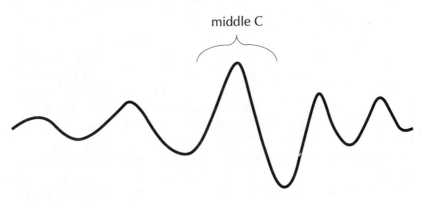

Figure 3.4 Middle C

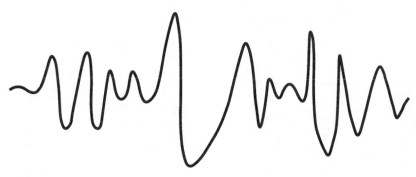

Figure 3.5 "Hello"

rubber band then vibrates at several places along its length in response to whatever frequencies are in the sound we hear. The hairs vibrate, stimulating all the connecting neurons, and messages begin to assault the brain. These messages contain the frequency content of the sound, which is then analyzed by the auditory cortex. The message is computed, and we've just heard someone say "Hello!"

Recalling the diagram of the middle C vibration, "Hello" might look something like Figure 3.5.

Figure 3.6 shows the frequency ranges of some often, and some not so often, heard sounds. Notice the breadth of frequencies included in a violin compared to a piano, a frog compared to a horse, and the range of the human voice.

This all may sound very complicated, and it is. Sound is a complicated impulse, and the mechanism required to interpret it, break it down into its component parts, send the appropriate messages to the brain, and regroup the messages so they can be understood is incredibly complex and requires all working parts to be in perfect condition. Otherwise, the message received will not be the message relayed. It's like the Telephone Game we all played as kids. Remember how you started with a short message and relayed it person to person via a whisper from one end of a line to the other. More often than not, the message reported by the last person in the line was significantly different from what the first person actually said. And that's why we played the game. It was fun to see how distorted the message could get.

But real communication is not a game, and it's not funny when messages are always distorted. The hairs along the basilar membrane begin to age, believe it or not, right after birth. Talk about premature

FREQUENCIES (IN HERTZ — "K" = 1,000)

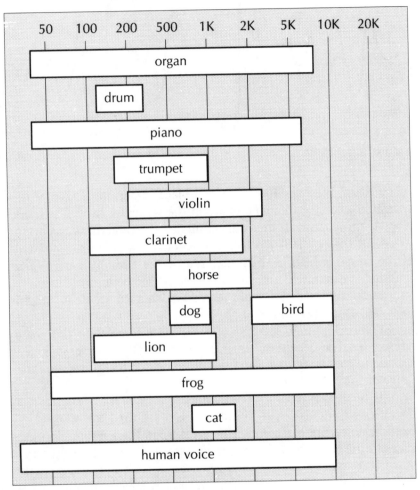

Figure 3.6 Sound vs. frequency chart

aging! There are many things that can compromise the integrity of these delicate little hairs—illness, aging, and noise are the most common causes. The end result in all cases, no matter what the cause, is that some of the hairs die at certain points along the rubber band—and they don't grow back. Once they're gone, they're gone forever. See Figures 3.7 and 3.8.

Figure 3.7 Intact hair cells, arranged in neat rows along the basilar membrane. Notice how each group contains three rows in a near-perfect half-moon.

HEARING AND LANGUAGE

Now let's take a minute to talk about language—words—and you'll see how this all fits together.

Language, any language, is made up of consonants and vowels. When analyzed for frequency content, we have found that, as a general rule, consonants are higher in frequency than vowels. When analyzed for decibel output, or loudness, we have also found that vowels are "louder" than consonants. It is important to remember here that frequency (or tone or pitch) is not the same as loudness. You can have a very soft middle C or a very loud middle C.

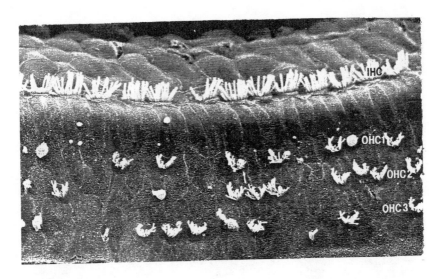

Figure 3.8 This photo shows damaged hair cells. Notice how the rows and groupings look straggly, almost like uncombed hair. Some are limp, and there are lots of empty spaces.

Photos taken with an electron microscope. From H. Engström, B. Engström, *The Ear*. Uppsala, Sweden. June 1988. Reprinted by permission, courtesy H. Engström, Uppsala, Sweden.

When language is analyzed further, we have found that it is the consonants that give language (at least the English language) its meaning. Try this little game with yourself. Figure out what the following sentence really says.

I ae o a y ai oi.

Can't get it? With all the consonants removed, this sentence has no meaning for you. In fact, it looks and would probably sound like a language you've never heard before!
Try this one.

hv t wsh m hr tnght.

It was probably easier this time. With a good language base, it's not too difficult to decipher the sentence "I have to wash my hair

tonight." Without consonants, our language is reduced to gibberish. We'd all sound like we were talking with our mouths full of marbles.

When only some consonants are missing, we could get into rhyming games. Let's take the sentence "The dish is in the sink." How could we change some of the consonants with rhyme to change the sentence? Why use rhyme? Because the words then sound alike— exactly what a hearing-impaired person goes through when trying to figure out a phrase in which the sounds have not been clear. We could use "The fish is in the drink." Two similar-sounding sentences, but two entirely different meanings. The first one makes sense. The second one could be quite alarming if you happen to be missing your pet goldfish.

Let's say that, for whatever reason, some of the hairs along your basilar membrane are missing. Because, in English, there are many more consonants than there are vowels, and each one is composed of several frequencies, the chances of these "bald spots" affecting consonant frequencies is about five to one. For someone with a hearing loss, that means the chances of misunderstanding a phrase are also about five to one.

This presents a frustrating situation. We need consonants to understand language, and it's consonants that suffer most from damage to the little hairs. Conversations seem to be filled with hundreds of tiny gaps. Other speech sounds are distorted. The message first entering the ear is not the one that reaches the auditory cortex, and now you have a real-life version of the Telephone Game—and a small inkling of what communication becomes for the hearing-impaired. The fence is weakened. There are holes in some areas; it's bent out of shape in others. The fence falls down. In language, communication falls apart.

A sensori-neural hearing loss causes distortion of a message due to damage to the cochlea and, specifically, the hair cells. What is heard, to a hearing-impaired listener, is similar to the appearance of an image when looking through frosted glass—fuzzy and unclear. The degree of distortion appears unrelated to the degree of hearing loss, except in cases of profound hearing loss (above 90 dB) when there is virtually always some distortion. Someone with a mild to moderate hearing loss may suffer extreme distortion, while another individual with a severe hearing loss may have only mild distortion.

This, in part, explains the differences in speech capabilities of children born with varying degrees of hearing loss. I've seen (or rather, heard) the phenomena over and over again. Someone I'd

expect to have good, intelligible speech sounded guttural and without inflection, while another boy (he was a man by the time I saw him) with a profound hearing loss spoke better than some hearing people I've known—and he didn't get his first hearing aid until he was in high school!

When hearing loss is profound, the deaf person hears a sound so distorted it would be unrecognizable as speech to a person with normal hearing. This is why the "speech of the deaf" sounds, to us, like a series of unconnected vowels or unrelated grunts, without inflection. But remember—they are only repeating what they hear. Some deaf people choose not to use their voice for varying reasons. Some realize their speech is unintelligible and figure why bother trying.

Although it is important for you to understand deafness as it relates to hearing impairment, this book is not about deafness. The scope is too broad, the effects and ramifications too impacting to be covered in just one or two chapters, let alone a few paragraphs.

UNILATERAL HEARING LOSS

There is one more notion that needs clarification. *One ear is NOT as good as two!* People with a unilateral (one ear only) hearing loss are at a distinct disadvantage in two critical areas.

- Localizing, or pinpointing the sound source, is dependent on binaural, or two-eared, hearing.
- Tuning out some sounds while attending to others is greatly enhanced by two-eared hearing.

Binaural hearing just sounds better—fuller. That's why people spend hundreds of extra dollars on woofers and tweeters and harmonic balancing to get a good *stereo* sound system.

Unilateral hearing loss *is* a problem and should be addressed in the same way as a hearing loss involving both ears. *Any* hearing loss is significant. Individuals with sensori-neural hearing loss live in an acoustic environment that is never quite tuned in. The sad part is there is *nothing* they can do to make sounds or words clearer. This aggravates the frustration, isolation, and sometimes extreme emotional effects of hearing loss, which we'll look at now.

CHAPTER 4

Silence Is (NOT) Golden

The Hearing-Impaired in a Hearing World

I am just as deaf as I am blind. The problems of deafness are deeper and more complex than those of blindness. Deafness is a much worse misfortune, for it means the loss of the most vital stimulus—the sound of the voice that brings language, sets thoughts astir, and keeps us in the intellectual company of men and women.[1]

Helen Keller

*T*he psychological and emotional effects of hearing loss are like an octopus. The tentacles wriggle and stretch into every corner of life. This is difficult to imagine until you have lived or worked with a hearing-impaired person. Even then, behaviors are unexpected. You, and they, must learn how to cope.

Communication is a learned behavior. "But everybody communicates!" you say. True. But few of us do it well. When communication breaks down, and we don't understand why, we also don't understand the rebound reaction. We *do* know how frustrating it is when *we* feel misunderstood!

Communication is vital to life itself. There's a story—perhaps just a folktale—about a fifteenth-century emperor who became curi-

---

[1] From *Helen Keller In Scotland: A Personal Record Written by Herself*. Metheun & Co. Ltd., London, England. 1933.

ous about the development of language. He devised an experiment involving all the newborn babies in his empire. He was the emperor, so of course he had complete cooperation. All the caregivers were instructed to carry on with the normal process of looking after their babies, but *they were not to talk to them—ever*. By doing this, the emperor figured the babies would devise a language of their own to communicate with those around them, and he would "study" that new language. Unfortunately, the emperor was never able to complete his study. All the babies died. Not from illness but from social deprivation.

Whether this is a true story or a folktale, the point is that we *have* learned how important it is for mothers and caregivers to communicate with babies, both physically and verbally.

Hearing is so important that it is the last of our senses to be affected by anesthesia (discovered when comments better *not* heard by patients were later repeated by them!). Consider the following statistics:

- Those without someone with whom to communicate are at a five times greater risk for cancer.[2]

- Those who are socially isolated are two to three times more likely to die prematurely.[3]

We've said it in jest before, but it's true. People *can* die of loneliness. We all need to communicate.

Psychologically, we define who we are based on our communication with others. From these interactions, we decide whether we are smart or dumb, pretty or plain, have a sense of humor or not. All of these traits are defined by the way others react to us.

Socially, communication gives us a sense of belonging. We gain a sense of control over our lives by our ability to influence others through communication. (We'd all like to think that the world is hanging on our every syllable. We need to feel that we can positively influence those around us, particularly our children.) Through communicating, we receive attention and respect. We gain self-esteem by

[2]R.B. Adler, N. Towne. *Looking Out/Looking In: Interpersonal Communication.* Holt, Rinehart and Winston. 1975.
[3]Ibid.

knowing that we matter to somebody. Life is a very practical matter as well. We have to go shopping, go to school, and use the telephone. We have to communicate with others to get our basic needs met.

Yet, several factors can choke our ability to communicate. There might be environmental effects, such as trying to listen with a fan in the background, or sitting in the last row in a concert hall with poor acoustics.

Physical factors can impede or destroy our ability to communicate. How eager are *you* to discuss refinancing the mortgage when you're tired or hungry? We know that the best time to ask the boss for a raise is *not* when she has a headache! And, of course, there's always hearing loss.

Finally, psychological interferences play a vital role in how well we do, or do not, communicate. Do you listen as well, as openly, to someone you dislike as you do to someone you're very fond of? Do you communicate as well when you're angry as when you're calm? How about when you're frustrated that your message isn't getting across? There's a saying that I once had hanging in my office. A reminder of the general frustrations in communicating that we all experience sooner or later, it said

> *I know that you believe that you understand what you think I said, but I am not sure you realize that what you heard is not what I meant!*

For most of us, these little interferences with good communication are an occasional experience, annoyingly more frequent when good communication is most important! For a hearing-impaired person, these interferences are a constant threat and often become the norm. Those trying to communicate with the hearing-impaired become victims of psychological obstacles—frustration, anger, intolerance, and ignorance. The hearing-impaired are victims of all three—psychological, physical, and environmental.

Remember the gas station attendant in Chapter 1? This is a *busy* person. In an attempt to give quick directions, he finds it necessary to stop what he is doing and read his inquisitor's questions and then, himself, write down each answer. If a point in the directions is misunderstood and requires further clarification, he must write even more. And all the while, he is thinking, "I don't have time for this!" As a result, he becomes increasingly agitated and the fuse on his

temper burns dangerously short. His reaction makes the "conversation" even more strained, adding to his frustration and growing impatience.

SOCIAL EFFECTS OF HEARING LOSS

Here's another common problem. For reasons that will be discussed in Chapter 7, it is *impossible* to *effectively* communicate with a hearing-impaired person from a different room. Room-to-room conversations are common in most households, right? We all do it. Mom's in the kitchen and calls to her son to please set the table for dinner. Dad is in the bathroom and asks for someone to please bring him a clean towel. Communicating from one room to another is standard operating procedure in, I would guess, most families.

So what happens when a family member is hearing-impaired? One person makes a statement. The hearing-impaired person doesn't understand and asks, "What did you say?" if he answers at all. The statement is repeated, but the television is on, the kettle is whistling, and the person still doesn't understand. So mom marches into her son's room and spits, "I SAID COME SET THE TABLE FOR DINNER!" Grrrrr. Dad finally snarls, "NEVER MIND! I'LL USE A WET ONE!" Grrrrr. Mom and dad are suddenly exasperated and angry. The unsuspecting son is now really bewildered. "Did I miss something?" he wonders.

Another example: Little Johnny has had an ear infection in both ears, on and off, all year. It is now March. One day he brings a note home from the teacher that goes something like "Johnny is having difficulty in class. He does not pay attention consistently and, as a result, misses assignments and important classroom discussions. Please talk to him regarding the importance of paying better attention in class." The teacher appears to have lost her patience. God knows she's tried. She has undoubtedly told Johnny at least once that he doesn't pay attention. She certainly can't teach him anything if he's not going to listen! On the way home, Johnny reads the teacher's note. "But I *am* trying!" he thinks angrily to himself. "Now Mom's really gonna be mad at me." The teacher is ready to throw in the towel, and what do you think has happend to Johnny's self-esteem?

Imagine this scenario. A hearing-impaired person goes to the

movie and chooses a seat. Someone else comes along and sits in the next seat, balancing a huge tub of popcorn. For as long as possible, the hearing-impaired person tries to tune out the crunch, crunch of his neighbor's snack. Soon, however, it gets to be too much. He's missing the movie, so he leans over and politely requests, "Can you please try to munch a little more quietly?" Some people really get into their popcorn! This exchange goes on, back and forth a few more times. "Munch! Crunch!" "Please!!" Finally, the Popcorn Person gets up, none too happy, and moves to another seat, muttering, "Gee whiz! Can't even go to the movies and get some peace!"

Anger. Hostility. Resentment. No mixed bag of emotions here. The reactions are clear, and they are negative. You may be thinking that it should have been the hearing-impaired person that changed seats. After all, it was his problem. On the other hand, have you ever said, "Excuse me" anticipating someone to move aside and allow you through? Or politely asked someone to "Shhh" while watching a movie or concert?

The point here is to demonstrate the *emotions* each party experiences. We'll talk about responsibility and who can do what in Chapter 7.

For adults, hearing loss is usually a gradual process. And often, the one with the hearing loss is the last to recognize it. Family members, co-workers, and close friends are often the first to perceive difficulty with understanding, because they are the ones who must repeat themselves. This starts with an occasional "What?" As time goes on, it becomes necessary to repeat more and more as the hearing loss becomes worse. This usually occurs over a period of years, but the impact is felt as quite sudden. Though slow, the progression follows an almost preordained path. The effects are tenacious and, without patience and understanding, can have irrevocable effects on everyone involved.

To illustrate, let's go back to when we were newborns. Once out of the womb, we are bathed in sound. We hear our own voice and that of others. Cuddling becomes reassuring from warmth and the sound of mother's heartbeat. Sound is identified with life and gratification of one's needs.

As we grow, we begin to be able to distinguish one sound from another; mom's voice and footsteps from dad's, sister's, and even the neighbor's; the sound the dog makes when someone is at the door; the sound the cat makes when you scratch behind its ears.

As we grow older still, sounds become warning signals. The sound of breaking glass—Oh, Oh! A horn honking—Get out of the way! The teacher's tone of voice—Somebody's in trouble!

Sounds become identifiers, symbols of the different aspects of life as it goes on around us. We are reassured by these sounds, because they give our life order and meaning, reassurance that life is going on and we are a part of it.

Background sounds are our feedback that life exists around us. Absolute quiet can be eerie. Have you ever been anywhere—in the country, let's say—when it was soooo quiet you actually stopped to listen? Soft music in the background is relaxing. The hum of the refrigerator is comforting—we know it's still working!

Subconsciously, we hear background sounds, and they soothe and allow us to feel secure. Consciously, we can tune them out, allowing us to attend to more important sounds or events while still being comforted by their presence. As we continue to grow into adulthood, background or random sounds continue throughout our life as reassuring reminders that life is around us.

Many events can affect hearing in adulthood, such as disease, illness, and aging. One way or another, hearing loss eventually plagues all of us if we live long enough. It is the nation's most common physical impairment, affecting more people than those with heart disease, cancer, blindness, tuberculosis, venereal disease, multiple sclerosis, and kidney disease combined.[4]

As you begin to lose hearing, the sounds with which you have come to identify life, to identify yourself, sounds that were once soothing and reassuring, begin to disappear, become distorted, or both. Because it is most often a slow process, the loss often goes unnoticed, initially, at the conscious level.

Little adjustments are made without really thinking about them: turning the television and radio up a little, an occasional "Pardon me?" As the hearing loss progresses, these "little" adjustments become bigger and more frequent, slowly accumulating like a fog rolling in. Suddenly (it seems), the television is blaring, and you realize you almost always have to say, "Pardon?"

You begin to consciously notice events that are inconsistent with experience (as a result of the hearing loss). You become con-

---

[4]Starkey Hearing Instruments.

fused, scared, and feel displaced because you may not understand why life is so unpredictable "all of a sudden."

What was easy conversation is now difficult. What was previously known to you as normal verbal communication no longer exists. Your ability to understand what is being said is compromised by the loss as well as by the background sounds that previously were so soothing. You begin to question whether you are growing "dumber" because of the increasing difficulty in understanding. You begin to wonder, "What's *wrong* with me?"

Because the acoustic feedback that you relied on when learning is now distorted, sometimes the ability to speak clearly also deteriorates. This only happens when the loss is extreme, but it does happen and can be quite devastating.

TINNITUS

Sensori-neural hearing loss is also often accompanied by tinnitus (tin-*eye*-tus), or noises in the ears. These noises have been variously described as a ring, buzz, or an all-out roar. For unknown reasons, the ear is manufacturing this noise, and no one else can hear it.

For some, tinnitus is simply another little nuisance. For others, the nuisance becomes extreme and can be so stressful that some clinics specialize in problems arising from tinnitus. For a few, tinnitus can be an annoying buzz that keeps them awake at night. For others, the roar in their head can interfere with carrying on a normal conversation. There is help for these problems, however, if they do become so extreme as to interrupt your daily routine. Along with the clinics mentioned before, help can come from a tinnitus masker.

So that we are not driven crazy by all the never-ending sounds in our environment, the brain has a clever way of tuning out some of them. This is only possible if the sound never changes in its loudness (intensity) or pitch (frequency). That explains why you don't constantly "hear" the hum of the refrigerator, even though it's always there. If you *want* to, you can listen for it.

Tinnitus, unfortunately, does not remain constant and so cannot be "tuned out" by the listener. A masker, which looks just like a behind-the-ear hearing aid, makes a sound that can be set to either high or low pitch. The masking sound does remain constant. For reasons that are not perfectly clear, after a few minutes the listener

is able to tune out the sound made by the masker *and* the sound of their tinnitus. This little device is so named because it works by "masking," or covering up, another sound.

For those whose experience is not so extreme but are bothered by the hum when trying to get to sleep, for example, turning a radio on might help. Tune it to some pleasant music, whatever that is for you, and set it low enough so that you can just barely hear it. By doing this, you give your brain something else to listen to and won't "hear" the buzzing.

PSYCHOLOGICAL EFFECTS OF HEARING LOSS

We are very adept at avoiding what is uncomfortable for us. The hearing-impaired person is no different. As difficulties and frustrations mount, the person withdraws little by little. Choosing to detach themselves from what has become uncertain and, as a result, threatening, they surround themselves in a "safety envelope" of solitude.

Inner turmoil mounts because, although they don't *want* to avoid communication, they feel they can no longer do it successfully and so *have* to withdraw. Insecurity grows because the reassurances of conversation, background sounds, and so on are gone.

What sounds like whispered conversations becomes fuel for feelings of paranoia. With reduced self-esteem and a feeling of no longer being in control, the hearing-impaired person becomes suspicious and withdraws further. Laughter once shared now generates feelings of apprehension and mistrust. The uncertainty of conversation magnifies the hearing-impaired individual's feelings of vulnerability, and apprehension, self-doubt, and paranoia escalate.

At this point, the individual feels totally out of control, that there is nothing he or she can do to improve the situation, and loses further desire to adjust—or try.

The universe of sound with which the hearing-impaired person has learned to identify, that has given his or her world direction, identification, meaning, and comfort, is now distorted and threatening. Depression often occurs, and it sometimes progresses to stages that seem disproportionate to the loss. Others around him don't understand, becoming frustrated and feeling helpless. Insecurity and discouragement creep into his daily interactions. Unexplained mood

swings occur. Family and social relationships begin to break down. The comfort of sound, conversation, and the hum of life become clouded and uncomfortable.

If allowed to progress this far without (1) identifying the hearing loss for what it is, and (2) seeking appropriate help and advice, the hearing-impaired person can become so despondent that withdrawal is almost total and self-perpetuating.

The following is a "short course" on the effects of hearing loss. These effects are totally unprejudiced, experienced by the educated and uneducated, male and female, adults and children.

- They experience the loss of social small talk and general information.

- They no longer find groups enjoyable; they stop attending church, theatre, bridge clubs, parties, and the like.

- They often "bluff" socially and then discover they don't know what is happening around them.

- They often feel confused and in the wrong, make mistakes that make them feel "stupid."

- They often feel anxious and depressed about everyday situations.

- Stress and fatigue often accompany a hearing loss. Guessing is hard work.

- Many feel less confident about managing their own lives and less certain about their own memories and judgment. They become dependent on others, creating additional stress.

- The hearing-impaired are often unaware of their own handicap, becoming cranky and impatient with others.

- Many become antisocial and alienated from others because of hearing loss. Other people are frequently unsympathetic and neglect the hearing-impaired.

- Hearing people are often impatient and make harsh judgments about hearing-impaired people.

- Hearing people tend to "talk down" to hearing-impaired people.

- Tinnitus may be very stressful.

Pretty depressing scenario? Yes, it is, and it gets worse if misunderstanding and ignorance continue. You may be saying to yourself, "Come on. It can't be *that* bad."

Believe me. It can be, and often is, due to lack of understanding about the complex problems of hearing loss. If something is so vital to life that without it we die, how could it *not* have such a profoundly emotional and psychological impact on one's life?

> *My misfortune pains me double, for*
> *inasmuch as it leads me to being misjudged,*
> *I must live like an outcast. If I appear in*
> *company, I am overcome by a fear that I am*
> *running the risk of letting people notice my*
> *condition . . . I was at the point of putting an*
> *end to my life—the only thing that held me*
> *back was my art.*
>
> Ludwig van Beethoven

There is help, though. Reading this book is a first step. Recognizing the signs and then using the techniques explained later will take much of the heartache and emotional pain out of hearing loss.

CHAPTER 5

Ears That Don't Work Right

Children with Hearing Loss

*E*ntire books have been written on the needs of hearing-impaired children at home and in the classroom, but precious little has been devoted to the emotional and psychological effects hearing loss has on children or their parents.

As with adults, how we handle any of the hurdles in our lives depends on several factors. For children, there are profound differences in adjustment and effect, depending on whether the loss is temporary or permanent and the degree of loss. In this chapter, I am confining my discussion to *general* effects, common to any degree of hearing loss. Whether the loss is permanent or temporary alters the emotional/psychological effects only insofar as whether those effects, also, are permanent or temporary.

All of the personality and emotional upsets mentioned in the previous chapter regarding adults can be, and usually are, present for children. Owing to the fragile development of personality and their sense of self, often even a mild hearing loss can have an intense impact.

This is largely dependent on how others in the child's life react to the hearing loss. Children are like little human photocopiers. They will duplicate behaviors and assimilate feelings they see demonstrated around them. As adults, we have acquired the knowledge of appropriate reactions and behaviors in many different situations. Children,

on the other hand, are still learning. Many times, they don't know how to feel, respond, or react to a given situation and base their actions and feelings on how others behave.

A young child, say between two and six years old, may be experiencing the nemesis of many youngsters at that age—recurrent ear infections or otitis media. For the child, no longer being able to share whispers with friends can blast a huge hole in conversational "technique." She feels isolated because of the inability to participate. Her friends may feel they are being ignored and so they ignore her. His friends may feel he is a snob, or really "dumb," and treat him accordingly. This is described better by a hearing-impaired friend recalling her childhood.

> *"Sometimes I felt lonely and left out. Sometimes neighborhood kids would organize a game, like baseball, and not include me. When the girls were playing jump rope, I could hear singing but didn't understand what they were saying.*
>
> *Nobody could tell me secrets because I couldn't hear whispering."*

This kind of cycle goes on for a couple of weeks and then the infection is gone and the child's hearing returns to normal. Now she can again hear the whispers that, by now, may not have been meant for her ears! Gradually, her friends accept her back as the friend they knew. Suddenly, another ear infection—and those earlier behaviors return.

Not from any fault or conscious effort on her part, this child's behavior has become inconsistent. As a result, her friends may misjudge this inconsistency as deceit, untrue friendship, or any number of incorrect assumptions. The result is the same. Her friends don't trust her. They don't understand why her behavior changes. These inconsistencies lead to misunderstandings in class and at home.

IN THE CLASSROOM

The *ideal* classroom has carpet on the floor, acoustically treated walls and ceiling, plenty of natural light, and a seating arrangement conducive to sharing the learning experience. *Most* classrooms have

tile or linoleum floors, cement or brick walls, flat ceilings, some natural light, and a seating arrangement whereby 2/3 of the class is looking at someone's back.

I'm not suggesting that a classroom should resemble our living room at home (well, maybe I am just a little). I am saying that the structure itself contributes greatly to *enhancing* difficulties experienced by hearing-impaired children. Ten years of testing experience tells me that at least one out of every five children between the ages of 5 and 10 is not hearing properly for several weeks of each of those years.

Why this age group? Because that is the age when otitis media (inflammation of the middle-ear cavity) is prevalent. The Eustachean tube, which allows air to pass in and out of the middle ear (and also serves as a kind of drain) is on a horizontal plane to the ground at this age. Because it is lying flat, the effects of gravity cannot aid in keeping the middle ear free of fluids, and the tissues, when aggravated by infection or allergies, have a tendency to swell the Eustachean tube shut more easily.

As the child grows, the Eustachean tube tends to become more angled in relation to the flat earth's surface. As a result, more drainage occurs, and infections usually resolve themselves before becoming incapacitating. The tube itself is also bigger.

Plugged ears mean plugged hearing. That means, in a fairly standard class of 30 to 50 students, 6 to 7 of those children are not hearing properly for extended periods of time. Considering that the basics of education are laid down during the first five years, you can easily imagine what the impact would be of missing out on many weeks of each of those critical years.

Kids look at teachers as authority figures. Kids are also, particularly at this age, taught to sit quietly at their desks, to "pay attention," and do what is requested of them without question. Notwithstanding the unsatisfactory acoustic environment in the classroom already placing the child at a disadvantage (reverberation or acoustic echo is a killer), the fact that these kids don't always *know* that they have missed instruction or have heard it incorrectly places them at a further disadvantage. They don't always have the confidence to raise their hand and say, "Could you repeat that please? I didn't hear you." The teacher doesn't always have the confidence that the child's request, if it does come, is innocent and genuine, often believing the child just wasn't listening. My hearing-impaired friend would tell me, *"I got punished for not hearing. Teachers didn't believe me. I didn't*

put my hand up in class because I didn't know what had already been said."

With constant interruptions like this, the lesson plan gets behind, the teacher begins to feel stressed and becomes angry at the next interruption. After awhile, the student accepts the situation and just keeps quiet.

In a survey conducted between 1980 and 1986 concerning the attitudes of teachers with hearing-impaired children in their classes, one teacher, in reporting her experience, noted, "*Be prepared to feel guilty about neglecting your other students . . . never being satisfied with your performance, and feeling extremely frustrated.*"[1]

So what if he missed an assignment? He can ask his friend, right? Often, however, frequent queries to friends regarding assignments or "What *was* that page number?" raise questions in the friend's mind as to the competency of this kid. So once again, he keeps quiet. Pretty soon, he's behind in class, the teacher thinks he's a daydreamer, and friends aren't sure what to think except that John or Jill isn't quite with it all the time.

Researchers in the field concerning the ramifications of mild hearing impairment (hearing levels between 20 and 40 dB) have aptly labeled these children as M.A.D. kids, or those with Minimal Auditory Deficiency. They are, or at least *someone* should be, mad about how much they are missing . . . if they only knew.

The age group of children most affected by minimal auditory deficiency is between birth and 8 years. They are missing critical language, vocabulary, and grammatical lessons, both in instruction as well as the simple act of listening. "The educational significance of a child's hearing problem is determined not only by the degree of loss, but by how much it has affected the child's language development, academic progress, listening behavior and overall ability to attend."[2] Because there are so many hearing-impaired kids between kindergarten and fifth grade, education regarding hearing loss *should* be part of the curriculum in training elementary school teachers. So they miss a little bit of kindergarten—big deal! How much do kids *really* learn in kindergarten besides social behaviors? Hopefully, you

---

[1] The Hearing-Impaired Child in the Mainstream: A Survey of the Attitudes of Regular Classroom Teachers. Susan Chorost. January 1988.

[2] "When a Child's Hearing Comes and Goes." Karen L. Anderson, *Principal*. November 1987.

will recognize this as a rhetorical question. Kids learn plenty in kindergarten.

The rudimentary rules of grammar they have learned at home become organized and built upon. The rules of language are expanded. And everything else that is taught is based on using language as a tool.

So they miss a little bit of kindergarten. They'll pick it up in first grade with review, right? WRONG! The delay or the learning lost in the first several years is carried over and over as the child moves from one grade to the next. "Children with histories of hearing problems during the first three years of life often continue to have problems with speech and language development long after the hearing fluctuations stop and they can hear normally."[3]

Instead of the missing parts being filled in, more missing parts accumulate as the child moves from one grade level to the next. Lessons in kindergarten that were critical for understanding some concepts in first grade were never grasped, so that learning, and additional knowledge that is based on it, is never absorbed. Then comes second grade. The foundation is weak, but more structures are added. Now, even broader concepts are introduced, supposedly building upon what was learned in first grade. And so on.

A little bit missed in kindergarten translates, often, to a severe delay in all learning areas by the time the child reaches third or fourth grade. What the child loses each year progresses exponentially—*if the problem goes unrecognized*.

Like most adults, kids are very good at doing what they have to do to get by. Perhaps they are even better at it than adults, as they feel incredible pressure to "fit in" or, conversely, to not draw attention to themselves. After all, nobody enjoys being singled out for poor or unacceptable behavior, and some are uncomfortable with applause. The hearing-impaired child must possess the following abilities to improve his situation:

1. The confidence to admit he needs help

2. The self-esteem to admit that she missed information

3. The ability to separate what is and is not under his or her control

------

[3]Ibid.

For a six-, seven-, or eight-year-old, this may simply be too much to expect. In fact, these children lose self-esteem because they are incorrectly labeled. They lose self-confidence because there is nothing they can do about their situation. They lose friends because their friends don't understand what is happening and why any more than the affected child does. What a dilemma for a six-year-old!

For older children, say high-school age, the dilemma is the same, but the methods of dealing with the problems are different. In this age group, reaction and coping methods often take one of two forms—the wallflower or the delinquent.

The wallflower is the one who quietly acknowledges his problem and does everything in his power to overcome it—alone. He doesn't want to draw attention to himself by asking for help, nor does he want to admit a weakness by virtue of needing help. Instead, he quietly endures, working twice as hard as his normal-hearing peers to accomplish the same goals.

After a seminar on hearing-impaired children for teachers, I was approached by a social studies teacher who questioned my statement that hearing-impaired children are *not* doing "just fine." He mentioned a student in his tenth-grade class. She was a "good" student, meaning her grades were slightly above average in all her classes. In his words, she seemed to be "getting by just fine." This was the kind of report from a teacher that worried me. I knew that *all* she was doing was, in fact, getting by.

Compared to math or science, social studies is usually a very vocal subject, with lots of class discussion and little work on the board. I began to ask some pertinent questions regarding this student's behavior in class, such as where did she sit, how was her reading, and how often did she *voluntarily* join in class discussions. (I knew the student, who was a client of mine, to be talkative but not a real extrovert, and she was intelligent. She had a permanent hearing loss of a moderate degree.)

As it turned out, she sat in the back corner of the class. Her reading, although adequate, was slow, and she *never* voluntarily joined in class discussions. When a question was asked of her, her answers were long enough to adequately answer the question but short enough to discourage further conversation.

You might say that, well, she was just a quiet girl—reticent by nature. And not everybody is a good reader. But this girl was also doing everything in her power not to call attention to herself and to

avoid discussions because she knew it would result in embarrassment at obviously missing points of conversation or details of a topic of discussion. If she responded incorrectly or said "something stupid," that would have been the ultimate embarrassment and opened wide the door to ridicule from her peers.

She may have had a meek personality to begin with. Her years of experience with her handicap probably intensified this aspect of her personality. Her social studies teacher did not necessarily agree with my suppositions, but he did leave with some food for thought.

Another teacher that I ran into after giving a similar workshop shared this experience with me. "You know, I tried the things you suggested, like moving my desk. It was amazing. All of a sudden, the lights went on!" Because of the layout of this particular classroom, window placement, and so on, it was easier for the teacher to move her desk and be seen more directly by the hearing-impaired student than it was to move the student's seat.

A hearing-impaired child in the classroom can be a rewarding, positive experience. In A Survey of the Attitudes of Regular Classroom Teachers, one teacher states "You must look beyond your own frustrations and failures and realize how frustrated the hearing-impaired child must be at times. Johnny has been a tremendous challenge, yet has brought so much to my life."[4]

Then there's the other extreme: the student who refuses to follow directions, denies adamantly that he needs help, disrupts the class, and is generally a pain in the neck. Deep down, this kid has become totally defeated. He's missed so much, he knows he'll never catch up, so why try? He also doesn't want to draw attention to himself, but in his attempts to cope with the effects of his hearing loss, does just the opposite.

He's fighting back, but he's attacking the wrong aggressor and using the wrong weapons. It's a classic example of beating your head against the wall. You finally figure out that it hurts, so you stop. This kid has been trying to succeed, but the constant insecurity, the incessant mistakes, and the overwhelming self-doubt have taken their toll. So he gives up.

For most of us, learning takes place all our lives but not without

---

[4]The Hearing-Impaired Child in the Mainstream: A Survey of the Attitudes of Regular Classroom Teachers. Susan Chorost. January 1988.

some effort, and effort can be tiring. A point often overlooked when dealing with the problems of the hearing-impaired child, no matter what the age, is that *hearing impairment is mentally tiring.*

Think of the last exam you had to take. Maybe it was to renew your driver's license, or to upgrade your credentials, or to test a newly learned skill. Remember how hard you had to concentrate while studying and while taking that exam? Think about having to maintain this level of concentration from the time you wake up until the time you go to bed—every single day! *A hearing-impaired adult or child must concentrate at this level all the time* if they don't want to miss out on anything.

With school-age children, let's face it—by noon they are exhausted. It's almost an automatic shutdown. The school, the time, the body all say, "Keep it up," but the brain says, very simply, "Sorry. No can do." It's often the last class of the day that suffers most. Unfortunately, while recommending course loads for students, counsellors rarely consider the differing needs of a hearing-impaired student (in all fairness, often because they just don't know), and they fail to recommend physical education, art, or another relatively non-taxing course as the last class of the day.

So as not to leave you with the impression that all hearing-impaired kids are nonachievers, riddled with self-doubt and low self-esteem, let me tell you about another teenage client I had. In a word, this girl was dynamite. She took charge of her life, identified her needs, and made sure they were met. Her speech was not good (she was born with a severe to profound hearing loss), but she didn't care how she sounded. Somehow, she made herself understood no matter how long it took. She was a superior student, an active member of the provincial athletic association for the deaf, and a competitive runner. I'm sure she will go on to climb more peaks, continue to be inspired, and strive to get all she can out of life.

There are many reasons why some kids choose to give up and why some fight back, why some conform and some rebel. Two hearing-impaired kids will respond in opposite ways to the problems they encounter. One thing is for sure: The better educated we become about their problems and difficulties, the better equipped we will be to help them become all they can be.

For those of you who are teachers, here is a list of signs and symptoms to alert you to the possibility of a hearing-impaired child in your classroom.

Physical Symptoms

- Frequent earaches
- Discharge from the ears
- Faulty equilibrium
- Complaints of "noises" in the ears (ringing, buzzing, hissing)

Speech and Voice Symptoms

- Omission of certain sounds in speech
- Mispronunciation of common words
- Habitually speaking too loudly or too softly

Behavior Reactions in the Classroom

- Frequent requests for repetition
- Turning of one side of the head toward the speaker
- Inattention during class discussions
- Habitually watches the speaker's lips/face
- Straining in an attempt to hear
- Frequent mistakes in following verbal directions
- Appears unaware when spoken to if not watching the speaker
- Inappropriate or irrelevant answers to questions
- Frequently watches others before beginning a task, with a tendency to imitate the actions of others

Other Signs That May Suggest Impaired Hearing

- Poor auditory discrimination skills
- Irritability
- The child may be more intelligent than his work indicates

- Frequent temper tantrums

- A tendency to withdraw or "daydream"[5]

These behaviors and symptoms may also be indicative of other problems, especially when viewed as separate entities. If any of these problems are present, it would be a good idea to examine them further and seek appropriate assistance and/or action where indicated.

If and when you do discover a hearing-impaired child in your class, the following should be helpful:

Preferential Seating for the Hearing-Impaired Child

- The child should *never be seated facing into the light*. The teacher must, therefore, be careful not to stand by the window when addressing the class; the speaker's face is then silhouetted.

- *The first row may be too close* to the front, especially if the teacher stands close to the front row of desks. When too close, the child must *constantly* look up to speech-read—a real strain on the neck muscles.

- The child should be seated so he or she *has a clear view* of not only the teacher but of the rest of the class. The hearing-impaired child needs to see others and to be seen by others.

- A hearing-impaired child should be *allowed to change or move his or her seat* when he or she can't see or hear well. This may be necessary in special-demonstration or field trip situations.

- The child should be *seated* in a place that *gets the best reception from the teacher and from most of the other children*. Distance from the speaker is a significant factor in the child's ability to understand. The farther from the source, the more difficult it is to receive the message.

---

[5]From a pamphlet *Hearing Impaired?*, distributed by the Elks Purple Cross Fund and Deaf Detection and Development Program. Reprinted with permission.

For more information on the Elks deaf education program, write or call them at:
Elks Purple Cross Fund and Deaf Detection and Development Program
108-438 Victoria Ave. E.
Regina, Saskatchewan S4N 0N7
306-586-6584

- *When there is a hearing loss in only one ear*, the child should be seated so that the good ear is toward the classroom and thereby receives the advantage.

- Whenever possible, the child should be seated *away from extraneous noises* such as fans, hallways, and open windows.

Suggested Seating Placement

In many cases, a good seat is with the *child's back to the window*.

The *second or third row from the front and toward the middle* gives the child a good view of both the teacher and some of the other students in class so as to get visual clues as to what is going on.

General Suggestions to Help the Hearing-Impaired Child

- The teacher should avoid writing on the board while talking. With her back to the class, speech reading is impossible.

- The teacher should try not to "pace" or move around a great deal while talking.

- Everyone should speak in a natural tone and loudness level. Don't exaggerate enunciation.

- All should take care not to make a social outcast of the child among his or her peers by singling him or her out with extra attention.

AT HOME

Living with a hearing-impaired child can be a lot like peering into a nuclear reactor when you didn't pass Fundamental Physics 101. You can't know what she's really feeling, and everyday life with kids is like that anyway. So you have "because they're a kid" problems *and* "because they're hearing-impaired" problems. Combine the two and you get extreme fusion!

We all remember how difficult it was just being a kid. It is easy to mistake hearing-impairment behavior for Obnoxious Preteen or Teenager Syndrome. As you now know (I hope), hearing impairment can, by itself, do strange things to one's psyche. Throw in a little

biological warfare and it's tempting to leave home . . . for about six years.

But it doesn't have to be that bad. Learning to communicate with anyone, especially a child, and *particularly* a teenager, is diffi-cult. Learning to communicate with a hearing-impaired person is, by comparison, a piece of cake. There are some communication pros and cons that we'll cover later. What I'd like to discuss here are the behaviors that manifest themselves as a result of being a kid who also happens to be hearing-impaired.

Those of us with children know that they never listen to us, right? Well, I hope you can sense the slight sarcasm there, but with a hearing-impaired child, this sense of being ignored gets exaggerated. Most of us say, "I can't hear you" when we don't quite catch what someone said to us. Good Communication Tip Number One: *Say what you mean.* If you didn't hear *anything*, how can you correctly respond, "I can't hear you"? We all do it, though, when what we really mean to say is "I heard you, but I didn't *understand* what you said."

There's a big difference here. A hearing-impaired person *often* doesn't *understand* what was said. It isn't because they weren't lis-tening but because the message sounded like gibberish. It's not their fault, and it's not yours, but it's important to understand that this occurs with regularity. To avoid the inevitable confrontations, accusa-tions, and defensive reactions, it's important to do everything you can to communicate *effectively*. We'll discuss how you can do that in Chapter 7.

Remember, however, that kids react to confusion in much the same way that we, as adults, do. They get irritated, angry, feel help-less, and do the wrong things. If you have a hearing-impaired child at home, try to give them the benefit of the doubt if they say they didn't "hear" you tell them to take out the trash—at least the first couple of times. Try not to laugh when they insist they've already taken a bath when you told them to let out the cat.

Kids really do want to please. Ask any child psychologist. Their sense of self is changing daily—sometimes hourly—and is fragile. Try not to get angry and hurl accusations when you've repeated something three times and they still don't understand. Count to 10 or backwards from 100 and start again. The fault was probably yours, which you will also learn about in Chapter 7.

Of course, like adults, there will always be kids who "use" their

impairment. Only you, as the parent, can know whether this kind of behavior is going on. *Start* by giving them the benefit of the doubt.

Hearing-impaired kids can feel extremely self-conscious if they wear hearing aids. They are as anathema as that first pair of glasses. (Although I've never heard of a hearing-impaired kid being called "four ears.") I have heard hearing aids variously described as "buckets behind my ears," "those awful THINGS," or "abnormal-looking growths on my ears." Girls and boys will want to grow their hair long to cover them up. (Men and women will do this, too.) They will wear hats. They won't come out of their room. Or they come home crying because the other kids at school have made fun of them. *Your* attitude about *their* hearing loss is critical. It can either be positive and nurturing or embarrassed and vain.

I had a client once, a boy who I saw between the ages of 9 and 12. During those years, I watched him become more and more sensitive about his hearing loss, more and more defensive about his classroom needs, and finally refuse to wear his hearing aid at all. (He had a hearing loss in one ear only.) His teacher, his aide, his mother, and I had several conversations about what would be the best approach.

I didn't truly realize where the problem was coming from until he talked about getting contact lenses. He didn't even wear glasses! I learned later that he needed glasses, but his mother wouldn't have it. He had to wait until he was old enough for contacts so they wouldn't "show." He wouldn't wear anything but an in-the-ear hearing aid because it didn't "show" as much, even though this type of aid wasn't powerful enough for his degree of hearing loss. Ralph (not his real name) didn't feel good about or hadn't accepted his hearing loss because—well, why do you think?

We are all models for our children. And their thirsty, growing little minds are ready to soak up most of whatever comes their way. If your child is hearing-impaired and you're not comfortable with it, your child will pick up on those feelings *even if you try to hide them.* They need to know that it's okay to be hearing-impaired, that, in spite of it, they are good, competent people. If not, their self-esteem will suffer, and they will carry that cross for the rest of their lives. If your child needed glasses, you probably wouldn't think twice about getting them. If your child needs hearing aids, your attitude should be the same.

Even if hearing aids are not an issue, hearing impairment can still make kids feel different. (There is further discussion of hearing

aids in Chapter 8.) Some people will have trouble communicating with them. Some people won't even try. They don't necessarily understand other people's reactions, so it's important for you, mom and dad and aunt and uncle and friend, to be as supportive as possible. Let them know that not being able to share secrets (because they are usually whispered) isn't the end of the world—even when they think it is. Suggest alternatives, like writing notes (except in class!).

Let them know that everybody makes mistakes without telling them that they make more. They already know that. Help them to understand their hearing loss, whether it's temporary or permanent. Tell them what is causing it and, if appropriate, that it won't last forever. Help them to identify their communication needs (Chapter 7) and how to let other people know what those needs are. Teach them to take charge of their hearing loss and not allow it to take charge of them.

The following is information you and your child may find helpful. The first section was designed by a hearing-impaired friend as a hand-out for our teen clients in an effort to acknowledge their feelings and let them know that those feelings were normal. The second outlines needs and expectations of various degrees of hearing loss.

HOW HEARING LOSS AFFECTS YOU

1. Your school effectiveness

- You miss important instructions.

- You find it difficult to be part of class discussion because conversation is hard to follow.

- Your classmates often do not understand your problem—they ignore you, and you get lonely.

- Straining to hear makes you tired and/or nervous.

- You are afraid to watch a film or listen to a tape because you miss so much of what is being said.

2. Your day-to-day living

- Mom and Dad get annoyed sometimes when you get instructions mixed up.

- Some people think you are "not too smart" or "snobbish" when you do not answer them properly.

- Background noise drowns out words.

You can help people talk to you by politely asking them

- to speak clearly and a little slower.

- not to shout.

- to speak face-to-face.

- to not cover their mouth or chew while talking.

- to rephrase a misunderstood sentence instead of repeating it.

- to not be afraid or embarrassed to use a pencil and paper.

- to not whisper in your ear—you need to speech-read.

And remember . . .

- Hearing loss is invisible.

- Hearing loss is not your fault . . .

- or your family's fault . . .

- or your friend's fault . . .

- or your teacher's fault.

- So don't be angry. Learn to live with it peacefully.

Effects of Hearing Loss in Children

Normal 0–20 dB	no special classroom treatment
Mild 20–40 dB	will have difficulty hearing faint or distant speech
	will have difficulty understanding if there is background noise
	listening may be more tiring than for the normal hearing child

may have effect on speech and language development (language will probably develop spontaneously but may have errors)

may require amplification (hearing aids)

may require special classroom considerations (preferential seating and/or auditory training equipment)

Moderate 40–65 dB	speech will sound muffled will depend on speech reading (including facial cues), especially in the presence of background noise will have difficulties in group discussions will often have speech/language delays (may develop spontaneously but with errors) will require amplification will require special classroom considerations
Severe 65–90 dB	may be able to discriminate vowels but not consonants (without amplification) may be able to identify some environmental sounds will always depend on speech reading group discussions will be extremely difficult to follow speech and language will not develop spontaneously and will be delayed without intervention will require amplification will require special classroom and teaching considerations

Profound
90 + dB

all consonants and most vowels *will not* be "heard" without amplification

will be able to identify only a few environmental sounds without amplification

vibrations may be perceived better than tonal patterns

will always depend on speech reading (vision may be the primary channel for communication)

group discussions will be extremely difficult to follow, if at all

speech and language will not develop spontaneously and will be delayed, perhaps even with amplification

amplification may or may not be beneficial for speech/language development due to extreme distortion caused by the hearing loss; still recommended, however, for gross sound perception

will require special classroom and teaching considerations, including one-to-one instruction

may require an interpreter and note-taker

CHAPTER 6

Advice for Parents of Hearing-Impaired Children

Heaven's Very Special Child

A meeting was held quite far from Earth.
"It's time again for another birth."
Said the angels to the Lord above,
"This special child will need much love.
His progress may seem very slow,
Accomplishments he may not show
And he'll require extra care
From the folks he meets way down there.
He may not run or laugh or play;
His thoughts may seem quite far away.
In many ways he won't adapt,
And he'll be known as handicapped.
So let's be careful where he's sent,
We want his life to be content.

Please, Lord, find parents who
Will do a special job for you.
They may not realize right away
The leading role they're asked to play.
But with this child sent from above
Comes stronger faith and richer love.
And soon they'll know the privilege given
In caring for this gift from Heaven.

Their precious charge, so meek and mild
Is Heaven's very special child."

Author Unknown

*T*his chapter is, as the title suggests, for parents of hearing-impaired children. The information is appropriate for any degree and type of hearing loss, but it is especially devoted to children with permanent hearing loss.

The Day arrives. Finally, after nine looooong months, mom and dad get to see their beautiful baby. They expect their child to be perfect in every way (unless there have been earlier indications of a problem). Their hopes are the highest; their plans are the greatest. They will raise, shelter, guide, and protect their baby the best possible way and do everything in their power to guard against their baby's suffering.

It doesn't always work out this way.

Sooner or later, *someone* will notice that something isn't quite right. Often, this someone is a friend, grandparent, or baby sitter. They voice concerns that the parents have possibly already had but were afraid to confront. The baby doesn't turn when someone enters the room unseen. He doesn't startle when in the kitchen and mom drops a pan on the linoleum floor. She doesn't seem to imitate sounds the way other babies do.

All too often, it is *not* the pediatrician or family doctor that observes any problems. And also, all too often, it is the doctor that dismisses mom's and dad's concerns, attributing them to any number of false pretenses—overreacting, expecting too much too soon. "He'll grow out of it." "She'll talk when she's ready." Oversimplifications such as these may cause the parents to feel even more anxious because, although they know what they observe at home, their doctor, whom they trust, is telling them there is nothing wrong. So they wait, continuing to notice little things that don't seem quite right, but still doing nothing.

The parents are being wrongfully judged, but the biggest injustice is done to the baby, who is losing precious rehabilitation time. The parents are also being robbed of emotional support that, in the beginning, is more critical than education in "life skills."

One mother expresses their search for credibility this way. "After a frustrating round of doctors who chose not to listen to a mother's concerns, we finally took her to a large medical facility in Boston where she was evaluated and diagnosed as hearing-impaired. We were fortunate, however, because the young doctor who gave us the diagnosis also gave us hope."[1]

I have had the experience of telling families that one of their children was profoundly hearing-impaired. This was not easy and, for me, did not get easier with each new case. Each family was different, to be sure, but initial reactions to this information are generally the same. In my eagerness to give these families as much hope and support, information and guidance, as I could, it was difficult to hold back and not try to do it all at once. I had to remember that, after initially hearing that their "perfect" baby was permanently hearing-impaired, *they really didn't hear anything else for awhile*. I had to give them time to react, time for the grieving process and time for themselves. In some cases, it was difficult for me not to cry right along with the parents.

I also had to realize, however, that parents deserve the privacy and confidentiality of our relationship and allow them to cry, in front of me if it happened that way. While I tried to give them hope and emotional support at this time, I had to refrain from my urge to give them all kinds of "helpful" information or get too technical regarding the nature of the hearing loss. There would be time for that later.

My own personal style was to schedule another appointment within two weeks and encourage the parents to call me sooner if necessary. At this next appointment, we dealt with questions (which the parents had been encouraged to write down over this period), "why's," more emotional support, and the beginnings of habilitation, which was almost always hearing aids. Although, in most cases, their

---

[1]From "Family Forum," presented in a paper at the SHHH convention: Judith Raskin, Rochester, New York. June 1988. Reprinted by permission. Excerpted from the *SHHH Journal*, 7800 Wisconsin Ave., Bethesda, MD 20814. Copyright September/October 1988.

baby was going to be hearing-impaired for life, there was a lot to accomplish—how to begin receptive language training, encouraging language expression, later speech development, and the lifelong task of bridging the gap between the hearing and the hearing-impaired world.

The "why's" were sometimes the hardest, because there wasn't always a clear-cut answer. "Why *my* baby?" "Why can't she hear normally?" Although initially it may help to understand if you know why, this generally will not change anything. You, as a parent, must be willing to accept, with or without an answer to "Why?"

Emotional support remains critical for an extended period of time—at least the first year. The needs of mom and dad may be different, and the clinician and/or doctor must be prepared to deal with this. Different emotional needs were profoundly apparent in one family I worked with.

JOSH

Bob was a scientist. His work took him outside a great deal, which he thoroughly enjoyed as he was not the "desk" type. He was highly educated and had a very analytical approach to life.

Martha had a college degree but was not working outside the home. Her approach to life was one of a realist, to more or less "roll with the punches." Bob and Martha had one child, a little girl. Bob's hope was that Martha's pregnancy would result in a baby boy with whom he could share his love of the outdoors, and who would perhaps follow in Bob's footsteps someday. Not an out-of-the-ordinary hope for many fathers.

Bob and Martha's baby was a boy. He was born with multiple abnormalities affecting nearly every system, physical and mental. Josh was also profoundly hearing-impaired.

Josh's rehabilitation needs were almost overwhelming they were so diverse and involved. Because he was an infant, motor skills were targeted as a priority, as well as receptive cognitive skills for his developmental age. Massive amounts of information were being given to the parents on how best to work with Josh, whose needs were so great.

He was fitted with two powerful, behind-the-ear hearing aids. We could only hope they were helping, because Josh displayed little

in the way of repeatable responses to sound. Clinical methods typically used to evaluate hearing in infants were inappropriate for him. His eyesight was also seriously impaired. His syndrome was a new experience for most of us on his team, and we all stumbled along when one thing didn't work and a new approach had to be devised.

Meanwhile, Bob was absorbing little of the educational information and advice. It seemed to me that while everyone was judiciously enlightening Bob on Josh and his regime, Bob's emotional needs were being sorely overlooked. His coping mechanisms were inoperative.

Martha was busy trying to adapt to a profoundly and unalterably changed life style, tending to her other child's needs and getting her own support when necessary. Bob's withdrawal from Josh created additional problems for Martha. I watched as each parent struggled to accept this child in their own way and finally decided to confront what I saw as a devastating cycle with Bob.

We started by talking about how he felt about Josh. This was difficult. Bob's initial approach was to analyze the syndrome and its effects on Josh's growth and development. He was intellectualizing everything. I had to remind Bob that we were supposed to be talking about the syndrome's effects on *him.*

The question as to whether Josh was epileptic came up. Further tests were ordered. As a result of these tests, Josh's cerebral functioning was determined to be very low. (He was not, however, epileptic which would have complicated his little life even more.) Bob was stuck in the grieving process somewhere between anger and despair. At the time, his technical mind would not let his emotional needs surface, be identified, and be met.

Bob was not able to interact with Josh on anything but a very superficial level, and this was difficult for Martha. She needed to know her husband loved their son, and she needed the very real relief of someone occasionally taking over for her. Until Bob could accept Josh the way he was, he was not able to help with the feeding, manipulation of limbs, putting on and taking off the hearing aids, and other requirements. Keeping the hearing aids on was a job in itself. Josh's ears were also not formed properly, and the aids would fall off with clockwork regularity while Martha was playing or working with him on the floor.

Eventually, over several counselling sessions intermixed with general follow-up sessions, Bob did work through his grief and realize that all his dreams for his son would not come true, and, in fact,

would not even come close. He eventually was able to stop looking for "answers" and to appreciate his son the way he was. Bob did have a need to love, hold, and nurture Josh, which he was able to do only after he had acknowledged and worked through his own feelings. He was able to learn coping mechanisms and was able to purposefully involve himself with Josh's increasing needs. The family gradually began functioning as a unit again, which allowed each one to support the other according to need. It was exciting to watch, especially their young daughter's developing interaction with her brother.

BRIAN

The Wilsons were not able to have children of their own, so they decided they would adopt. Their first adopted child was, as one would hope, cherished and loved. Typical childhood problems appeared, but otherwise it was smooth sailing. The Wilsons decided to adopt another child.

The second child, a boy, was adopted also as an infant. All went well until, at the age of two, Brian contracted meningitis. He recovered from this potentially deadly disease, but he was left with a profound hearing loss.

The Wilsons did obtain hearing aids for him, but they were of little help in Brian's speech development due to the degree of hearing loss. As the years went by, Brian learned to sign, but the Wilsons did not. They eventually had two more children of their own, but none of the kids in the family learned to sign fluently. Brian was unable to communicate with his own family.

Brian was eventually placed in a special school for the deaf. In this atmosphere, Brian was with others with whom he could connect, peers and teachers alike. There were, however, severe behavioral and social-interaction problems. Even though he was finally among what was for him his first peer group, Brian had never learned "correct" social behaviors. He did not "know" the unwritten rules for interacting with peers and adults that most normal-hearing children learn at home and in the early elementary-school years. Brian was also lagging behind educationally, and he was physically small for his age.

The years of not being able to communicate at a regular school or at home had been psychologically excruciating for Brian, depriving him of the social and emotional support he desperately needed for

self-esteem, nurturing, and positive growth. He was asked to leave the special school, with socially destructive behavior given as the reason.

By now, Brian was 13. He came home but was unable to fit in at the regular neighborhood school and, again, he found himself in an environment at home in which he could not communicate.

It would seem that the Wilsons never received the appropriate emotional counselling and support crucial to their acceptance of the result of a disease over which they had no control. Perhaps they blamed themselves. Perhaps they were afraid, or angry. The only sure thing is that they were never able to adequately deal with their feelings, and Brian became an outcast.

After a short while at home, Brian was placed in a foster home with a family of two deaf parents and a hearing son close to Brian's age. Everyone in the family signed. Brian was finally with a family who could communicate with him as well as understand the problems of deafness.

But there were those who said it was too late. Brian's behavior was still a horrendous problem, and appeals were made to the special school to take Brian back, contingent upon his receiving appropriate counselling. He began refusing to wear his hearing aids, partly due to the influence of his foster father, who felt that hearing aids on a "deaf" person were useless.

While Brian was with his foster family and appeals were being considered by the special school, the Wilsons were making an appeal of their own. They went to court and were successful in *unadopting* Brian. He became a ward of the court. He was 15.

The lesson here is that a hearing-impaired child is not an isolated and separate entity. She or he is part of a family whose needs— first and foremost, in my opinion—are emotional. The family, especially the parents because they are the role models, *must* successfully work through the grieving process and deal with any guilt, feelings of loss, and a whole range of other emotions *before* they can accept their child and absorb information that is critical to language development, educational choices, and communication choices.

If you are now or become the parent of a hearing-impaired child, please, please, please, get the help you need for yourself first, or at least at the same time the "professionals" are working with your child. An excellent book on the grieving process is *On Death and*

Dying by Katherine Kubler-Ross. Don't be misled by the title. Although Ms. Kubler-Ross does address death, the book's focus is on *loss*. Parents who have a hearing-impaired child do experience feelings of loss, whether the baby is born hearing-impaired or loses hearing later in life. (If this does occur later in life and the child is mature enough, this book would also be excellent reading for them. They, too, have experienced a great loss and need help in coping with their feelings.)

Nobody likes to feel they are "going it alone." As social beings, we derive satisfaction, a sense of belonging and sharing, by discussing problems with others who have "been there." Some perceptive people were keen to recognize this, and support groups sprouted up. Alcoholics Anonymous (AA) is one such group. There are support groups for parents of Sudden Infant Death Syndrome victims, for women who have had a mastectomy, for parents who lost a child, *and* for parents with hearing-impaired children. These groups can be an incredible source of comfort. You will be among people who genuinely do "know what you are going through" and who can provide a wealth of ideas. Check in your area to see whether there is such a group. If not, start one! Believe me, even in a small town, you are *not* the only parent with the problem of a kid who doesn't hear well!

Support groups can also be a powerful tool. There is strength in numbers. Sometimes one family, approaching a "professional" about an unmet need can feel like they've run into a brick wall (or at least an individual with brick ears). This may be particularly true with educators. All too often, when approached with the needs of a particular child in the classroom, the teachers feel that you are encroaching on their turf and that *they* really know best. Don't allow yourself to be intimidated and become an inconspicuous parent. Teachers are the experts on education. You are the expert on your child's disability and how to best ensure that he is getting an education. Be charming. Be informed. Be helpful. *Be persistent!*

It always helps to have someone else along who shares your needs. This is one area where another parent or family from the support group can be instrumental in getting needs met. Try to present your requests as "needs" rather than demands. But think of them in your head as demands, and don't settle for less, particularly where money is involved. This can get sticky because invariably, there won't be any money for what you want. Count on hearing "It's not in the budget."

Believe me, there's money out there for hearing-impaired kids. You've just got to find it—also easier when there is more than one person looking. In the appendices of this book, you will find advice on setting up a parent support group and the warning signs of possible hearing loss.

In the meantime, here are some areas to address when dealing with the needs of a hearing-impaired child in the classroom, no matter what their age.

- Any hearing-impaired child needs to sit in the front of the class. If they have a hearing loss in only one ear, they need to sit on the side of the classroom favoring their good ear, so if the loss is in the left ear, the child should sit in the second or third row and on the left side of the room. The first row is not the best because it then becomes difficult to see other classmates and get clues as to what is going on ("Now take out your reading book."). If the hearing loss is temporary or fluctuating, the child should sit in this place in the classroom any time his hearing is impaired, and he should tell the teacher where he needs to sit if the teacher is not aware of the hearing loss.

- Hearing-impaired children need most verbal information supplemented in writing. New vocabulary needs to be visualized as well as heard. Assignments need to be written on the board for copying. A teacher may complain that this takes more time, but even more time will be devoted to "catching up" or tutoring if these new pieces of information are not understood the first time and require repetition.

- Classroom discussions need to be monitored for "speed." This may sound peculiar, but it takes a few seconds longer for a hearing-impaired child (or adult, for that matter) to figure out who is doing the talking. If a discussion is allowed to proceed at its regular pace, the new speaker will be halfway through whatever is being said before the hearing-impaired child figures out where it's coming from!

- Visual feedback is important. It is helpful if the teacher introduces each new speaker ("Okay, Sam. What would you like to say?" "Jane, what would you say about that?"). Most children know where their classmates sit and can cue in faster when they

hear the name than when trying to figure out where a voice is coming from.

- The child should be seated away from sources of external noise, such as fans and hallways. This background noise only further garbles what is already an unclear message.

- We all have difficulty concentrating and seeing the speaker's face when looking into direct light. The teacher should avoid teaching while standing in front of windows or artificial lighting that is not overhead. If the classroom seating arrangement is not in traditional rows, the hearing-impaired child should be seated so that the light from windows is *behind* him.

- Any hearing-impaired individual depends on visual feedback. This is especially true for children who are trying to learn. Discuss this need with the teacher(s), gently suggesting that they avoid talking while writing on the blackboard, that their face is unobscured by a book, paper, or their own hand when speaking, and to remain as stationary as possible while delivering lessons. This can be tough if your child gets a teacher whose style involves roaming.

- Acoustics in most classrooms was last on the list of building considerations. Hard walls, hard floors and ceilings, and unmuffled fans create a riot of sound. Information reverberates from one surface to another, adding echoes and distortion to an already difficult listening situation for a hearing-impaired child. Getting necessary materials, such as carpeting and acoustic ceiling tile can be tricky because it usually involves the "C" word—cash.

But don't despair! If you are firmly told there is no money in the school budget for such "amenities," seek donations of money or materials. Many organizations are devoted to serving the handicapped—United Way, Kiwanis, the Lions, and the Elks, to name a few of the larger organizations. And don't forget the suppliers. If you need carpeting, go to a dealer. She may have remnants, roll ends, or outdated stock that she might be persuaded to give away. Point out that she may be able to use the donation as a tax write-off for the business. Sometimes individuals have carpet that they want to unload after remodeling.

Be creative! Anything you can do to add sound absorption to the room will help. Curtains for windows can be made fairly easily. Get together with other members of your support group and whip some up together. Ask the store where your material is purchased for a donation or discount.

Egg cartons make wonderful sound absorbers, and the class can become involved in decorating them. You'll need lots, but almost everyone eats eggs. Arrange for a central drop-off place, someone's house or a store willing to cooperate, and get on your local radio station. Most have some time allotted to public service announcements where you can ask for almost anything. In this case, tell the world you need their egg cartons and where to drop them off!

These are basic needs. There are many other, subtler areas that get overlooked. For instance, it is very difficult for a hearing-impaired student to learn a foreign language. His own language sounds foreign to him! Because of the additional distortion created by second-hand speech (from a tape), this method of teaching is particularly unsuccessful. Explain this problem to the teacher and ask that insult not be added to injury by demanding "perfect" performance. Sometimes, learning from a tape is simply not a choice, and alternatives need to be explored.

Learning is a mentally tiring process at the best of times. In order to keep up, a hearing-impaired student must concentrate much harder than you or I and for much longer periods of time—every waking minute if they want to be sure not to miss anything. The younger students tire more quickly than those in their second year of high school. Discuss this with the teacher. Explain why Janice daydreams (or so it seems) now and then. Explain why John is a real dynamo at 10 A.M. and a total slug at 2 P.M. Check out the possibility of manipulating the schedule. Perhaps tests can be given in the morning.

Once again, look for and ask for alternatives. *Always* remember to *express* support and appreciation for those teachers who do go the extra distance, and think of them as *partners* giving additional time and effort.

Once your student arrives home, mom and dad, try to avoid conversations any deeper than explaining what's for dinner for awhile. Your son or daughter is "listened-out," and you need to be able to accept that they need some time just to be mindless.

Through all of this, maintain a positive attitude. Don't expect

less from your child just because she is hearing-impaired. Don't predict failure before effort and don't let anyone else either. I've often wondered how I would react if a doctor told me I would never walk again. I like to think I have the gumption and determination to say, "Ha! That's what you think!" and I'd walk just to spite the diagnosis.

But not everyone is like this. Well-intended pieces of advice from "experts" can sometimes be prophecies of doom, and we believe them because, after all, this is the enlightened advice of experts. One mother's search for information led to this experience:

> *"At one of these residential programs, we were counseled by a psychologist and told not to expect so much from her. Didn't we understand that hearing-impaired children couldn't talk, learn or do the things hearing children could? We needed to lower our expectations and not put so much pressure on her and us. . . . Obviously, he thought hearing-impaired children and their families were inferior and of limited intelligence. Was he wrong!"*[2]

Be realistic, not fatalistic.

Above all, remember, your child is a child first and hearing-impaired second. Give them all the love, support, and encouragement you would any child. Teach them to take risks. Let them know they're okay, whoever and whatever they are. This same mother expresses it best when she says, "When I have tried to analyze what has made the difference between my daughter and other hearing-impaired students, one thing continues to surface—our expectations for her were always great."[3]

Judith Raskin, the mother quoted above, goes on to advise, "Parenting a hearing-impaired child requires a major commitment of time and energy. Parents need to

- Get a good diagnosis and have regular evaluations from hearing care professionals [*audiologists*].

---

[2]Ibid.
[3]Ibid.

- Explore communication methods that seem right for the child and family.

- Choose a program (from a sometimes confusing array of choices) or create an appropriate program if none exists.

- Identify and communicate the child's strengths to the professionals.

- Establish a program of services and follow through with a commitment to make that program work.

- Learn all they can about the child's method of communication. Face the hard-of-hearing child, speak clearly and slowly and encourage cooperation from the entire family.

- Make a commitment to use assistive devices which help the child and enhance communication.

- Monitor the child's reactions, growth, services, etc., and build on successes.

- Demand the absolute best from the child. Parents must expect the best performance from their child in regard to language, reading, schoolwork and behavior.

- Plan ahead. Identify what the child wants to do and do not close any doors to him. Focus on the child's skills and strengths. Look at what the child will need for the future and supplement what he gets in school.

- Enrich the child's educational and social experiences.

- Work with the community to open opportunities for hearing-impaired children as well as adults.

- Make the child aware that he is responsible for his actions and that he realizes the dignity in taking risks and setting goals.

- Help the child to look for positive role models.

- Demand integration rather than segregation in school and social situations.

- Strive for excellence."[4]

---

[4]Ibid.

CHAPTER 7

Louder is Not Better

Learning How to Effectively Communicate

*N*ow that you know why communication is so difficult for the hearing-impaired, *what do you do*? Stop talking to them? Write notes?

I have a friend who had a laryngectomy, the removal of his voice box. Until he had additional surgery to implant a mechanical voice box, he had to write down everything he wanted to say. I jokingly told his son one day that he would know when his dad was yelling at him if he wrote in VERY BIG LETTERS.

Why is it that when we feel the most need to get our point across, we raise our voice? Some people even find themselves talking louder than normal to someone who is blind.

Reprinted by permission: Tribune Media Services.

DON'T DO THAT!!! For the majority of hearing-impaired people, and certainly for those classified as deaf, louder is not only *not* better, it's a waste of time. Shouting at a hearing-impaired person is insulting and annoying to them, as well as hard on your own vocal cords. It's irritating to anyone else close by, and frustrating because it doesn't work.

Why doesn't it work? Remember, with the most common kind of hearing loss (sensori-neural), not only is there a loss of loudness but also a loss of clarity. Everything sounds distorted. When your radio strays from a station, and all the "s's" sound fuzzy, and all the "t's" have that annoying little click, do you turn the radio up louder? Most likely, you would retune the station so that it comes in *clearer*.

The unfortunate problem here is that a hearing-impaired person can't retune their ears. Just like with the radio station, turning up the volume doesn't make the garble any *clearer*; you just get *louder* garble.

Learning to communicate, or relearning to communicate, with a hearing-impaired person is a thoughtful process. That is to say, it requires some, and often a lot, of effort. Old methods don't work, and it's hard to break old habits.

When you are talking to a hearing-impaired person, above all, remember this:

I know you believe that I understood what you think
you said, BUT I am not sure you realize that what you
said is not what I heard!

Your chances of successful communication depend on your realizing that you have a 50-50 chance of being understood. With these odds, it becomes necessary for you to do *everything* you can to insure good, effective communication the first time around.

The most important rule to remember is that you *must* look at a hearing-impaired person when you speak to him or her. Notice that I did not say "should" or "sometimes." There's no gray area here. If you want to communicate effectively, save a lot of repetition and frustration, you *must* look at the person. (This implies, too, that the person is also looking at you!)

To do this, you must think about logistics and set up the scene to everyone's best advantage. This may sound like too much to do for one or two sentences, but I can guarantee that if you don't pay

close attention to detail and look directly at the person while talking, you *will* have to repeat yourself. So, first of all, you must get the hearing-impaired person's attention.

Most people, even in the worst of listening situations, will recognize their own name being called. Even when you *don't* want someone to hear a message, if you use their name and they're within 100 yards, they'll hear you. We seem to have special little receptors in our ears that are tuned strictly for this sound.

So now you have their attention. Now you must look directly at them and deliver your message. If they are in a different room, someone has to move! It is my belief that, because you are the one with something to say, this is *your* responsibility. Don't expect your audience to come to you.

I've just thrown a major glitch into the communication network of most households. We *all* talk from room to room on a regular basis. In fact, probably several times a day because it's convenient. But, think about *why* it's convenient. You can convey a message without interrupting what you are doing at the time. Dad doesn't have to interrupt his newspaper reading to get a soda when he can call mom, who's already in the kitchen, and ask her to please bring him one. Sister doesn't have to miss a crucial segment of her television program to fetch her brother from his bedroom to come watch.

But when communicating with a hearing-impaired person, this no longer works. Dad asks for a drink, and mom, knowing he's reading the newspaper, thinks he said something about the sink and goes on with whatever she was doing. Meanwhile, Dad is still waiting. Sister yells to brother to come quick, and he thinks she said something about him being pretty thick and a fight breaks out.

In the long run, you save much time and aggravation by putting aside the newspaper or jumping up for a minute and *going to* the other person to communicate your message. After all, we do like to be able to see the person with whom we're communicating, even when our hearing is normal.

Picture yourself at dinner. You're at a chic restaurant, with beautiful china and a lovely centerpiece in the middle of the table. If you sit across from one another, what do you do with the flowers? It's awkward to converse while gazing through the petals and baby's breath. The flowers, lovely as they are, play second fiddle to your conversation and get moved to one side so you can see each other.

The reasons why it is so important for a hearing-impaired person

to be able to see the face of the speaker are many. Let's talk about lip reading first and perhaps dispel some myths.

First of all, lip reading isn't all it's cracked up to be. Of the thousands of English words, only one in every three is actually identifiable by what is reflected on the lips alone. That leaves room for two-to-one odds of being wrong, and a lot of guessing.

This is not to say that lip reading is impossible. On the contrary, hearing-impaired people depend on it, but not all by itself. There are courses taught in lip reading, and there are different methods of teaching it. One approach is to learn to recognize small groups or "clusters" of words. Another approach is to learn to identify each word by itself. Each method has its pros and cons, but neither method is fail-safe.

Because so much more goes on in visual communication than just the movements of the lips, lip reading has gone through a transition and is now referred to as speech reading. When a hearing-impaired person watches your face, she isn't just watching your lips. Your eyes, your facial expression, and, believe it or not, your throat all add subtle input to your message that enables the hearing-impaired person to integrate each bit into a whole, meaningful byte of communication.

For these reasons, there are some additional points to remember. "Oh no," you groan. "By the time I think about all I have to do, I'll have forgotten what I wanted to say!" Well, it may seem that way at first. But remember, old habits *can* be changed. These are "try to's" or "try not to's." If you remember them, they will add to the success of your communication.

- Try to keep your hands away from your mouth and face while you talk. I know some people that, if they couldn't use their hands, would become mute. Some people's hands seem to be a direct physical extension of their vocal cords. That's okay. Just keep them away from your face.

- Try not to chew gum while you talk. All that extraneous lip flapping and jaw movement confuses the message.

- Try not to shroud your face in facial hair. Don't get me wrong. I like beards. But beards and moustaches seriously get in the way of detecting critical lip movements, throat action, or facial expressions. If your contact with hearing-impaired people is

rare, there shouldn't be much of a problem. Just remember all of the other communication tips and you should be okay. If, on the other hand, you live with someone who is hearing-impaired and are also the proud owner of a perfectly groomed beard or moustache that has taken you years of pruning to get just right, I would seriously consider . . . shaving it off. Yes, it's that important.

- Try to manipulate lighting. If someone has to look into or toward the light, be it a window, the sun, or a bright lamp, try to have it be you and *not* the one who is hearing-impaired. *You* can still talk while you squint, but it is difficult for the hearing-impaired person to get all that important visual information when their field of vision is narrowed to tiny little slits.

I hope I have convinced you of the importance, and the reasons why, the Golden Rule of communicating with someone who is hearing-impaired is that they must be able to see your face when talking to them. Now we'll move on to some other necessary, albeit difficult, habit changes.

No one enjoys being patronized, especially if they know they have a problem. And no one likes being talked down to. When having a conversation with a hearing-impaired person, speak in a normal tone of voice and at a normal rate (unless that rate is like my friend's—about 200 words per minute). Don't exaggerate certain sounds or slow down your speech so that you sound like an old victrola that needs rewinding. You may think you're trying to help, but it comes across as further distortion to what is already distorted, and slightly condescending.

Some of us have had the pleasure of visiting a foreign country while not knowing the native tongue. French is French. Russian is Russian. No matter how the language is spoken to you—fast, slow, in a monotone, repeated over and over—if you don't speak the language, it doesn't matter. It all sounds Greek to you. The hearing-impaired person experiences much the same feelings of helplessness with his own language. Suddenly, familiar phrases sound different. Sounds that once were familiar are suddenly unrecognizable.

No matter how many times someone says to you in Russian, "The restaurant is over there," if you don't speak Russian, you'll stay hungry. No matter how many times you say to a hearing-impaired

person, "You're here for a hearing test," he will hear that he's there for a urine test. (This actually happened, much to the chagrin of the technician and relief of the client when he learned it was only his ears we were interested in.)

When a hearing-impaired person misunderstands what you've said, *reword* your sentence. Don't continue to repeat the same phrase. Some words are easier to understand than others. Some are easier to "read" on the lips. So get creative! If "I'm going out to get the mail" is misunderstood, try "The mailman was just here. I'll see if there are any letters." Without turning your statement into a paragraph, the more information you can give, the easier your message will be to understand.

The real nemesis for hearing-impaired people is *background noise*. I am using "noise" in a generic sense here and not for what most of us would consider noise, like the hum of the refrigerator or a lawn mower outside. To a hearing-impaired person, anything going on in the background of a conversation that is not a part of that conversation is noise. The gist of the idea here is simple. If you want to carry on a conversation, turn off or get away from anything and everyone that is making noise in the background. The Bach symphony that you consider soothing background music is irritating interference to the hearing-impaired. The television may not bother you, but it is competing with everything you say to a hearing-impaired person.

This conveniently brings us to different situational problems. Anyone who has lived with a hearing-impaired person notices that, as the hearing loss progresses, the hearing-impaired person often becomes more and more of a recluse. They simply do not want to go out anymore. There are just too many difficulties, too many pieces to organize into an understandable byte of communication. But there are ways to manipulate the situation to their best advantage (or yours, if you're the one who is hearing-impaired).

It's four o'clock. You've had a long day and, next to hiking the Sahara, the last thing you want to do is cook dinner. So you suggest that the family go out to eat. "Yay!" shout the kids. "No thanks," quips your husband. (I don't mean to be picking on men, but there are more hearing-impaired males than females.) Carrying on a conversation in a restaurant is too demanding and frustrating for most hearing-impaired people. It's not relaxing—until you know what to do.

Consider first the place. *Don't* go to a place that you know is always loud, either with people or music. Some eateries have great

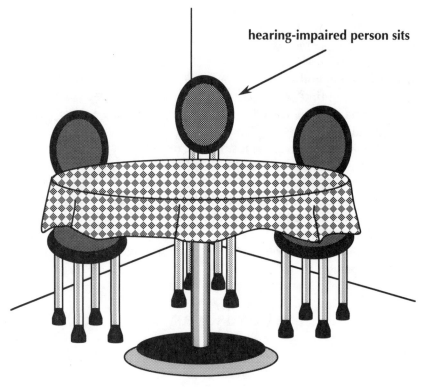

hearing-impaired person sits

Figure 7.1

food but lousy acoustics. When you arrive, there is often a hostess that will cheerily greet you and proceed to seat you where she thinks you ought to sit, based on either the waiter's turn or the first table she comes to. *Be assertive.* Ask to sit, first, in a corner. And allow the hearing-impaired person to have the seat at the table that backs into the actual corner. Look at Figure 7.1.

In this way, two things are accomplished. The walls, coming together as they do, act as an acoustic arena to capture all the conversation, not allowing it to spread and radiate throughout the room. Second, with the rest of the diners facing into a corner, there is less tendency to gaze about the room while conversing, thus allowing the hearing-impaired person to always (we hope) see your face.

Let's say the cheery hostess apologizes, but there is no available table in the corner. If you haven't time to wait, ask for a table along

the perimeter of the room, *away from the door, kitchen, and/or bus stands*. These are the biggest noise generators in the place; avoid them like the plague!

If this type of seating is also not available, and your goal is to have a relaxing and enjoyable meal, go somewhere else to eat. This may take more time, but chances are you'll enjoy yourselves and not come home with at least one member experiencing severe stress-related indigestion.

Speaking of conversations, having one of these with more than one person is also very difficult for the hearing-impaired and another reason why they begin avoiding parties or meetings or having company over for dinner. These are typical situations that foster paranoia.

Most discussions move rapidly from one person to the next. It's this lively exchange of words that keeps a conversation interesting, and it is also why it is very difficult, if not impossible, for a hearing-impaired person to follow.

this is Harry

Figure 7.2

Remember our recent discussion of the Golden Rule—how important it is to see the speaker's face? For those of us with normal hearing, we can quickly shift focus from one speaker to another, without having to see the first words out of their mouths. We can understand them in those first few seconds it takes to look from one person to another and easily carry on with what's being said. For the hearing-impaired participant, these first few seconds are critical to understanding what comes next. Harry (who is hearing-impaired) encounters this problem at a meeting (Figure 7.2).

Five people are sitting around a table, discussing the new manufacturing plant that's coming to town. Joe begins the conversation. Because Joe is the first to speak, Harry is "tuned in" from the beginning (Figure 7.2).

Then John jumps in with a point or two about the effect the plant will have on the community. By the time Harry looks from Joe to John, he's lost the first few words of John's remarks (Figure 7.3). While John continues talking, Harry is listening but trying to piece together what he missed in the beginning so the conversation makes sense and he can add some intelligent remarks.

Figure 7.3

Figure 7.4

Bob pipes in with a comment, and Sam responds quickly to what Bob has said. Harry completely missed what Bob said, and, in the process of trying to refocus on what Sam is saying, he misses several seconds of Sam's reply. Harry is still trying to figure out what Bob said to make sense of what Sam is saying (Figure 7.4).

Then John and Joe, simultaneously moved to add something, both speak up at once. By this time, Harry is so lost he doesn't know where to look, on whom to concentrate, and he has lost enough of the gist of the conversation that he feels left out and unwilling to contribute for fear of saying something inappropriate (Figure 7.5).

One of two things will likely happen next. Harry will force himself to be content to sit on the sidelines, hoping no one asks for his opinion, or he will excuse himself and leave. This isn't any fun for Harry.

The best way to handle a multiple-speaker conversation involving a hearing-impaired person is to try to slow things down. Try to lengthen the time between one speaker and the next by only a second or two. Assuming you're the next speaker, don't jump in quite so fast. This is tempting, I know, because we all feel that what we have

Figure 7.5

to say is very important. Because it *is* very important, slow down just a bit so that *everyone* catches what is being said.

Remember, too, that your rate of speech tends to accelerate when you get excited or really immersed in a topic. Try to keep it normal, not too fast and not absurdly slow.

If you are hearing-impaired, choose the seat that best enables you to see everyone's face. For those of you who often find yourself in meetings, there are several types of assistive listening devices that will greatly enhance your listening pleasure (see Chapter 8 and Appendix 5). If your meetings are always held in the same one or two rooms, consider "looping" the area as explained in Chapter 8.

Outside the confines of the home, most listening situations will require some degree of manipulation. Once you know what to do and get the hang of what's necessary, it will all become second nature. It's sort of like water skiing on a slalom ski. Being dragged along an often bumpy surface at warp speeds while standing on one foot, as your arms are slowly being wrenched from their sockets, knowing

that if you fall, this otherwise forgiving surface will embrace your body with the impact of a cement wall is not everyone's idea of fun. But, if you stick with it (assuming all your body parts stay intact) with practice, you *will* stay up.

Likewise, these suggestions will become, with time, second nature—a piece of cake.

If you have ever had the opportunity to watch two or more people sign to each other, you know how fascinating it is. Most people find it hard to look away. These people use their whole body to talk! I find it almost like watching a dancer, and I especially get a kick out of watching two signers telling a joke or having an argument. Their bodies come alive with expression and meaning.

All these body gymnastics have a purpose. They serve to clarify, emphasize, point out, identify—all the things we normally do with tone of voice or inflection. Because much of what a hearing-impaired person "hears" is highly dependent on guessing, using all the body language you can (while maintaining your personal definition of propriety) will enhance the conversation for both of you. Body language can be fun!

If you are aware that a particular hearing-impaired person has a hearing loss in only one ear, or a substantially greater hearing loss in one ear than the other, try to avoid speaking to him or her from their weaker side. Sometimes you can tell without actually being informed by the way they tilt their head. If they consistently turn their head to one side during a conversation, this is a good indication that one ear hears better than the other. Observe their body language. If you're lucky, they'll tell you that one ear is better. Don't be embarrassed to change positions. This says you care and your actions will be appreciated.

Let's say that you've dutifully memorized all the "try to's" and they have become routine for you. You're having a conversation with a hearing-impaired person and using everything you know, but you're still having trouble. "What do I do now?!" you agonize.

Don't despair! If you've deftly tried everything you know and your conversation is still going poorly, *ask*. Admit that you're having trouble, and ask what you can do to improve the situation. That may sound like an oversimplification, but we often assume and forget to ask.

Remember, too, that in communicative situations, we don't perform as well when we are tired, hungry, or not feeling well. The

same is true, only more so, for the hearing-impaired. For them, listening requires effort and is to some degree stressful at the best of times. This stress becomes pronounced when they are at a physical or mental low. In these circumstances, more is better. Do all you can to make listening easier and more effective.

COMMUNICATING WITH THE DEAF

I have been talking about how to make communication easier for the hearing-impaired. What about communicating with a deaf person?

All of the tips for successful communication with a hearing-impaired person also apply when communicating with a deaf person. They also need to see your face. Since most deaf individuals have some degree of residual hearing, background noise can be a problem and something to monitor. Rephrasing is as useful for the deaf as for the hearing-impaired. Body language and facial expressions are always important. There are additional aids, as well, that can be used with the deaf that may not be appropriate with someone only moderately hearing-impaired. (I use the word "only" as compared to deafness.) Sign language is the most obvious.

When most of us refer to sign language, we are talking about American Sign Language or ASL—the language of the deaf. Linguistic authorities have studied ASL and determined that it is, in fact, an independent language, just like French and Polish. ASL is governed by its own set of grammar and syntax. It has slang. It has thousands of vocabulary expressions. And it is difficult to become fluent in ASL. Often, when a hearing person attempts to learn sign language, their expressive sign will progress faster than their receptive ability to understand. What most people do not know is that there are at least five different sign languages or, more appropriately, five different ways of signing. ASL is the only one that is a language unto itself.

Signed English, Seeing Essential English (SEE 1), and Signing Exact English (SEE 2) were created in the early 1970s by educators attempting to teach English to deaf students. They are still used in varying degrees; however, most educators teaching in special schools for the deaf will use ASL. Sometimes, a child will learn SEE 1 or SEE 2 in school but use ASL at home. There remains a great deal of controversy between the deaf community and the hearing educators as to which method best serves a child's needs.

The deaf community feels that a deaf child should not be prevented from learning her own language (by virtue of it not being taught in school). Some hearing educators of the deaf feel it is important that deaf children correctly learn the English language. (I emphasize the word *hearing* educators because virtually all deaf educators of the deaf already use ASL and share the belief that a deaf child should learn the language of the deaf.)

This is—understated—a difficult argument. Some educators believe in a strict oral approach, meaning that any kind of sign language is not taught. Emphasis is placed on speech reading, speech rhythms, intonation, and so on.

My own bias is for what is called Total Communication. Simplified, this means whatever works, use it. Sign language, auditory cues, pictures, writing—any and all of our methods of communicating are utilized in total communication. Gratefully, more educators are coming around to believe in total communication because it does not force a child into a no-win situation. Some deaf children will never have understandable speech, no matter how hard they try or how much they practice.

Signed English, or SEE 1, is a translation of grammatical English into Sign. Most signs are based on meaning, however. There are different signs for synonyms, homonyms, adjectives, and adverbs, depending on how the word is used. In other words, English is translated into Sign in a grammatically correct manner, using all word endings, usually verbatim, while preserving context. For example, in ASL there is no sign for "coming" in the sentence "I am coming." Tense is established by time-based words such as "now" or "before." In ASL, "I am coming" would be signed something like "Come now I." In Signed English, "I am coming" would be signed "I am come" with an additional sign tacked on the end for "ing." In the sentence "I am too tired to see two movies tonight," there would be different signs for "too" and "two," and the "to" in "to see" might be left off.

Signing Exact English, or SEE 2, is word-based rather than dependent on meaning. Signing Exact English means just that—a word for word, verbatim translation of English into Sign. In SEE 2, "I am too tired to see two movies tonight" has only one sign for the words "to," "too," and "two," no matter how they are used. In ASL, this sentence would translate something like "Tired I. Not want see two movies tonight." In both SEE 1 and SEE 2, contractions, prefixes,

and suffixes, such as the "ing" in "coming," are denoted by signs called "markers." There is no such designation or distinction in ASL.

Adverbs are not used much in ASL. Most, if not all, of the "wordettes" of English, such as a, an, the, and to simply don't exist in ASL. The language is saturated with pointing or "indexing" to indicate who is expressing what and to whom the speaker is talking. Adverbs we so commonly use to add detail to our language are considered extraneous and redundant in ASL, only getting in the way of what is being said.

Pidgin Signed English or PSE is a combination of ASL and Signed English. Signs are based on meaning, and expressions swing from more ASL-like to more English-like. Normally, before one becomes really fluent in ASL, the sign language used will be Pidgin Signed English. The indexing and phrases common to ASL will be used, but word order will resemble that of English. (This is the way I sign because I use it infrequently, and so I have not become fluent. When signing with someone, I am constantly asking them to "slow down please!")

Signs can vary according to the method of sign, much the same as dialectal differences make it difficult for someone from northern Germany to understand someone from southern Germany. Sometimes, the differences are subtle. At other times, the differences are so drastic that someone having ASL as their first language may not understand someone speaking to them using SEE 2, and vice versa.

If you are faced with a choice as to which sign language to learn, this can be a gut-wrenching decision. Undoubtedly, you will be getting advice from all manner of "experts"—some who know what they are talking about and some who do not. I have already shared my opinion with you, and I would argue against the oral approach until there are no more deaf children. I, too, can only suggest to you which might be the best way to go. The following are some factors you should consider before making your choice.

Is This an Adult Who Has Become Deaf?

In this case, he or she already knows the English language and, consequently, doesn't have to be taught the right and wrong way of using English. And, because sooner or later most individuals with a handicap want to spend time with others who have a similar handicap, this adult will keep company with the deaf community. In this case,

this adult and all those who regularly associate with him should learn ASL. You don't learn Polish in order to communicate in France.

Is This an Infant or a Young Child?

The decision is not so cut and dried in the case of a baby or youngster who is deaf and hasn't yet learned English. Again, I must state my belief in Total Communication, and you must do whatever it takes to get a message through to this child. I also believe the child, and her caregivers at the very least, should learn ASL. But should you also teach English? I guess that depends on your purpose for doing it.

Will the child be taught in a school for the deaf? If so, they will probably use ASL. Will the child still learn to read? Yes, if reading is supplemented with sign. And don't forget: Many children learn to read long before they ever have their first class in grammar.

Were I in the position of having to make a decision, I think I would choose to have English taught along with math, science, and social studies. But, unequivocally and without reservation, I would allow the child to *communicate* using ASL.

Are Your Chances of Communicating with a Deaf Person Remote?

What do you do when the situation suddenly appears? That's easy. Use all the techniques you've learned to use with the hearing-impaired, and don't be afraid to write things down. If this is a deaf person who has made the choice not to use his voice, he will be writing notes to you, so don't be embarrassed to respond in kind.

TIPS FOR CAREGIVERS AND HEALTH PROFESSIONALS

There are some situations that require certain expertise and careful attention to communication. The one that comes to mind first is a hearing-impaired or deaf patient in either a doctor's office or the hospital. These patients deserve the same respect and information that hearing patients receive. Unfortunately, either through ignorance or time constraints, or embarrassment or simply not knowing,

many hearing-impaired patients experience extreme anxiety in the company of their caregivers.

If you are a doctor, nurse, or other caregiver, communicating with a hearing-impaired or deaf patient *does* mean extra effort and time. This will, however, ultimately pay off in the deliverance of *quality* care.

First, there should be a standard method of alerting those involved with caring for the person that he or she is hearing-impaired or deaf. Some hospitals already use the symbol of an ear with a line through it in the form of a sticker applied to the patient's chart. Further notes should be made as to how this patient regularly communicates. Do they have intelligible speech? Do they sign and speak? Do they only sign? Can they speech-read? All of this information can be obtained just as easily as determining whether the patient has any allergies, and it should be noted on the chart where it commands attention.

Remember that hearing-impaired or deaf patients do not communicate nearly as well when ill. They are where they are because they want to get better. Don't complicate the healing process by making communication more difficult or by not communicating at all.

The following is just one experience of a deaf patient.

"I was hospitalized two years ago, and I will never forget the experience. I told the doctor I was deaf when he came in to examine me. He said nothing, examined me, and then left the room without a word. Later, my wife told me he'd ordered a test . . .

After the test, I was moved into a room with another man who was also a patient of my doctor. Later, our doctor came in, went directly to the other man's bed, and they talked for some time. The doctor then left the room without even glancing at me. My wife came in about an hour later and told me what the doctor had told her about the test."

This patient's reaction? "I am deaf, but I'm not dumb. And I don't like being treated like an idiot."[1]

---

[1] From *RN*, "The Deaf Patient," June 1976.

There are those who consider deaf and hearing-impaired people as mentally slow or completely oblivious. There is *no* physiological link between the brain and the ears that affects intelligence.

While many hearing-impaired people seem to seek isolation, there is also a fear of it. Placed in unfamiliar surroundings, this fear is magnified. For the deaf, there is a lot to be afraid of—afraid of what's wrong with them, afraid of not being able to make oneself understood, afraid of not understanding others, afraid of procedures, and afraid of strange surroundings. These are fears we all experience. But *our* communication is not dependent upon the willingness of others to communicate with us in the same way it is for the deaf. This dependency creates additional anxiety. So, here we go with some more "try to's" or "should do's."

First, when you enter the room of a deaf patient, *and they did not see you enter*, don't walk up behind them to give a reassuring pat on the shoulder. Chances are, you might receive a professional right jab from their startled response to suddenly being touched. Touch is good, but make sure they see you first.

The same is true for talking. Don't march into the room and immediately launch into the day's routine. By the time the patient realizes he is being spoken to, if at all, most of what you've said has been lost, and you'll have to start all over again.

Be careful in your expectations regarding speech reading. Some hearing-impaired and deaf people are better at it than others. And remember, many words look the same. You may be conveying a message completely different from what you intended, and it's not always funny. For example, "Suffering much?" and "son of a bitch" look nearly identical on the lips.

Don't leave understanding to chance, or assume that because you've followed all the rules the patient has understood. It never hurts to supplement information or instructions in writing. The patient may be embarrassed to tell you he didn't understand, especially if it is obvious that you are trying your very best. Just because they say "Yes" to "Did you understand that?" doesn't always mean they did. Few people will voluntarily allow themselves to look like fools, whether it be real or imaginary.

A congenitally deafened adult is sometimes the same as a child with regard to vocabulary. Be careful not to use medical terminology or "big words" when explaining procedures, tests, or a diagnosis.

Ray Krock, founder of McDonald's, said it best in espousing

his approach to the public—Keep It Simple, Stupid—which has affectionately become known as the "KISS" principle. Don't be afraid of using too many words. In communicating with the hearing-impaired and deaf, more is better. Just be mindful of the particular words you are choosing.

There are times, especially in a crisis situation, when an absolute understanding of what is going on is necessary. At these times, an interpreter should be present. Every hospital should make themselves aware of a person in the community who is fluent in sign, especially ASL, and is willing to be on an on-call contract with the hospital. In large urban centers, it is not difficult to find a handful of individuals fluent in ASL. In smaller, more rural areas, this can be a problem, but every attempt should be made to find someone. The advent of computer-assisted telephones, where we can simultaneously see the person with whom we are talking, will make the proximity of an interpreter irrelevant, but that technology is only on the horizon for most of us.

Take the time to learn a few simple, relevant signs, such as the ones for doctor, nurse, medication, pain, feel good, feel bad, and name. Commit them to memory. Learn the manual alphabet. Make it a fun family project. It's a great way to admonish your kids in a public place without disturbing anyone! (There are several books on signing. One is *The Complete Book of Sign*. Another is *A Basic Course in manual communication*, published by the National Association of the Deaf. Their address is at the end of this chapter and in Appendix 6. You'll find the manual alphabet in Appendix 7.)

If you know a patient wears hearing aids, keep them in a place the patient can easily get to, and make certain they are on (both physically and mechanically) before you begin a conversation.

Particular care should be taken when caring for a deaf or hearing-impaired child. A frightening experience at the best of times, a child with hearing loss can find the hospital or doctor's office experience so terrifying that it may have long-term effects. One mother relates how her three-year-old deaf son had such a horrible experience while in the hospital for a tonsillectomy that he wouldn't go near the Good Humor man for an entire summer!

Do everything you would do for a hearing-impaired or deaf adult, only more. There is no better time to practice being a surrogate mother, so give an Oscar-winning performance.

So that you don't have to grab this book and reread this whole

chapter every time a communication situation with a hearing-impaired person comes up, you will find in the appendices a "quick reference" of communication tips. Copy it. Hang it on your refrigerator or in the bathroom. Take it to bed with you. Your hearing-impaired friends and patients will thank you.

Finally, if you are a caregiver and would like more information on establishing a deaf patient care program at your facility, the following places would be delighted to help you.

> Director and/or Nursing Supervisor
> Gallaudet College Student Health Services
> Florida Ave. and 7th St. NE
> Washington, DC 20002
>
> The National Association of the Deaf
> 814 Thayer Ave.
> Silver Spring, MD 20910

To obtain a list of registered interpreters in your area, write to:

> Registry of Interpreters for the Deaf
> PO Box 1339
> Washington, DC 20013
>
> The National Association of the Deaf, above.
>
> The Canadian Hard of Hearing Association
> PO Box 5559 Station F
> Ottawa, ONT K2C 3M1
>
> The Canadian Coordinating Council on Deafness
> 294 Albert St., Suite 201
> Ottawa, ONT K1P 6E6

CHAPTER 8

Assistive Listening Devices

HEARING AIDS: THE IMPORTANCE OF REALISTIC EXPECTATIONS

In the medical industry, hearing aids are thought of as a prosthetic device, requiring medical approval to be fitted, rather than assistive listening devices. In fact, though, that's exactly what they are—a device that assists, not a cure, a solution, or a "miracle."

Hearing aids have come a long way since the bell horn of the 1800s, but they cannot now, or perhaps ever, duplicate the intricate responses of a real ear. When one goes to purchase a hearing aid, the importance of having realistic expectations cannot be overstated. Otherwise, as a consumer, one will feel her money has been wasted. As an individual with a handicap, she will feel frustration in the dissatisfaction of false hope.

Hearing aids are not like eyeglasses. They do not restore perfect hearing. Yes, in many, many cases, the help obtained from hearing aids is tremendous, but the inner ear is still damaged. A hearing aid doesn't change that. Speech is difficult to understand for the hearing-impaired at the best of times. Our language is so intricate and has so many acoustic nuances that the characteristic quality of some sounds is certainly difficult, and perhaps impossible, to duplicate convincingly.

A hearing aid user will still experience some degree of distortion and *will still rely on the communication aids discussed in the previous chapter.* Listening will become immeasurably easier, less stressful, less fatiguing, and, as a result, more enjoyable. But it still won't be perfect—not the way it "used to be."

Realistic expectations are equally important for those with normal hearing who interact with a hearing-impaired person. When your dad is fitted with hearing aids, don't expect him to hear perfectly again. You will still need to look at him when you speak. You will have to monitor background noise, and never, *never* raise your voice or shout at anyone wearing hearing aids.

Hearing aids are "fitted" like any other prosthetic device. They are fitted to the individual's hearing loss by degree of loss and, to a lesser extent, degree of distortion. A hearing aid, in the hands of a competent audiologist or hearing aid dispenser, can be "tuned" to compensate for those frequency areas where the loss is the greatest and to diminish distortion. Some hearing aids have as many as four or five internal controls that govern loudness, response to pitch, range, and the reduction of sudden, loud sounds.

This is one definition of a hearing aid.

A hearing aid is an ultra-miniature, electrico-acoustical device that is always too large. It must amplify sounds a million times but bring in no noise. It must operate, without failure, in a sea of perspiration, a cloud of talcum powder, or both. It is a product that one puts off buying for 10 years after he needs it but cannot do without it for 30 minutes when it has to be serviced.

There are many hearing-impaired people who should but do not wear hearing aids. Only between 8 and 18 percent of all those with hearing loss have at least one hearing aid. Because our society is so beauty conscious, compared to a wart hearing aids are less preferred. People who wear hearing aids try to hide them by growing their hair longer, by wearing hats, and by choosing an aid based on size rather than suitability to hearing loss. There is no age barrier to the dread felt by the approaching purchase of hearing aids. For this reason, many people who would otherwise find the quality of their lives immeasurably improved shy away from hearing aids. "I don't need one" (yet). "It's not me. It's the way you talk." "I'm *not* wearing one of *those*!" Period.

Suggesting to someone that they may benefit from hearing aids often has the same effect as recommending Charles Manson as your next caretaker: absolute horror. For many, the purchase of hearing

"We implant this behind your left ear and you won't even know it's there."

aids is admitting to a hearing loss, which, for them, is synonymous with a confession of weakness, incompetence, or inadequacy. It is easier *for them* to ignore the problem and force *you* to accept it as is.

The elderly are especially susceptible to this pattern of thinking, which is often unknowingly fostered by our reactions to them. "Grandma says such silly things" (because she hasn't been able to follow the conversation). "Grandpa keeps right on talking even when others are speaking" (because so little penetrates the barriers of isolation and insecurity).

It is critical that the recommendation of hearing aids be made

in a gentle, nonaccusing manner. Point out the *positives* of what they are missing—"Wouldn't it be great to hear the birds again." "You would be able to spend more quality time with Jenny, Grandpa." Try to make the hearing-impaired feel good about doing something for themselves, rather than trying to make them feel guilty about *not* doing something for others. Then everyone ends up a winner.

Another area of concern that I have, relative to the consumer, is misleading or blatantly presumptuous advertising.

You are hearing-impaired and thumbing through one of your favorite magazines when your eye is caught by huge letters shouting about some "miracle" hearing aid. The ad might go on to tell you how wonderful you will *feel* about wearing one of these hearing aids (most people *accept* hearing aids but don't *feel* any better when wearing them). Sounds will be *so* much clearer and speech easier to understand (with the subtle implication that it will seem like a "miracle"). They also emphasize that no one will know you're wearing hearing aids because they are so small (subtly suggesting that identifying yourself as a hearing aid user by wearing *visible* hearing aids is somehow negative).

The antithesis of what is implied and what *isn't* alluded to is that

- the hearing aid in this or any other ad is *not* an antidote for hearing loss. There are some things a hearing aid cannot do for your hearing;

- you will still experience some degree of distorted listening; and

- the size of a particular hearing aid determines how powerful that hearing aid is and its application to varying degrees of

Reprinted with special permission of King Features Syndicate.

hearing loss. Size has *nothing* to do with how "good" it is. The only "miracle" ears are the ones we are born with.

Yes, any improvement may seem like a miracle to some. It's the majority who are disappointed with less than a miracle that I am concerned about—for both their satisfaction and the resultant reflection on the hearing aid industry. The rule is—let the buyer beware, and don't expect perfection. In general, one should not be too quick to respond to flyers received in the mail, flashy ads, commercials on television or radio, and telephone solicitations regarding hearing aids.

TWO IS BETTER THAN ONE

I have so far referred to the individual who wears hearing aids. By far, if one has a hearing loss in both ears, one should wear two hearing aids. God did not give us two ears by mistake or because there were lots left over. Normal hearing is always two-eared or binaural. Equal input from both sides of the head is necessary due to the complex interaction of nerve impulses traveling up to the brain from the inner ear.

A stereo or two-channel system is necessary for several acoustic events. Determining where a sound is coming from (localization) cannot be done without a balanced system. Hand in hand with localization is our ability to estimate the distance from the source, also dependent on a balanced system. We can attend to more than one sound at a time, and we are able to "tune out" or selectively listen to one stimulus over another with balanced acoustic feedback. (A lot of hearing-impaired people are wrongly accused of "selective listening." If they only have one hearing aid, they *can't* be selective.)

Speech discrimination in noise—always a problem for the hearing-impaired—is enhanced by a balanced system. Listening is plainly easier, and sound quality is better. Parents of children fitted with two instead of just one hearing aid have noted such things as increased localization and an increase in the distance over which the child is able to understand speech.

Research and personal experiences abound supporting binaural

amplification. Statements like "Binaural hearing is the optimal method of rehabilitating hearing-impaired individuals," "Binaural amplification should be the rule rather than the exception," and "Children with binaural aids seem to do better in school" are not uncommon. Users, comparing the experience of one versus two hearing aids report that, in all, their auditory performance, social encounters, and personal enjoyment of life were enhanced by changing to binaural amplification.

All the wonderful things our ears are constructed to do are dependent on two, balanced ears. When you wear only one hearing aid, the system is thrown severely *off*-balance. The *ideal* hearing aid has been described as "an instrument (or instruments) which give the wearer the same perception of external stimuli as a normal hearing person would have."[1] That being the case, it would seem that all dispensers of hearing aids would recommend two, but they don't.

I'm not sure why. There are only rare instances where people lose their hearing in only one ear. I think part of the reason is the poor attitude surrounding the wearing of hearing aids. If one is bad, two might be seen as unacceptable. There is also the cost factor. There usually is not a discount for the second aid, so the price doubles. Some dispensers will recommend starting with one and then obtaining the second aid later, presumably feeling that it will be easier to adjust to one-sided amplification than preserving the balance of the system as it was intended. Adjusting to wearing hearing aids takes a bit of time. Beginning with one first and then getting another only serves to double that adjustment period, not to mention being potentially disappointing before getting the true appreciation for binaural hearing.

My own personal experience, as well as research, strongly dictates the fitting of two hearing aids from the beginning in nearly all cases of binaural hearing loss. There are always exceptions. A very few people may have what is unpleasantly referred to as a "dead" ear. This phrase generally refers to an ear that has no measurable hearing at the loudest levels an audiometer is capable of producing, usually 110 to 115 dB. In these cases, a hearing aid will not help. A few people have such severe distortion that two hearing aids seem to magnify

---

[1]Libby, E. Robert. "Binaural Amplification—State of the Art." *Ear and Hearing* 5, September-October 1981, p. 183.

rather than help the problem. Even in cases of an asymmetrical loss, when hearing is not the same in both ears, a hearing aid for each ear should be the rule.

If you have a hearing loss in both ears, ask for two hearing aids right from the start. Don't arbitrarily assume you cannot afford two. Many hearing aid dispensers have flexible payment plans. If your dispenser recommends against two, and the reason falls into one of the previously mentioned exceptions, then fine. Go with one. If not, get a second opinion.

TYPES OF HEARING AIDS

The most common hearing aids on the market are in-the-ear hearing aids and behind-the-ear hearing aids. There are also "body" aids, so called because the aid is worn on the body, usually somewhere on the chest, and "connected" to the ears via receivers that snap into the earmolds. These are *very* powerful hearing aids and generally restricted in use to those individuals with a profound hearing loss, especially children (see Figure 8.1).

In-the-ear aids (commonly referred to as ITEs) come in various sizes. Those that "fill up" the entire space of your outer ear are the biggest. Some just fit in the ear canal, not sticking out any farther than is necessary for you to reach the volume control with the pad of your finger. This is called a "canal" aid. Figure 8.2 shows both types.

Behind-the-ear hearing aids (commonly referred to as BTEs) also come in various sizes, but they all are worn behind the ear, coupled to the ear canal via an earmold which is a separate piece of equipment. Both ITEs and the earmolds for BTEs have a canal portion that should be kept scrupulously clean. Learn how to do this from the very beginning.

An earmold is a relatively innocuous piece of equipment. There's not much you can do to hurt it short of cutting or melting it. Cleaning the canal portion of an ITE hearing aid requires a bit more expertise but is easily learned. I have had more than one client bring me their hearing aids claiming that the aids were defective ("Yes, I tried a new battery!"), only to find the canal of the earmold or ITE impacted with ear wax. The hearing aid was working, but no sound could get through! At the end of this chapter, you'll find information on how

BODY HEARING AID

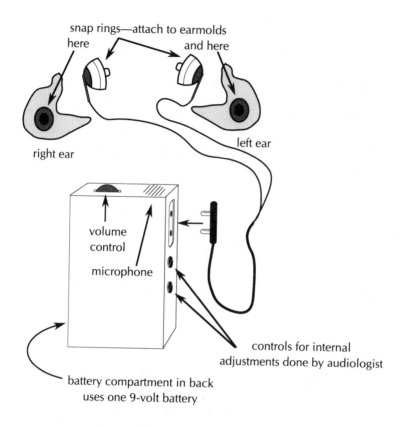

snap rings—attach to earmolds
here   and here

right ear   left ear

volume control

microphone

controls for internal
adjustments done by audiologist

battery compartment in back
uses one 9-volt battery

BEHIND-THE-EAR HEARING AID

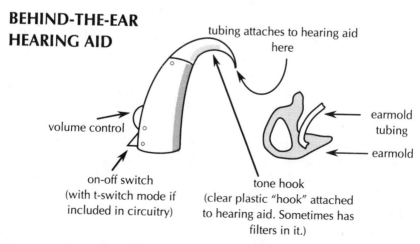

tubing attaches to hearing aid
here

volume control

earmold tubing

earmold

on-off switch
(with t-switch mode if
included in circuitry)

tone hook
(clear plastic "hook" attached
to hearing aid. Sometimes has
filters in it.)

Figure 8.1

to care for your hearing aids and earmolds, and troubleshooting exercises if your hearing aids are giving you problems.

Much of the advertising for hearing aids impacts the consumer in the area of size. The manufacturers or at least their marketing departments want you to believe that the size of a hearing aid is the main ingredient to its success and that smaller is better.

IN-THE-EAR HEARING AID (FULL)

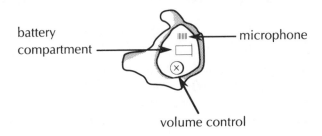

(In-the-ear hearing aids generally do not have an "on-off" switch due to size and circuitry limitations—the only way to turn them "off" is to take the battery out.)

CANAL HEARING AID

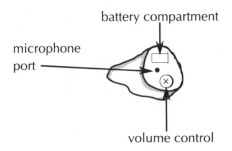

So called because it rests in just the ear canal and does not extend into the "bowl" portion of the outer ear as the full in-the-ear hearing aid does. A much smaller hearing aid and, as such, very limited in the circuitry that can be included. Good for those with only a mild hearing loss.

Figure 8.2

Smaller only means less visible, not "better" insofar as your own particular hearing loss is concerned. Unfortunately for the consumer, all too much emphasis is placed on cosmetic appearance.

The complex circuitry and power output of a hearing aid is limited only by the imagination of its creator—and its size. No matter how you stuff it, you can't get 10 pounds of potatoes in a 5-pound bag. A tiny hearing aid is not necessarily a bad hearing aid, but it is limited in its circuitry (you can only get so many chips into a given space), as well as its ability to make sounds louder. You simply cannot place a powerful amplifier very close to a microphone and not have feedback.

In simple terms, a hearing aid has three main components—a receiver, an amplifier, and a microphone. The receiver picks up the sounds, sends them through the amplifier, and it all comes out through the microphone. When you put a big amplifier too close to a microphone, you get that awful feedback squeal. The solution is to move them farther apart or turn down the volume. With its limited size, it is often not possible in an ITE to move the microphone farther from the amplifier, and turning down the volume means that you then don't have enough loudness.

If you have only a mild or borderline moderate degree of hearing loss, an in-the-ear hearing aid might be just fine for you. It might have the power to give you just the boost you need. (I should clarify here that the power output of a hearing aid is not dependent on where the volume is set. I am talking about internal power capabilities, just as some stereo speakers are more powerful than others. Think of it that way.)

On the other hand, if your hearing loss is more toward the extremes of moderate or into the severe range, an in-the-ear hearing aid *probably* will not have the powerful boost to its amplifier that you need. Once your hearing loss is well into the severe range and on into a profound degree, ITEs are no longer appropriate simply because they do not have space for all the control settings that you need, nor do they have the necessary power output capabilities.

Unfortunately, many hearing aids are fitted on the basis of size and not suited to the hearing loss. I should also mention that often a consumer will *demand* a certain style of hearing aid whether it is appropriate or not. This type of demand is often based on misguided information and, in the long run, he will be the loser. If you're going to spend between $1,000 and $1,500, don't you owe it to yourself to

spend it on what will *help* you the most instead of what will be *seen* the least? (The *average* cost of one hearing aid is generally between $500 and $750.)

You can try to hide your hearing aids, but you cannot hide your hearing loss. In the end, you will be straining just as much, missing just as much, and getting more tired by using a hearing aid that is inappropriate for your degree of loss. My advice to you is not to get caught up in the advertising and cosmetic value a given hearing aid may have. Get the best aid for you and your hearing loss.

Some Pros and Cons of In-the-Ear Hearing Aids

Pros

1. Location of the microphone most naturally duplicates the natural ear.

2. There is less movement during participation in sports.

3. Wind noise is generally less irritating.

4. Sometimes, but not always, more comfortable while wearing eyeglasses.

Cons

1. Appropriate for limited degrees of hearing loss.

2. Not compatible with assistive devices used in classrooms (auditory training equipment).

3. Electronics and circuitry are limited by the size of the ear. Often, there is not room for desired controls and extras, such as a T-switch. (See page 119.)

4. Controls are smaller and difficult to handle for someone with limited finger dexterity, such as those with arthritis.

5. A loaner cannot be supplied if the hearing aid must be sent away for repair.

6. Any changes to the external ear or ear canal require the aid to be recased in a new earmold—a problem for growing children and older individuals.

7. Little reserve power or flexibility to circuitry should the user's hearing change.

8. Often requires more testing than a behind-the-ear aid in the fitting process.

9. Historically requires more repairs than behind-the-ear hearing aids.

BEING AN EDUCATED CONSUMER

Once you have made the decision to get hearing aids, there are a few guidelines to follow.

If at all possible, purchase your hearing aids from a certified audiologist. They have more training than a hearing aid dispenser. More is better. If you do go to a dispenser, make sure he or she is licensed. In most states, licensing requires several months of training and up to two years of working under the tutelage of another licensed dispenser. Certification is obtained from the American Speech-Language and Hearing Association and requires that an audiologist spend one year working under the supervision of a certified audiologist *after* completing a master's degree. Once this year is successfully completed, the audiologist is awarded the Certificate of Clinical Competence, or three "C's." This is recognizable by the letters "CCC-A" after their name. CCC-SP means this person is a certified speech pathologist, and CCC-SP/A means this person is certified to practice both speech pathology and audiology. Licensing, on the other hand, is granted by each state, often with variable requirements between states. Many states require a certified audiologist also to be licensed to sell hearing aids.

Do not allow someone to fit you with a hearing aid without having had a *complete* audiometric evaluation, which includes hearing *and* speech discrimination. Remember, hearing aids are, or should be, fitted to the hearing loss, not personality type, size, or hair color.

Ask if there is a money-back guarantee or the option of another fitting if these particular aids don't work out. Any reputable manufacturer and dealer will give a consumer their money back if he or she is not satisfied. In the case of hearing aids, there may be a dispensing fee subtracted from the refund, but there should be a provision of

receiving *most* of your money back in the event you have tried other fittings and are really unhappy with the product.

Find out what to expect and what not to expect. There will be an adjustment period, just like getting used to a new pair of glasses. Before hearing aids, you experienced a gradual hearing loss and got used to the way everything sounded. After hearing aids—*wow*! Your quiet little world suddenly explodes with sound. Bombs are going off right next to your ear. Niagara Falls is suddenly in your kitchen sink! Sounds will be very different and, most notably, louder. This takes getting used to, but you will adjust quickly. Most dispensers will recommend a gradual "break-in" period—a few hours the first day, a little more the second, even longer on the third, and so on. If you want to avoid being assaulted by noise and ripping off the aids before you've really had a chance to get used to them, *do not wear them out of the dispenser's office!* Start out wearing them at home, where sounds are familiar and the atmosphere is notably quieter than on the street or in a mall.

Get to know your hearing aids and earmolds, if you have them. Fondle them, caress them, speak kindly to them. They don't bite, although they sometimes will squeal. As with many types of electronic instruments, some people are afraid to do more than just look at them. You must become comfortable with your hearing aids, and touching is part of the process.

Keep in mind that hearing aids are electronic instruments and, as such, do not stand up well when immersed in water or subjected to great variances in temperature. I once had a client who accidentally

Reprinted by permission of NEA, Inc.

washed one of her hearing aids. She was too embarrassed to call the clinic to find out what to do, so she tried to dry the aid out—in the oven. Believe me, people do some pretty crazy things with their hearing aids.

Some hearing aids have as many as four or five internal controls. Anyone with a little manual dexterity and a tiny screwdriver can peer into the bowels of a hearing aid. I know you think you are saving the dispenser's time or the cost of an appointment, but, in all kindness, you will probably make matters worse. The only controls you, the hearing aid wearer, should manipulate are the on-off switch and the volume. Period.

Helpful Hints for Hearing Aid Users

1. Always try to face the individual you want to hear.

2. Move away from sources of background noise to have your conversation.

3. In a restaurant, sit in a corner with your back to the wall. When this is not possible, sit along the perimeter, away from the door, kitchen, and bus stands.

4. In a theatre or at a play, when not using an assistive listening device, sit near the front of the auditorium or in the front of the balcony. Avoid a seat in the middle of the auditorium or along the back wall.

5. If background noise is a real problem in a certain situation, try turning your hearing aid *down* slightly.

6. When talking on the telephone, turn *off* the hearing aid on the ear you are not using. If you wear behind-the-ear hearing aids, hold the end of the receiver through which you *listen* next to, but not directly on top of, the microphone of your hearing aid, *not* at your ear where you used to hold it before you started wearing hearing aids.

7. Allow people with normal hearing to set the volume on the radio, television, and so on. You can then adjust the volume on your hearing aid and/or change positions.

8. Make certain your hearing aids are turned off when you are not wearing them. Opening the battery case a little when you take them off insures that they are off and also prevents accidental battery leakage into the aid.

9. Always check that you are using a good battery each time you put your hearing aids on, even if it was only an hour ago that you took them off. Batteries can be unpredictable and go from good to bad very quickly.

An easy and quick way to do this is to turn on the hearing aid and push the volume control up all the way. When you cup your hand over the ear canal portion of the aid or earmold, the hearing aid should whistle. If it doesn't, install a new battery. A battery tester is also a good investment (especially if you're concerned that you won't hear the whistle!).

Be sure to turn the volume back down and turn the aid off before putting it on. Otherwise, it will scream in your ear as you insert it into the ear canal!

10. Hearing aids do not like hair spray, mousse, or gels. Put your hearing aids on *after* fixing your hair!

Remember, many listening situations that you find difficult are also difficult for those with normal hearing. Just do your best, and let those around you know what they can do to help.

WORKING WITH YOUR HEARING AID DISPENSER

It is your dispenser's responsibility to educate you about all of your options with regard to hearing aids. Size may be one; so is color. For dark-skinned individuals, hearing aids can be ordered in a dark brown rather than the more common "flesh" color or light tan.

Once the hearing aids are fitted, appropriate to the degree of loss and distortion, your dispenser should then "test" you in a controlled setting (the clinic), simulating different listening situations. That is, you should be tested with regard to your speech discrimination in both quiet *and* in the presence of background noise, and your tolerance to loud sound should be checked. Only then can the two of you

determine that the fitting is appropriate, that no further internal adjustments need to be made, and that you're off to as good a start as possible.

As a hearing aid user, you also have some responsibilities to the dispenser. If you are dissatisfied *for any reason*, make another appointment. Simply becoming disgruntled and throwing the aids in your dresser drawer does a disservice to you, your dispenser, and the industry. This is one of the reasons why hearing aids have the bad reputation of being ineffective by so many people, including those who have never worn one! Even if you think the problem is just you, or some trivial little thing not worth bothering anyone about, *make another appointment*! Most problems can be solved either through slight adjustments the dispenser can make to the internal controls or, when necessary, a new fitting. Sometimes it takes a while to get the earmold to fit just right. But these and most other problems are generally solved easily, *if the dispenser knows about them.*

Recruitment

Many, in fact most, hearing-impaired people suffer from an acoustic condition known as "recruitment." Because of the damage to the inner ear and hair cells, the range of comfortable hearing is reduced and the ear's ability to react and judge the loudness of sounds is impaired. For an individual with recruitment, one sound may be perfectly comfortable, while another, only slightly louder, may sound like a jet taking off *directly* overhead. This is a real phenomenon and not to be laughed at or taken lightly.

Recruitment is one of the biggest problems a dispenser must face when fitting hearing aids. For this reason, many aids also come equipped with certain circuitry that allows the hearing aid to compensate for the abnormal loudness balance. For the wearer of an aid equipped with this circuitry (often called AGC—Acoustic Gain Control), a loud sound will be softened within milliseconds after reaching the receiver and before exiting the microphone. There are some very specific tests for recruitment, but if you think you may have this problem, discuss it with your dispenser before deciding on an aid.

OTHER ASSISTIVE LISTENING DEVICES

Although hearing aids are the first to come to mind when it comes to devices to help the hearing-impaired, there are many, many more "gizmos" that fall into the general category of "assistive listening devices." Some, if not most, are dependent on a certain circuitry within your hearing aid, which brings us to another choice you have to make when purchasing your aids.

A Great Little Circuit: The "T-Switch"

Initially designed to be used with the telephone, this circuitry is commonly referred to as a "T-switch." Since its development, however, its application in the area of assistive listening devices has been greatly expanded. In simple terms, a T-switch changes the input mode on the circuitry of a hearing aid so it is compatible with electronic devices external to the hearing aid electronics.

The T-switch is an optional feature to hearing aids and will add a bit of cost to the aid. (This cost generally runs between $50 and $100, but it depends on the dispenser and type of hearing aid.) In my mind, it is money well spent because having this capability opens many doors to the hearing aid wearer to augment their listening environment even further. I'll explain shortly.

Too often, though, the dispenser will neglect to mention this option, and, once the aid is ordered, it is too late (unless you want to pay for another brand-new aid). Any hearing aid can be equipped with a T-switch, providing there is enough room internally for the wiring and externally for the switch (another limitation of some ITEs).

In public places, such as airports, bus stations, and some theatres, you'll sometimes see pay telephones that are a little different than usual. Instead of a black piece of rubber where the metal phone cord connects to the receiver, this piece of rubber will be bright blue. This means that this telephone has been equipped with the circuitry compatible with the T-switch in a hearing aid. When you use these telephones, with your hearing aid switched from the "O" for "On" or "M" for "Mic" to the "T," which stands for "telecoil," your ability to hear more clearly on that particular telephone will be greatly enhanced. The next time you're in a public area like those mentioned, look for these phones. I'll bet you'll say, "Hmmmm. I never noticed

that before." Unfortunately, there are a great many devices available to the hearing-impaired that they do not even realize the uses for, and they are not educated sufficiently by those of us in a position to do so.

In large theatres, such as the Shubert in Chicago, the Paramount theatre in Seattle, or the Queen Elizabeth theatre in Vancouver, hearing-impaired audience members can rent, usually for only a few dollars, a piece of equipment that looks a lot like small headphones. When used in conjunction with the T-switch on their hearing aids, they will hear the performance quite well, often better than their normally hearing neighbors, no matter where they sit in the auditorium!

Some churches have had members of the congregation get together and "segregate" a portion of the seating area by way of a simple wiring system on the floor that surrounds the seats. When hearing-impaired members of the congregation sit inside this "loop" with their T-switches on, they won't miss a syllable of the sermon. The only catch is that the pastor or priest must use a microphone with this type of "loop" system.

There is another accessory that you can easily attach to the television, and someone with a T-switch on their hearing aids can independently control the volume of the television by the volume control on their hearing aids. This device alone could be responsible for saving hundreds of marriages—no more being literally driven out of the room by volume just so your loved one can hear the action.

T-switches have many, many applications. Without one, a hearing aid user greatly restricts his or her options. With one, for the little bit of extra money, there are lots and lots of new toys that will further enhance their listening environment and, consequently, their lives. In the appendices you will find a list of various suppliers of Assistive Listening Devices. Write for their catalogs. You'll be surprised what's available, *if* you have a T-switch.

"Man's Best Friend"

Although not typically thought of as a "device," I consider this aid worthy of mention. Man's best friend has attained a position of importance with the hearing-impaired, too. There are seeing eye dogs. There are also hearing ear dogs.

Specially trained to respond to specific needs and situations of

the hearing-impaired, these dogs can make life immeasurably more rewarding and less fearful for many severely and profoundly hearing-impaired people, both young and old.

Imagine the young, severely hearing-impaired or deaf mother. She may be alone for long periods of time with her baby. How does she know when the baby cries? Rover comes to get her! Trained to alert this young mother that something requires her attention, the dog will come and "take" her to the baby. No more worries! (Well, not as many. *All* moms worry.)

Imagine a young couple walking arm in arm down the street, completely absorbed in each other and unaware of a vehicle honking at them. Good 'ole Rover to the rescue! By special training, the dog alerts this couple to danger *before* it is too late. The same situation is equally possible for a young child.

These dogs are companions as well as servants and share the same privileges in public as seeing eye dogs. They act as alarm clocks, butlers, retrievers, guards, and friends. Most often, due to need as well as supply, they are matched to individuals having severe to profound hearing losses and the deaf. Often, they can be obtained without charge, but not always.

If you are interested in learning more about these dogs or perhaps obtaining one for yourself or your child, write to any of the following. They will be happy to explain their program and application process.

Dogs for the Deaf
10175 Wheeler Rd.
Central Point, OR 97502
503-826-9220 (Voice or TDD)

International Hearing Dog, Inc.
5901 East 89th
Henderson, CO 80640
303-287-3277 (Voice or TDD)

Hearing Ear Dogs of Canada
1154 Highway W
Ancaster, ONT L9G 3K9
416-648-1522
416-648-2262 (TDD)

Caring for Your Hearing Aids and Earmolds

1. Turn the hearing aid off or open the battery compartment slightly every time you take it off.

2. Check to make sure the battery is still good each time you put the aids on by turning the volume up to high and cupping your hand over the canal—it should whistle.

3. Clean the canal portion of the hearing aid or earmold—nightly if you have heavy ear wax, every two to three days if you don't. If you did not receive a special tool from your dispenser for doing this, use one end of a paper clip or any other small, *blunt* instrument, and be gentle. The canal portion of the hearing aid or earmold is fragile.

4. Every two to three days, take a damp, not wet, cloth and gently wipe off your hearing aids and earmolds. *Never* submerse your hearing aids in water, and remember to take them off before showering or bathing! Never use anything but water to clean your hearing aids.

5. Every two or three days, remove your earmolds from the hearing aids and wash the earmolds in warm water using a *mild* detergent. It is all right to get your earmolds wet because they do not contain any electronic parts.

   The best time to wash your earmolds is in the evening just before going to bed. Once washed, gently blow the water out of the tubing, using either an instrument you obtained from your dispenser for this purpose or your mouth. Then set the earmolds in a warm, dry place to dry overnight. In the morning, check to make sure there is no lingering condensation in the tubing, as this will affect sound transmission. If necessary, blow through the tubing again until dry.

6. Individuals who perspire heavily sometimes have trouble with moisture building up in the hearing aids. Check with your dispenser for products such as "dry tube" and "dry pack" available for this problem.

7. Try to keep all your hearing aid items together in one place, such as a small box or drawer. (A fancy little box for this purpose makes a great present!)

8. Batteries should be stored in a cool place. The refrigerator is best. *Never* put your batteries in the freezer!

9. Earmold tubing (the part that attaches to the hearing aid) should be soft and flexible. When the tubing gets stiff (actually, *before* it gets *stiff*), take the earmold to your dispenser to have the tubing replaced. This should normally be done every four to six months.

TROUBLESHOOTING PROBLEMS

Many problems users experience with hearing aids are related to the battery. Even if you have recently put in a new battery, this is the first item to check, always.

Problem:	Sounds are weak.
Possible Causes:	The battery is weak. Replace with a new battery.
	The hearing aid switch is not on "M." Make sure the on-off switch is on "M."
	The earmold canal is clogged with wax. Clean per instructions.

If, after checking all these areas, you still have the same problem, take your hearing aid(s) and earmold(s) back to your dispenser. (Always make an appointment unless you have been told it's okay to just drop in.)

Problem:	Sounds are intermittent or on-again, off-again.
Possible Causes:	The battery is weak. Replace with a new battery.
	Earmold tubing is kinked or collapses with head movement. Make an appointment with your dispenser.

In all cases of intermittence, unless the problem is the battery, you should make an appointment with your dispenser.

Problem:	There is no sound.

Possible Causes: The battery is dead. Replace with a new battery.

The wrong type of battery is being used. Check your initial instructions regarding battery type against the battery you are using.

The battery is in backwards or upside down. Remove and replace properly—the " + " should always be facing *up*. (Often, the battery compartment drawer will not close easily if the battery is upside down. Don't try to force the drawer closed if it doesn't slide shut easily. There's usually a reason for it.)

The hearing aid switch is on "T" or "O." Make sure the on-off switch is on "M."

The earmold is impacted with wax. Clean per instructions. Sometimes, the wax has hardened and cannot be removed without soaking the earmold in warm water for a bit. If yours is an in-the-ear hearing aid with wax impacted in the canal, it is best to make an appointment with your dispenser.

There is moisture in the earmold tubing and/or canal. Blow out and allow to dry, overnight if possible. If you have "dry pack," put your earmold in that overnight. Do not attempt to "quick dry" the earmold by placing it on or in a source of heat, such as the oven.

If you have checked the above areas and still get no sound from your hearing aid, the problem most likely can't be taken care of at home. Make an appointment with your dispenser, and take *all* your equipment in with you.

Problem: The hearing aid "hisses."

Possible Causes: The on-off switch is on "T" if you have a telecoil. Set switch to "M."

If this does not solve the problem, see your dispenser.

Problem:	The hearing aid whistles or has "feedback."
Possible Causes:	The wrong type of battery is being used. Check your initial instructions regarding battery type and make sure you are currently using the correct battery.
	The earmold is not properly "seated" in your ear or ear canal. Putting the earmold in takes practice. Check in a mirror or have someone who knows how it should look check for you. (Ideally, husbands and wives should accompany each other to the first counselling session when the aids are picked up, just for instances like this.) Reinsert the earmold if necessary.
	The volume is too high on the hearing aid. Turn the volume down slightly.
	There are holes or a crack in the earmold tubing. Make an appointment with your dispenser for replacement.
Problem:	You can no longer get the volume you need from the hearing aid without having problems with feedback.
Possible Causes:	The battery is weak. Replace with a new battery.
	The earmold or ear canal is clogged with wax. Clean per instructions.
	The earmold does not properly fit your ear due to changes in your ear or length of ear canal. Make an appointment with your dispenser.
	Your hearing has changed. Make an appointment with your dispenser.

Once you have hearing aids (or if you know you have a hearing loss but don't have hearing aids . . . yet), an annual hearing check is a good idea.

Problem: Sounds are distorted.

Possible Causes: The battery is almost dead. Replace with a new one.

The volume on the hearing aid is too high. Turn the volume down slightly.

There is moisture in the earmold and/or hearing aid. Blow out the earmold (*not* the hearing aid) and put both in their regular place to dry, preferably overnight. If you have a "dry pack," put both hearing aid and earmold in there overnight.

If you have checked all these areas and continue to experience the same or perhaps a different problem, make an appointment with your dispenser. Do not try to change the shape of your earmold yourself or attempt to open the casing of any hearing aid. Do not change any of the internal controls.

CHAPTER 9

Before You Lose It

Preventing Hearing Loss

*W*e are a society bombarded by noise, sometimes judiciously controlled, at times abusive. As a health practitioner, I don't like seeing the end result when it could have, should have, been prevented. None of us can avoid the effects of aging, but we can do something to protect our hearing from deteriorating due to external sources, namely noise.

Noise is the most common causal factor of hearing loss between the ages of 20 and 40. Some 20 million Americans are exposed to damaging noise levels on a daily basis. Almost ten million Americans have noise-related hearing problems. Audiologists are seeing more and more noise-induced hearing loss between the ages of 10 and 20. That's right. Ten years old. Pretty sad, because this young person will go through life with a hearing loss that should never have happened. I know of audiologists who have seen clients as young as 8 with a noise-induced hearing loss.

Because of the physical layout of the inner ear and the place on the basilar membrane (remember the rubber band in Chapter 3?) where sound first makes contact, a noise-induced hearing loss shows up clearly on the audiogram by the configuration, or shape, and location in frequency of the hearing loss.

Remember those tiny hairs in Chapter 3, and that in responding to an incoming sound they vibrate? In simplified terms, the intensity with which they vibrate is wholly dependent on the intensity of the incoming sound. If the intensity is too great, or goes on for too long,

Figure 9.1 A healthy cochlea

(such as 45 minutes with a chain saw), the hairs get tired and start drooping. In the case of a blast, they simply explode, ripped completely off the membrane. Over the course of several exposures, more and more hairs are worn down and disintegrate—and *they don't grow back*. (There is some current research in animals that suggests hair cells may be able to regenerate. This has not been documented in human ears yet.)

Noise also damages the base cell structure of the hearing mechanism. It can block the vascular (blood and other necessary fluid) supplies by causing tissues in the capillaries to swell. This swelling causes tiny tears in the delicate membranes of the organ of hearing. The hearing lost from the destruction of these hair cells is often permanent, no matter how old you are. The amount of damage

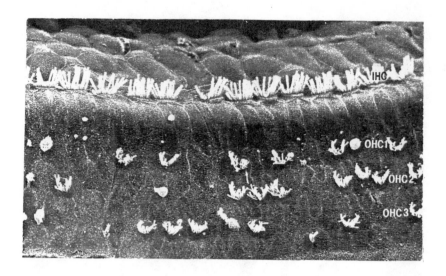

Figure 9.2 Hair cells withered and missing

and whether it is permanent or temporary depends on the loudness (intensity) and duration of exposure.

Let's look again at the photos you saw in Chapter 3. Figure 9.1 shows a healthy ear, with the rows of hair cells arranged in neat little bundles. Figure 9.2 shows how the same hair cells, or what's left of them, might look after varying levels of noise exposure. Figure 9.3 shows how the cochlea would look following exposure to extremely loud noise or after years of exposure to noise—the hair cells are gone completely.

Try to tell a teenager (or a 10-year-old!) that they are killing their little hair cells by listening to too loud music and you immediately become identified as completely out of touch. But ask how many of them have left a dance at school with their ears ringing, and nearly all of them will acknowledge the experience.

Now, I know that these kids are smart, but because they can't *see* the damage and don't *feel* any different, they don't listen to what their bodies are trying to tell them. They're just like we were at that age. Indomitable, omnipotent, and blessed with immortality and the

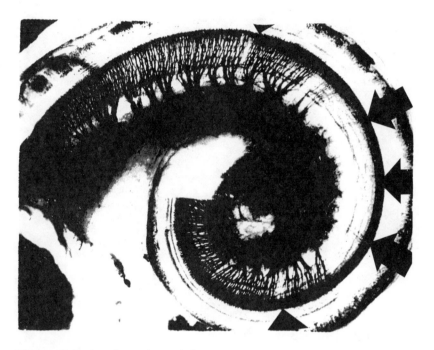

Figure 9.3 Another view of the basilar membrane, showing "bald" spots (arrows) at several places along the coil. Other areas show noticeably fewer strands in each group.

Reprinted with permission, courtesy of Goran Bredberg, M.D. Associate Professor, Director, Dept. of Audiology, Sodersjukhuset, Stockholm, Sweden.

knowledge of the ages. Unfortunately, they don't realize what is happening until it is too late.

But it's not just music. Many toys and recreational games kids engage in have potentially damaging noise levels. So do many tools and guns. The next time dad goes out to target shoot and junior tags along, consider this. The impulse noise from a high-powered rifle measures approximately 170 dB sound pressure level. There are NO hearing protection devices available today that will adequately protect your ears from this level of noise. Some degree of permanent damage is almost certainly guaranteed. (We can lose up to 30 percent of our hair cells before a hearing loss is perceived.) A cap pistol can measure as high as 125 dB sound pressure level.

Ears ring in response to many things. Too much noise is one. Your ears are trying to tell you they have been bruised, which is

helpful of them since we can't peer into our inner ears and see a black and blue mark. A persistent ringing in the ears should get our attention.

The longer or more intense the exposure, the longer the ears ring until it never goes away. (I use the term "ring" in a generic sense. The "noise" has been variously described as a ring, a buzz, a hum, a click—all manner of sounds.) It is the nemesis of many hearing-impaired people. It may come and go, but it comes much more often. Tinnitus, or "noises in the head," is caused by more than just noise. If you are bothered by persistent tinnitus, or if the noises you experience suddenly sound different, see your physician. A feeling of "fullness" in the ears after excessive noise exposure is also a warning sign that at least temporary damage has occurred.

Teenagers are not the only ones who often choose not to protect their hearing. Do you wear hearing protection when mowing the lawn, when running a chain saw, at work? *Any* time you're exposed to loud noise? Too often, especially around the home, we think, "Oh, it's only for a minute or two. That can't do any harm." Well, yes and no. It depends on how loud the noise is, how long is a "few" minutes, and, most importantly, how often the activity is repeated. If you engage in an activity that for five minutes is not harmful, but you repeat this five-minute procedure regularly, the noise becomes potentially damaging.

Many studies have been done on the effect of noise on the ears, resulting in a table used by industry and the watchdog of industry— OSHA (the Occupational Safety and Health Act. In Canada, it's WCB—Worker's Compensation Board). These tables specify what noise levels are safe for unprotected ears and for how long. Exposure to noise in the workplace has strict regulations regarding the provision of hearing protection, according to the Hearing Conservation Act of 1983. As aptly put by one director of hearing conservation, "It should be conservation, not compensation. A man should not have to sell his ears because he makes paper, cloth, or automobiles. Hearing conservation is feasible and practical, and really not expensive."[1]

As you look over the table on the following page, notice that for each rise of 5 dB, the safe exposure time is cut *in half*. These exposure

---

[1]Dr. R. B. Maas, Director of Hearing Conservation in Wisconsin (date of statement unknown).

times reflect safety limits *without* hearing protection and are not carved in stone for everyone. The safest ceiling to use when considering hearing protection is anything over 80 dB for more than a few hours. Noise can affect you in other ways besides destroying hair cells, which I'll discuss later.

Noise Level (dBA)	*Exposure Time*
85	16 hours
90 *(table saw)*	8 hours
95	4 hours
100	2 hours
105 *(lawn mower)*	1 hour
110 *(chain saw)*	½ hour
115 *(18-wheel truck)*	¼ hour
120 + *(rock bands)*	0 hours
140 *(jet engine)*	0 hours

Now let's look at the loudness levels of some common environmental sounds—the kind we all experience every day.

Noise Level (dBA)	*Source*
40	average living room noise
50	average conversational speech
60–70	average business office
70–80	vacuum cleaner, dishwasher, washing machine and dryer
80–90	average street traffic, blow dryer, food blender, alarm clock, garbage disposal
90–100	video arcade, talking doll, orchestra
100–110	personal stereo at ½ volume, power tools, chain saw, snowmobile, leaf blower
110–120	personal stereo at full volume, rock concert, subway train screech, power boat, some baby squeeze toys, cap gun
130 +	rifle shot, firecracker, jet engine

Any time exposure exceeds these limits you run the risk of doing permanent damage to those little hairs. The maximum allowable level in industry, before hearing protection is *required*, is 90 dBA in the United States. The *strongly recommended* level is 85 dBA. (The "A" represents a certain scale of measurement. In this case, when sound is measured on the "A" scale, the low frequencies are "rolled off" below 1000 Hz at a rate of 3 dB per octave. Low frequency noise is less common in industry than the high-pitched whine associated with many types of machinery, so the lower pitches are weighted less heavily.)

Now let's apply some of this. From the tables, we can say that your living room is pretty safe. Operating a table saw for 1/2 hour isn't going to hurt you unless you are a carpenter, who probably repeats that 1/2 hour frequently. If it takes you longer than one hour to mow your lawn, you should be wearing hearing protection. (Actually, that also depends on the type of lawn mower you have. Without accurate measurements, I would venture to say that some of the bigger riding mowers pump out enough sound to make the limit 1/2 hour. It is better to be safe than sorry; unless you have a postage-stamp-size lawn, wear hearing protection.) With average street traffic being between 80 and 90 dB, it's no wonder people in the city get a little surly.

How many truck drivers do you think spend just 15 minutes driving every day? Most of them tell me that they can't wear hearing protection because (1) the DOT says so (Department of Transportation), and (2) it interferes with their ability to listen to their truck and hear what is going on on the highway—horns honking and the like. Actually, neither of these is true.

The DOT does not forbid wearing hearing protection while driving. Although noises sound "different" with earplugs in, once you get accustomed to the new way your environment sounds, it is generally easier to hear over background noise with hearing protectors than without (unless you have a moderate or greater degree of hearing loss). Custom-made earplugs are available that, by way of a vent and filters, manipulate the higher frequencies a bit and somewhat enhance the frequencies that are important to the understanding of speech and the variances in the whine of an engine.

What the DOT does specify is required hearing levels of "perceives a forced whispered voice in the better ear at not less than five

feet with or without the use of a hearing aid" and "does not have an average hearing loss in the better ear greater than 40 decibels at 500 Hz, 1,000 Hz and 2,000 Hz with or without a hearing aid."[2]

The DOT does require the wearing of hearing aids when "a driver whose hearing meets the minimum requirements of 391.41(b)(11) of this subchapter only when he wears a hearing aid."[3] The Code goes on to require that the driver in this case "shall wear a hearing aid and have it in operation at all times while he is driving. The driver must also have in his possession a spare power source for use in the hearing aid."[4]

By *not* stating anything specifically about hearing protection, the inference is that drivers should have the specified hearing—a forced whisper at not less than five feet—*with* hearing protection should they choose to wear it. The unfortunate reference here is "forced whisper." This is subjective to the point of ruling out validity. For a measurement to be "valid" it must be consistently repeatable over time. My forced whisper would not be the same in loudness or pitch as yours, your neighbor's, or your doctor's. The reference needs to be definitive and objective to be credible, such as "able to hear speech noise at a level of 30 dB from a distance of five feet."

The other reference that, as stated, can actually work in favor of supporting hearing protection is that of "the better ear." Most truckers have a hearing loss either in only one ear or one that is decidedly worse in one ear—usually the left. That's the ear that receives the brunt of noise from the street, traffic, air brakes, and wind through the open window.

With a custom plug, for example, in the left ear only, the right ear then becomes the "better ear," and the trucker need only satisfy the specified hearing levels for that ear. Again, nothing in the Code prohibits the wearing of hearing protection. For truckers, this is a very real issue because most of them in the business for a few years will acquire a hearing loss *without* hearing protection.

Personal stereo systems are another area of concern, involving great numbers of the population. Most of our kids and many adults

[2]Code of Federal Regulations—Title 49 (Transportation): Federal Motor Carriers Safety Regulations, para. 391.41(b)(11).
[3]Ibid., para. 392.9b.
[4]Ibid.

own one. From the table, we know that at a volume setting of 5 (given the range is 0–10), after a half-hour we risk permanent damage to our ears. At 115 dB, full volume, we're exterminating some of those hair cells. The person in his car with the brand-new 150-watt stereo with the latest electronic technology, blasted at full volume with all the windows rolled up is at an extreme risk of noise-induced hearing loss.

Interestingly, at least one manufacturer is responding to the research on noise. Sony has come out with a personal stereo called "My First Sony." Sort of like child-proof bottle caps, it has a limiter on it that can be set by the parents with a screwdriver. According to Sony, with the override system on, output cannot exceed 85 dB.

And then there's the issue of rock music or, in general terms, dance bands. As far as anybody's *ears* are concerned, if ears could talk, they're *all* too loud. With repeated exposures, the teens, preteens, and their chaperones all risk serious and permanent damage to their ears.

Unfortunately, the music industry would like us to believe that their music *sounds* better when it is louder. There are also some who believe teenagers opt for louder music because it is more "exciting" and fits in with the animated environment.

It's all very aesthetic. When analyzed on an oscilloscope, a "C" is a "C," whether it's played at 70 dB or 120 dB. The major difference is that the notes tend to distort before 120 dB.

My message to teenagers: When your ears are ringing, it's their way of telling you that they need a break and they've suffered a lot already. If it's not cool to say, "Turn it down!", is it cool to say, "Huh? Pardon me?" all the time?

By permission of Johnny Hart and NAS, Inc.

There is some good news, though, for both kids and parents. A company called HEAR has developed hearing protection they feel is attractive to kids. Custom made and "decorative," they are called "Earshades." To locate a distributor in your area, you can call HEAR at **800-635-EARS**, or write to them at **PO Box 460847, San Francisco, CA 94146**. Who knows? You may start the next trend in your area of day-glo ears. Hot pink . . . Lime green . . .

There is also some research that suggests that the amount of damage done is subjectively related to your enjoyment of the "noise." The level of noise necessary to cause a temporary shift in your hearing can vary by as much as 30 to 50 dB, researchers say, from one person to the next. The implication is that your kids are more apt to suffer damage from Bach, and you parents are more likely to experience hair-cell death from New Kids on the Block. Interesting hypothesis— I would guess at least partially stress-related, which can have all sorts of nasty effects on our bodies. The research is still going on, though, so the fact that Guns N' Roses played at 120 dB doesn't bother you is *not* a good excuse to avoid hearing protection!

HEARING PROTECTION DEVICES

I've talked a lot about hearing protection. So what's good and what's not? How much is enough? Again, it depends on how much noise you are "in." All types of hearing protection come with a Noise Reduction Rating, or NRR, number. This number generally ranges anywhere from 10 to 34 dB. An NRR of 18 suggests that the noise level reaching your inner ear will be reduced by 18 dB when wearing this particular hearing protection device. I use the word "suggests" because these numbers do not reflect accurate protection when used in the field. To best judge the degree of protection you are receiving with any given hearing protection device (HPD), take the NRR number and cut it in half.

To apply this to your own particular situation, let's say your working noise environment has been measured at 105 dB. With the above HPDs, giving you 9 dB of *reliable* protection, your exposure is reduced to 96 dB (105 minus 9). From the table, you know this is safe for about 1¾ hours. If you are in this noise environment for more than this time period, you need HPDs with a higher NRR—at least 30—for 8 hours.

Every style of HPD is different insofar as noise reduction capabilities, depending on material and the presence or absence of filters. The rating has virtually nothing to do with size. When in doubt, go all the way. Rated A, B, and C, Class A earmuffs are the best hearing protection available (NRR of 30 or higher).

Then there are custom-made earplugs. Much the same as an earmold for a hearing aid, they can be specially modified or "tuned" with filters, vents, and the like to protect your hearing while not reducing everything to imperceptible. These are becoming so popular, in part because they are very comfortable, that many musicians are now wearing them. The more modifications, the more the cost as well as changing the NRR. Some can run upwards of $250 a pair. But aren't your ears worth it? These custom-made plugs are generically known as "noise blockers" and can be obtained from any person or business that sells hearing aids.

There are sponge or foam rubber earplugs, rubber earplugs, silicone earplugs, and a host of other materials, falling into the general categories of disposable and nondisposable. Any of the foam rubber or spongy plugs fall into the disposable category, and you should do just that with them as soon as they get slightly dirty—and I do mean slightly. Before you use a pair, look at them and ask yourself whether you would put them *into your mouth*. If the answer is "yuck," throw them away and get a fresh pair.

All hearing protection is good if it is used or inserted properly and is appropriate for the amount of noise you are working in. The disposable yellow and the white foam plugs are actually as good as some muffs but only when they're used properly.

Earmuffs come in different types and styles. The muff must fit snugly all the way *around* your ear, with no gaps, to be maximally effective. Don't try to "squeeze" your ear under the muff. This will rapidly become *very* uncomfortable, but it will also prevent the proper seal getting all the way around your ears to block the noise. If you wear glasses that may get in the way, get the best seal you can and consider wearing plugs under the muffs. You can't overprotect your ears.

Always try earmuffs on before buying a pair. Each style sits a little differently and everyone's ears and heads are different. At work, your employer should provide more than one style for just this reason. One type of earmuff does not fit everyone.

Your earmuffs should be kept scrupulously clean, in the same

manner as hearing aids, earmolds, and nondisposable earplugs. Periodically wipe them off with a damp cloth and mild detergent. Avoid subjecting the rubber to extremes of heat or cold and they will last that much longer. When the rubber rings around the earholes do become cracked or hard, replace them. You needn't throw the entire muff out because the outside rubber ring is cracked. And never, never use any alcohol-based product to clean your earmuffs (or hearing aids) or earmolds.

Earplugs come in many shapes and sizes, but for any of them to be effective, there are certain steps to follow when inserting them into your ear canal. Foam plugs are the most notorious for not being inserted properly.

Between your fingers, *roll* the plug down to compress the air. Do not fold, twist, or bend the plug to compress it. Your ear canal is cylindrical in shape, and that's what you want the earplug to be after compressing it. While it is compressed all the way, reach around *behind* your head with your opposite hand (always insert the plug with the hand on the same side—left ear, left hand) and pull your ear back and slightly away from your head.

Then quickly insert the plug until you encounter resistance. Let go of your ear, but *hold the plug in place with your finger for at least five seconds* (eight is better). Otherwise, as the foam rubber is expanding in your ear canal, it will also be expanding *out* of your ear canal. I can't tell you how many factories I've been through and seen almost everyone there with little yellow or white antennae sticking out of their ears. When inserted properly, these foam plugs should only be just barely visible.

If using the plastic or other molded plugs, just remember to reach around behind your head and pull your ear out before insertion. There's no compression or expansion to deal with. (The process of reaching around behind and pulling your ear back and away from your head serves to straighten the ear canal. Having a curve to it, this procedure allows the plug to form a good seal against the canal wall as it expands.)

Earplugs may get uncomfortable when worn for many hours, especially when not inserted properly. If this is a problem you have experienced, first examine whether you are going through the proper insertion steps. If so, then you probably want to consider muffs or custom-made plugs. These are preferred by many because of their custom fit and convenience. They are appropriate for just about any

noise you may generate at home (unless you're in the habit of operating a jackhammer in your back yard) and for the noise levels in most factories. Prices range from around $40 a pair up to $250 or higher for some of the highly modified sets.

Those of you who live in noisy environments, such as New York City, and consider wearing earplugs to bed, that's okay, providing you haven't also worn them for eight hours or longer at work that day. Your ear canals do need ventilation. Wearing a solid plug in your ear for hours on end, day after day, may lead to fungal infections or other skin irritations in the lining of the ear canal.

Protecting your hearing is as easy to remember as brushing your teeth. Don't wait until you can no longer hear the water running to know that it's too late.

NOISE AND STRESS

I mentioned that noise can affect you in other ways besides slaughtering hair cells. The fact that we escape to the shore, campgrounds, and hiking trails by the thousands throughout the year says something about the daily environment most of us reside in. We are seeking peace and . . . *quiet*.

Noise is a stressor. It contributes to cardiovascular changes in our bodies (namely increased heart rate and decreased blood flow— a deadly combination) and fatigue. Irritability and tension are compounded by noise. Noise levels that may not be physically damaging to our ears can still cause havoc with the rest of our bodies.

This phenomenon occurred in one company when a group of employees began complaining of headaches and feeling generally surly. An acoustical expert, who happened to be a professor of mine, was called in to do a "noise study." One of the first things he noted was that the work area was located directly off the boiler room. Noise level measurements were taken, and it was discovered that (1) the noise was not loud enough to be hazardous insofar as hearing was concerned, and (2) much of the noise was concentrated in the low-frequency range.

Dr. Frank's ultimate analysis and recommendation? These people were being physically "rattled" by large and continuous sound waves passing through and/or being absorbed by their bodies! Their work area was moved, and within days, all symptoms disappeared.

The constant, low growl of machines or whine of equipment or buzz of traffic may not be loud enough to kill hair cells, but it is doing a number on your body and head. Even if you don't work in an environment that dictates hearing protection, try it anyway and see how much more relaxed you are at the end of the day.

> *For mine own part, I could be well content*
> *To entertain the lag-end of my life*
> *With quiet hours.*
>
>   Shakespeare
>   *King Henry IV*

PERCEPTION OF HEARING LOSS

And now, as promised, here's the Perception of Hearing Loss quiz again. After completing it the second time, compare it to your answers before reading this book. If I have succeeded, at least some of your answers should be different, as will, hopefully, your attitude and approach toward the next hearing-impaired person you encounter.

1. On a scale from 1 to 10 (10 being *very*, 5 being *moderately*, and 1 being *not at all*), how disabling would you rate hearing loss? (Circle one number.)

   1 - 2 - 3 - 4 - 5 - 6 - 7 - 8 - 9 - 10

   As compared to blindness?

   1 -2 -3 -4 -5 -6 -7 -8 -9 -10

   As compared to an amputated limb?

   1 - 2 - 3 - 4 - 5 - 6 - 7 - 8 - 9 - 10

   As compared to Alzheimer's disease?

   1 - 2 - 3 - 4 - 5 - 6 - 7 - 8 - 9 - 10

2. What percentage of each age group do you think is affected by hearing loss?

   - Newborns _____%
   - Age 1 mo.–5 yrs. _____%
   - Age 6–11 _____%
   - Under 18 _____%
   - Age 19–44 _____%
   - Age 45–64 _____%
   - Age 65–74 _____%

- Age 75 +   _____%
- Total population   _____%

3. Would you rather be hearing-impaired or blind? (Circle one.)

4. While conversing with a hearing-impaired person, I find that I will . . . (Circle your answers.)

   - raise my voice   yes   no
   - talk through another person, if
     present   yes   no
   - overarticulate   yes   no
   - get frustrated/discontinue the
     conversation   yes   no
   - try to avoid communicating at all   yes   no

Warning Signs of Hearing Loss in Children

Before 6 Months:

1. The child does not startle in some way (body jerk or blinking eyes) or change immediate activity in response to sudden, loud sounds.

2. The child does not imitate sounds such as gurgling or cooing and shows no response to noise-making toys.

3. The child does not exhibit responses to or is not soothed by the sound of mother's voice.

By 6 Months:

1. The child does not "search" for sounds by shifting eyes or turning the head from side to side.

By 10 Months:

1. The child does not show some kind of response to his own name. You may note a *reduction* in the amount of vocalization behaviors.

By 12 Months:

1. The child shows no response to common household sounds such as running water, silver rattling on plates, or footsteps from behind.

2. The child engages in loud shrieking vocalizations or prolonged vocalizing of vowels.

3. The child does not respond to someone's voice by actively seeking the source—turning head and/or body in all directions.

By 15 Months:

1. The child is not imitating many sounds and trying to produce simple words.

2. One has to raise his/her voice *consistently* to get the child's attention.

At Any Age:

1. The child frequently says "Huh?" or "What?" when spoken to at any age after talking has begun.

2. The child seems to respond inconsistently to sound, sometimes hearing and sometimes not.

3. There has been a history of chronic ear infections.

4. Mother had rubella (German measles) during pregnancy, especially during the first trimester.

5. There is a history of blood incompatibility, pregnancy disorders, or frequent high fevers.

6. There is a family history of hearing loss, the onset of which was *before* the age of 20.

7. The child seems to intently watch the speaker's face.

8. The child exhibits behaviorisms that seem to favor one ear, such as always tilting the head to the left or right when listening.

9. There are chronic complaints of hurting ears.

10. The child seems to prefer either low-pitched or high-pitched sounds.

11. There is a change in the loudness level of speech—the child begins talking softer or louder than is customary.

12. The child regularly turns the radio or television up louder than other family members require.

Other factors that may contribute to or cause hearing loss include the following:

- Viral infection or other fetal distress early in pregnancy

- Bleeding during the first trimester of pregnancy

- Some drugs, especially belonging to the "mycin" group or those containing quinine

- Prematurity and/or birth weight 1500 grams or less

- Prolonged, sudden, or difficult delivery

- Injuries to the child's head, especially blows to the head or directly to the ear

- The child having mumps or *viral* spinal meningitis

- Congenital malformations of the ear, lip, or palate

- Multiple birth abnormalities

- An Apgar score of 1 to 4, and/or apnea and cyanosis at birth

- Bilirubin of 20 mg/100 ml or more at birth. (The baby appears "yellow.")

Taken in part from *A Handbook for Prevention and Early Intervention of Communicative Disorders*. Curtis E. Weiss, and Harold S. Lillywhite. C. V. Mosby Co., St. Louis, MO. 1976. Reprinted by special permission of Curtis E. Weiss, Ph.D.

Warning Signs of Hearing Loss in Adults

- Sounds are loud enough, but not "clear."
- "Soft" sounds, such as your watch ticking or its little beeper, some birds, and voices from another room are very difficult or simply cannot be heard anymore.
- People often seem to be "mumbling" or talking too fast.
- Understanding what is being said is very difficult when there is *any* background noise.
- Group conversations are becoming increasingly difficult to follow.
- You notice some people are easier to understand than others.
- You experience more than the very occasional ringing in your ears.
- Meetings, groups, movies, parties, and so on aren't fun anymore.
- "Small talk" is a *big* burden.
- Loud sounds seem more annoying than before.
- Your hearing is "good" when you're fresh and rested, but it seems to deteriorate quickly.
- You notice that you often "favor" one ear over the other.
- You find yourself asking for repetition frequently.
- Your family tells you that the television and radio are uncomfortably loud for them.

Starting a Parent Support Group

Granted, the great majority of parents want to educate themselves as best they can when it comes to dealing with a problem involving their children. Demands of our fast-paced global life style can sometimes inhibit the best-intentioned parent. In order for parents to *want* to become involved, a foundation of careful planning must precede actually forming a group.

Goals must be outlined. What is the purpose? Is it general support, a forum for sharing experiences? Is it educational, covering current topics in deaf and hearing-impaired education with possible guest speakers? Is it to act as a lobbying group, bringing issues such as access of hearing ear dogs to the attention of local, state, and perhaps federal legislatures?

Is it all of the above? Some of the decisions as to what direction to take may rest with how many are projected to be involved. Just remember the lion and the mouse. It is possible for a few to accomplish a lot. Will your energies be directed solely at the hearing-impaired, or is your purpose also to educate the hearing public regarding hearing loss? Are there other, similar, groups in the area with which to network or get ideas?

Will it be a formal or informal group? Will there be a president, vice-president, and so on? Will there be dues? What will the money be used for? How often will you meet? Will you need to keep minutes of each meeting? (Money and minutes require a treasurer and a secretary.)

Once you have at least a general idea of the structure and purpose of the group, you can begin to organize your first meeting. At this time, you will probably want to solidify the group's purpose by outlining some goals and defining responsibilities. If this is going to be a group with an executive staff (president, secretary, treasurer, committee heads), the responsibilities will vary among the staff and members and need to be outlined. For instance, some executive responsibilities might include the following:

1. Leading the group in discussions

2. Providing requested information or suggesting alternate resources

3. Arranging meeting times and locations

4. Arranging for guest speakers

5. Suggesting fund-raising events

6. Bringing important issues before the membership

7. Maintaining confidentiality regarding sensitive or personal information that may be shared during meetings

Parents and other family members of the group should also have some outlined responsibilities, such as the following:

1. Commitment—coming to meetings regularly

2. Maintaining confidentiality in the same manner expected from the executive staff

3. Contributing ideas and information

4. Participating in outside activities when/if required, such as fund raising, writing letters for lobbying, and so on

During the first one or two meetings, if the group is a large one (say, more than 15), you might want to break up into small groups for a short time to brainstorm the group's purpose (putting it down in writing), establish immediate short-term goals, and propose topics to cover, specific concerns, fees, and so on.

Once you've got this great group off and running, it's time to think about the regular meetings. Tedious as this part may be, each

meeting should have a game plan. Presumably, you're not just getting together to "chat," so someone should be responsible for setting each meeting's agenda. Ideas can come from the group or from unfinished business from the last meeting, but one person (or maybe two, but you know what they say about too many cooks . . .) should be responsible for putting it together in some kind of order. When planning this material, one must consider the length of the meetings. One and one-half to two hours is best. This gives enough time to get your teeth into the topics discussed, but it is not so long that people are likely to get restless, bored, tired or, worst of all, stop coming.

Keep in mind that one of your goals is getting people to come, and that should include the whole family. Scheduled meetings in the evening allows those who work and go to school during the day to come. By choosing a time that is convenient for most people, you also let them know that you *want* them there!

In the process of getting started—outlining your purpose, goals, areas of interest—you may find the ideas and concerns slightly overwhelming. If a support group like this has not existed before, you may find yourself surrounded by support-hungry parents throwing out ideas the same way a starving man approaches a banquet table. You may have to say "Whoa!" and set priorities. This doesn't mean that you can't or won't get to all the ideas—only that it can't be done in the first two or three weeks. It is important that everyone's concerns are addressed in a way that emphasizes their relevance, but the group as a whole should decide what is the Number 1, 2, or 3 issue. In this way, everyone sees their needs as important, as being met, and this will keep the members coming.

Finally, guard against stagnation. If the same people always do the same thing, it gets old—for them and for the other members. Encourage everyone to take a leadership role at one time or another. Let everyone know how important their presence and input are. Get new blood into the group whenever the opportunity presents itself, either by recruiting new members, inviting guest speakers, or maybe embarking on a "field trip." It also helps to plan some outings just for fun—a summer barbecue, a winter cross-country skiing day. The ideas are limited only by the members of the group. You all need and deserve some time out from the regular purpose. Take it and enjoy life.

Appreciate the comradery that can come from a support group, and good luck!

Tips on Achieving Effective Communication with the Hearing-Impaired

1. Make sure you are facing the person!

2. Use inflection, but avoid dropping your voice at the end of a sentence.

3. Speak at a moderate to *slightly* slower rate.

4. Avoid overarticulating.

5. More is better. Use as much information as you can when asking a question or making single statements. Be careful not to overdo it, though. Keep it simple, too.

6. *Do not* attempt a conversation or any communication from one room to another. It just doesn't work.

7. Monitor background noise. Turn it off or avoid communications while close to whatever is making the "noise."

8. Change to a new topic with a key word or phrase and at a slower pace.

9. Do not try to converse with anything in your mouth or while covering your mouth.

10. *Don't shout* or otherwise raise your voice.

11. If light must shine on someone's face, arrange yourselves so that the light is *behind the hearing-impaired individual(s).*

12. Remember physical and mental stress negatively affects communication abilities for all.

13. Rephrase instead of endlessly repeating.

14. Use body language to facilitate understanding.

15. Remember that some words are easier to understand than others. Don't accuse a hearing-impaired person of "hearing what they want to hear."

16. Stand or communicate from the better side if the individual has a "better" ear.

17. Don't be afraid to ask what you can do to improve communications.

18. Remember that hearing aids do not restore 20/20 hearing. Keep your expectations realistic.

Here are some special tips for communicating with a hearing-impaired or deaf patient.

1. Assess the scope of the communication difficulties, and make obvious and easily seen notes on the chart.

2. Identify the patient as hearing-impaired or deaf with a special sticker on the front of the chart.

3. If the patient wears hearing aids, make sure they are always within reach. Whenever possible, before beginning any communication, be sure the hearing aids are physically and mechanically turned on.

4. Do not try to communicate using an intercom system.

5. Don't assume the patient has understood you. Supplement important information by writing it down.

6. Know how to reach an interpreter if necessary, and don't be embarrassed to do so.

7. Always have paper and pen near the bedside. This may come in handy for both your and the patient's use.

8. Learn a few basic signs.

9. If the patient wears glasses, make sure they are always within reach. Many people don't "hear" as well when they can't see well.

10. Keep communications simple and direct but complete.

11. Remember that the stress of a hospital visit is magnified for a hearing-impaired or deaf patient. Do all you can to let him/her know you *want* to communicate with them.

12. Never do anything, especially unexpected, from behind.

13. Explain sudden changes to the routine or care.

14. Assess the patient's response to what you are saying. If there is *any* doubt that you are being understood, begin again.

15. Do not leave the patient in darkness. If necessary, use a night light.

16. Do not restrict the patient's hands unless this is absolutely necessary for a certain procedure. Do not leave the hands restricted, in this case, for any longer than is absolutely necessary, and try to avoid restraining both hands at the same time.

17. Try to make exceptions where visitors are concerned. Few rules are carved in stone.

18. Use all the communication tips for general communication situations with the deaf or hearing-impaired!

Sources for Obtaining Assistive Listening Devices

Suppliers have been listed by state. For those of you new to the ALD arena, I would suggest writing to a few to find out what is available. One supplier often will not have everything, so writing to a few will give you a good general idea of what's out there. If you have something specific in mind, ask! If one supplier doesn't have it, perhaps they know who does.

California
Beep-Alarm Wrist Radio Co.
13222-B Admiral Ave.
Marina del Rey, CA 90292

Eckstein Brothers, Inc.
4807 West 118th Place
Hawthorne, CA 90250-2797

Krown Research, Inc.
10371 West Jefferson Blvd.
Culver City, CA 90232

Menlo Scientific
39 Menlo Place
Berkeley, CA 94707

Connecticut
Earmark, Inc.
1125 Dixwell Ave.
Hamden, CT 06514

Phonic Ear/Phonak
Canterbury Advertising
PO Box 122
Plainfield, CT 06374

Georgia
SEHAS, Inc.
533 Peachtree St. NE
Atlanta, GA 30308

Illinois
Jay L. Warren, Inc.
PO Box 25413
Chicago, IL 60625

Maine
Oval Window Audio
78 Main St.
Yarmouth, ME 04096

Wilner-Green Associates
449 Forest Ave. Plaza
Portland, ME 04101

Maryland
Nationwide Flashing Signal Systems
8120 Fenton St.
Silver Spring, MD 20910

Massachusetts
National Hearing Aid Distributors, Inc.
145 Tremont St.
Boston, MA 02111

UNEX
PO Box 574
3 Lyberty
Westford, MA 01886

Michigan
HARC Mercantile Ltd.
PO Box 3055
Kalamazoo, MI 49003-3055

Minnesota
Telex Communications, Inc.
9600 Aldrich Ave. South
Minneapolis, MN 55420

Williams Sound Corp.
5929 Baker Rd.
Minnetonka, MN 55345-5997

Missouri
Audio Enhancement
932 Spoede Rd. North
St. Louis, MO 63146

New Jersey
AT & T National Special Needs Center
2001 Route 46 East
Parsippany, NJ 07054-1315

Phone TTY, Inc.
202 Lexington Ave.
Hackensack, NJ 07601

Siemens Hearing Instruments, Inc.
10 Corporate Place South
Piscataway, NJ 08854

Wheelock, Inc.
273 Branchport Ave.
Long Branch, NJ 07740

Hear You Are, Inc.
4C Musconetcong Ave.
Stanhope, NJ 97874

Precision Controls, Inc.
14 Doty Rd.
Haskell, NJ 07420

New York
Hal-Hen Co.
35-53 24th St.
Long Island City, NY 11106

Julian A. McDermott Corp.
1639 Stephen St.
New York, NY 11385

Telephone Extension Corp.
83 East Central Ave.
Pearl River, NY 10965

Pennsylvania
Camp Laboratories
PO Box 200
Fredonia, PA 16124

Texas
Audex
713 No. 4th St.
Longview, TX 75601

Radio Shack
300 One Tandy Center
Fort Worth, TX 76102

Washington
Heidico, Inc.
625 Peace Portal Dr.
PO Box 3170
Blaine, WA 98230

Wisconsin
Quest Electronics
510 So. Worthington St.
Oconomowoc, WI 53066

Ultratec, Inc.
6442 Normandy Lane
Madison, WI 53719

Canada
Western Institute for the Deaf and Hard of Hearing
2125 West 7th Ave.
Vancouver, BC V6K 1X9 Canada

General Information Sources

For sign language gifts, write to (include an SASE for free catalog):

> "Evergreen"
> PO Box 20003
> Alexandria, VA 22320

The Voice (magazine)

Good general information source and interesting articles on current/ relevant topics to the deaf and hearing-impaired.

> PO Box 2663
> Corpus Christie, TX 78403-2663

American Speech-Language and Hearing Association

This is the national governing body for certification of training programs in speech pathology and audiology, establishing and policing policies, code of ethics and practices of both professions and a host of other functions.

To find a certified audiologist in your area, you can call the ASHA helpline at **800-638-TALK** (in Alaska, Hawaii and Maryland: **301-897-8682**).

> 10801 Rockville Pike
> Rockville, MD 20852

HEAR NOW

A nonprofit organization whose purpose is to raise funds for financially needy hearing-impaired people, enabling them to access hearing aids and other equipment. To obtain an application or participate in funding, write or call:

> 4001 S. Magnolia Way
> Suite 100
> Denver, CO 80237
> 800-648-HEAR (voice and TDD)

The Alexander Graham Bell Association for the Deaf

Publishes much in the way of general and specific information for parents and educators. Has two major publications: the *Volta Review*, geared more toward professionals and published 7 times a year, and *Newsounds*, geared toward the lay person and published 10 times a year.

> 3417 Volta Place NW
> Washington, DC 20007

Better Hearing Institute

Has brochures and posters relating to hearing and hearing loss.

> 1430 K Street NW, Room 200
> Washington, DC 20005

Canadian Coordinating Council on Deafness (CCCD)

A general clearinghouse for information and current laws pertaining to hearing loss. They can also supply addresses of provincial agencies and associations.

> 294 Albert St., Suite 201
> Ottawa, ONT K1P 6E6

The National Information Center on Deafness, c/o Gallaudet College

Gallaudet College is the only liberal arts college in the United States for deaf students. They can provide information on various aspects of deafness as well as information about the college.

Kendall Green, NE
Washington, DC 20002

International Association of Parents of the Deaf

Has their own set of publications and is a good arena for networking.

814 Thayer Ave.
Silver Spring, MD 20910

National Association of the Deaf (NAD)

Acts as a clearinghouse for information about deafness and problems concerning the deaf. Supplies pamphlets, brochures, and films. Publishes *The Deaf American*.

814 Thayer Ave.
Silver Spring, MD 20910

Junior National Association of the Deaf (JNAD)

Similar to the NAD, this is a student organization. With chapters in many secondary schools and programs for the deaf throughout the United States, JNAD holds national and regional youth conferences each year for students to learn more about their options, potential, and for networking.

814 Thayer Ave.
Silver Spring, MD 20910

National Center for Law and the Deaf

Offers legal counselling for individuals with hearing loss, not restricted to the "deaf." Sponsors workshops on law around the United States.

> c/o Gallaudet College
> Kendall Green NE
> Washington, DC 20002
> 202-651-5454 (TDD)

National Council of the Churches of Christ in the U.S.A.

The Council provides assistance with specialized ministries, including Christian Education and the Hearing-impaired.

> Division of Education and Ministry, Rm. 708
> 475 Riverside Dr.
> New York, NY 10115

SHHH—Self-Help for Hard-of-Hearing People, Inc.

Publishes a bimonthly journal. Deals with issues that are current and meaningful to the hearing-impaired population. Offers excellent problem-solving suggestions and carries well-written, timely articles.

> 7800 Wisconsin Ave.
> Bethesda, MD 20814
> 301-657-2248

Silent News

Published monthly, this is a newspaper devoted to issues relating to the deaf community.

> PO Box 584
> Paramus, NJ 07652

The World Around You

Published twice a month, September to May, this magazine is devoted to those issues of interest to and affecting deaf and hearing-impaired youth.

> MSSD
> Box 5N
> Gallaudet College
> 800 Florida Ave. NE
> Washington, DC 20002

Deafpride, Inc.

An organization promoting positive issues relating to deafness, as well as current topics relevant to the deaf community.

> 2010 Rhode Island Ave. NE
> Washington, DC 20018

House Ear Institute

Conducts research in many areas relating to hearing loss and deafness. Has extensive library resources, including audiotapes and videos. Publishes the *Parent-to-Parent Resource Catalog*, which is the most complete compilation I have ever seen. Categorizing available information by books, pamphlets, and audiovisual materials, the topics include: "Initial Concerns," "Medical Information," "Audiological Information," "Communication Methods," "Child Development," "Educational Programs," "Support Services," "Assistive Devices," and "General Reading."

An invaluable resource guide for anyone living with or around hearing loss, and an especially good way for parents of newborn hearing-impaired children to begin learning about hearing loss.

> 256 So. Lake St.
> Los Angeles, CA 90057
> 213-483-4431 (voice)
> 213-484-2642 (TDD)

Other organizations addressing general interests of the hearing-impaired and deaf include:

Consumers Organization for the Hearing-Impaired
PO Box 8188
Silver Spring, MD 20907

Suzanne Pathy Speak-up Institute, Inc.
525 Park Ave.
New York, NY 10021

Washington Area Group for the Hard of Hearing
PO Box 6283
Silver Spring, MD 20906

There are also many, many excellent nonfiction and fiction books in print on the subjects of hearing impairment and deafness. Consult your local library's catalog listing—and happy reading!

The Manual Alphabet

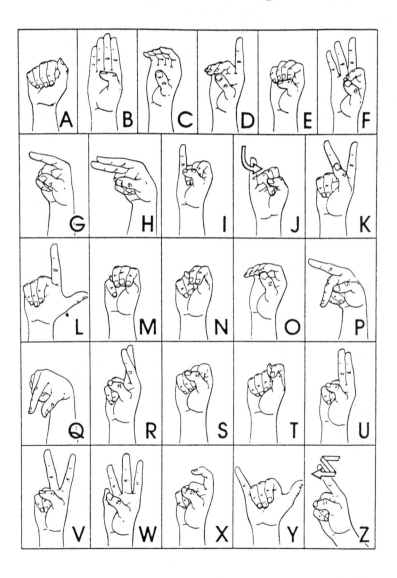

Glossary

Amplitude: The physical intensity of a sound (subjective impression of "loudness").

ASL: American Sign Language. The language of the deaf, having its own set of grammatical and syntactical rules.

Attenuate: To decrease the amplitude (loudness) or energy of a signal.

Audiogram: A graph of a person's threshold hearing levels.

Audiologist: An individual trained to the master's degree level, responsible for testing and evaluation of hearing and hearing loss, and the administration of habilitation and rehabilitation programs involving hearing loss.

Auditory nerve: The eighth cranial nerve that transmits information from the cochlea to the auditory cortex in the brain for interpretation.

Basilar membrane: The central membrane in the cochlea upon which the hair cells rest; contained within the Organ of Corti.

Bilateral: Referring to both sides.

Binaural: Referring to both ears.

Bony labyrinth: The system of interconnecting pathways of the inner ear.

Cerumen: Ear wax; from the Latin, meaning wax.

Cilia: The "hairs" within the cochlea.

Cochlea: (the "snail") The spiral organ in the inner ear that receives sound waves from the middle ear and transmits that information to the auditory nerve.

Conductive (hearing loss): When hearing is affected by anything that impedes the passage of sound through the outer and/or middle ear sections—prevention of the effective conduction of sound from the outer ear to the inner ear.

Congenital: Present at birth. Not necessarily hereditary.

Deaf/deafness: Little or no measurable hearing.

Decibel: Abbreviated dB. Technically, one-tenth of a bell. A relative measurement of sound intensity or pressure, based on a logarithmic relationship between two sources where one serves as the reference. Reference 0 dB hearing level would be the baseline "norm."

Degrees of hearing loss:
Normal—thresholds are better than or equal to 20 dB.
Mild—thresholds are between 20 dB and 40 dB.
Moderate—thresholds are between 40 dB and 65 dB.
Severe—thresholds are between 65 dB and 90 dB.
Profound—thresholds are above 90 dB.

Eustachian tube: The tube connecting the middle ear to the oral cavity allowing for equalization of pressure (equal to atmospheric pressure) in the middle ear.

Filter: Acoustically, a device that allows the passage of certain frequencies and attenuates others.

Frequency: Cycles or number of complete vibrations per second. Expressed in Hertz (Hz).

Hearing-impaired ("hard of hearing"): Any degree of hearing loss. (Those with deafness are hearing-impaired, but one who is hearing-impaired is *not* necessarily deaf. See def. of deaf/deafness and Chap. 2.)

Hemi-: A prefix meaning one-half.

Hertz: Designation for frequency, named after the German physicist Heinrich Rudolf Hertz.

Incus: ("anvil") The second in the chain of three middle-ear ossicles.

Left-corner audiogram: Measurable hearing only at the frequencies of 125 Hz, 250 Hz, and 500 Hz. Thresholds are usually above 70 dB.

Localization: The ability to determine the source or direction of a sound.

Loudness: The subjective impression of "amplitude" or the intensity of a sound.

Malleus: ("hammer") The first of the three middle-ear ossicles.

Minimal Auditory Deficiency (M.A.D.): A hearing loss generally of only 10–15 dB; thresholds between 20 and 30–35 dB.

Noise: Physically, the production of random, erratic sound waves. Psychologically, any unwanted sound.

NRR: Noise Reduction Rating. The amount of attenuation possible from a particular type of hearing protection device. Methods of measurement in obtaining NRR numbers require that number to be halved when applied in actual use.

Octave: A two-to-one relationship of frequencies. (1000 Hz is one octave above 500 Hz.)

Organ of Corti: That part of the cochlea containing the hair cells.

OSHA: The Occupational Safety and Health Agency, responsible for administering industrial safety standards set by the Occupational Safety and Health Act.

Ossicle: Any small bone, but especially those of the inner ear.

Otitis: An inflammation involving some portion of the outer, middle, or inner ear.

Otitis media: Inflammation of the tissue lining the middle-ear cavity.

Otoscope: An instrument used to examine the external ear canal and eardrum.

Pinna: The external ear (auricle).

Pitch: The subjective impression of frequency.

Presbycusis: Gradual hearing loss, especially in the high frequencies, from aging.

Recruitment: abnormally rapid increase in the sensation of loudness.

Sensori-neural (hearing-loss): When hearing is affected by abnormal function of the cochlea and/or auditory nerve. Often referred to as "nerve deafness." (Use of deafness here is in the vernacular. Refer to def. of deaf/deafness and Chap. 2.)

TDD: Telecommunication device for the deaf.

Threshold: The lowest level of measurable hearing where a response occurs 50 percent of the time.

Tinnitus: Subjective perception of noises in the ear(s). Variously described as ringing, buzzing, humming and clicking.

Total Communication: An approach to communicating with the severely and profoundly hearing-impaired that includes simultaneous use of sign and speech, sometimes supplemental written information; as opposed to, say, the "oral approach," wherein speech is used exclusively.

Tympanic: Referring to the middle ear.

Tympanum: The middle-ear cavity.

Index